AF600233

METROPOLITAN TRAGEDY

Genre, Justice, and the City in Early Modern England

Metropolitan Tragedy

Genre, Justice, and the City in Early Modern England

MARISSA GREENBERG

UNIVERSITY OF TORONTO PRESS
Toronto Buffalo London

Toronto Buffalo London
www.utppublishing.com

ISBN 978-1-4426-4880-7

Library and Archives Canada Cataloguing in Publication

Greenberg, Marissa, 1976–, author
Metropolitan tragedy : genre, justice, and the city in early modern England / Marissa Greenberg.

Includes bibliographical references and index.
ISBN 978-1-4426-4880-7 (bound)

1. English drama – Early modern and Elizabethan, 1500–1600 – History and criticism. 2. English drama – 17th century – History and criticism. 3. English drama (Tragedy) – History and criticism. 4. Theater and society – England – London – History. 5. Literature and society – England – London – History. 6. Justice in literature. 7. London (England) – In literature. 8. London (England) – Social conditions. I. Title.

PR658.T7G74 2015 822′.05120903 C2014-907705-X

University of Toronto Press acknowledges the financial assistance to its publishing program of the Canada Council for the Arts and the Ontario Arts Council, an agency of the Government of Ontario.

University of Toronto Press acknowledges the financial support of the Government of Canada through the Canada Book Fund for its publishing activities.

For my parents

Contents

Illustrations

Acknowledgments

Writing a book on tragedy is in many ways an exercise in gratitude. As I read about the suffering of others, I found myself profoundly thankful for the support of so many people. I am indebted to the mentors and colleagues whose rigor and generosity fundamentally shape my scholarship. Jean E. Howard advised me when I was an eager undergraduate, and in the years since, she has fostered my work in more ways than one. Stephen Cohen saw in me a promising scholar when I was a green graduate student. I am at a loss to express my gratitude for his sincerity and ardour. At the University of Pennsylvania, I was privileged to work with Margreta de Grazia, who first encouraged me to think about genre; Cary Mazer, who helped me to identify my scholarly community; and Phyllis Rackin, who urged me to find my voice, and, when I could not see the path ahead, offered candid and heartfelt advice. The Medieval-Renaissance Seminar provided me with my first and still some of my best readers, including Jennifer Higginbotham, Michelle Karnes, Kurt Schreyer, and Elizabeth Williamson. I am particularly grateful for the sustaining friendship of Jane Hwang Degenhardt, whose acuity and encouragement saved me from floundering more than once.

At the University of New Mexico, I found another supportive community, in particular Cathleen Cahill, Helen Damico, Jonathan Davis-Secord, Barry Gaines, Scarlett Higgins, Matthew Hofer, Gail Houston, Aeron Hunt, Anita Obermeier, Charles Paine, Mary Quinn, Andrew Sandoval-Strausz, and Melina Vizcaíno-Alemán. Jane Slaughter guided me through bureaucratic straits, and Lorenzo Garcia, Jr, provided assistance with my little Latin and less Greek. Jesse Alemán has graced me with his clear-headed, diligent, and enthusiastic mentorship. I am blessed in my fellow early modernist Carmen Nocentelli, who has become a cherished ally and friend. She read this book in its entirety at a crucial moment in its evolution, and it benefited immeasurably from her uncompromising integrity, expertise, and clarity of thought.

Earlier versions of portions of this book were presented at meetings of the Shakespeare Association of America, Renaissance Society of America, and Modern Language Association, and to the Five Colleges Renaissance Seminar, the University of Connecticut Renaissance Seminar, George Washington Medieval and Early Modern Studies Institute, and the University of Pennsylvania Medieval-Renaissance Seminar. The final version benefited in innumerable ways from the comments of my interlocutors, in particular Clare Costley King'oo, Alan Dessen, Theresa DiPascale, Doug Eskew, Jonathan Gil Harris, D.J. Hopkins, Jonathan Hsy, Brendan Kane, James Mardock, Greg Semenza, Bruce Smith, Paul Stevens, Will West, Paul Yachnin, and Mimi Yiu. In timely conversations, Jeremy Lopez and Richard Preiss provided much-needed encouragement. I am beholden to Laura Lunger Knoppers, who, upon hearing my ideas on Milton and the Great Fire at a conference at the University of Hull, graciously offered her insights on chapter 4.

Several grants and fellowships supported my research and gave me time to write. A National Endowment for the Humanities Award for Faculty at Hispanic-Serving Institutions allowed me to dedicate a full year to the book. Grants from the University of New Mexico's Research Allocation Committee funded archival research, and along with funds from the Department of English and the Office of the Associate Dean for Research, assisted with the costs of publication.

My thanks go to the British Museum, British Library, London Metropolitan Archives, Bridgeman Images, and Library of Congress for permission to reproduce images and manuscript materials. For permission to reprint an excerpt from Erin Gendron's "In the House on Olympia Street," published in *The Maple Leaf Rag IV* (2010), I thank the poet and Portals Press. A version of chapter 1 appeared previously as "Signs of the Crimes: Topography, Murder, and Early Modern Domestic Tragedy," in *Genre* 40.1 (2007): 1–29 (Copyright © 2007 by University of Oklahoma. All rights reserved. Reprinted by permission of the present publisher, Duke University Press. www.dukeupress.edu). A version of chapter 3 and elements of the Postscript appeared as "The Tyranny of Tragedy: Catharsis in England and *The Roman Actor*," in *Renaissance Drama* n.s. 39 (2011): 163–96 (Copyright © 2011 by Northwestern University Press. All rights reserved. Reprinted by permission of the present publisher, The University of Chicago Press. www.press.uchicago.edu).

I am grateful to the editors and current publishers of these journals for rights to reproduce parts of those articles here.

My heartfelt thanks also go to Suzanne Rancourt at University of Toronto Press, who steered this book through a difficult process. I appreciate the scrutiny of my readers, which helped me to refine my argument and strengthened my resolve in its contributions.

My friends and family know how much I have needed them through the writing of this book. Betsy Raz has been unflagging in her support. Eliza Ferguson fed my body and soul more times and in more ways than I can count, and I aspire to come to life's banquet with her fearlessness. Erika T. Lin has read every page of this book numerous times with both compassion and care, and I remain in awe of her ability to illuminate what I am trying to do. Time and again, her insights set me on track and her confidence saw me through my doubts. I would not and literally could not have written this book without her.

One of the pleasures that the publication of this book affords is that I may make good on a promise: to dedicate this book to my parents, Cynthia and Lloyd Greenberg. They instilled in me a love of theatre, encouraged my desire to brush up my Shakespeare, and gave up so much so that I might achieve my goals. I am incredibly lucky to have an extended family that has loyally followed the progress of this book: Sarah Greenberg, Andrew and Debby Greenberg, Phyllis and Steve Lyons, Dena Lyons, and especially Helaina and Paul Bardunias, for always listening. Adam Lyons has stuck by me despite the crazy and helped me write a life replete with comedy, adventure, melodrama, but never tragedy. Leam and Jamy serve up daily bottles of perspective simply by being their brilliant, affectionate, exuberant selves. They remind me of all I have to be grateful for each and every day.

Note on Texts

Unless noted otherwise, all quotations from Shakespeare's plays are taken from *The Norton Shakespeare,* ed. Stephen Greenblatt, Walter Cohen, Jean E. Howard, and Katharine Eisaman Maus (New York: W.W. Norton, 1997). When quoting from early modern printed texts and transcriptions of manuscript sources, I have retained early modern spellings and typography, with the exception of the long *s*, which I have silently modernized, and superscript letters and tildes marking omitted letters, which I have lowered and italicized.

METROPOLITAN TRAGEDY

Introduction

CLOWN: We have found her.
ISABEL: Hah, whom?
BONAVIDA: The pride of Nature, and of Love;
 Beautie and Vertue in most high contention
 Which should exceede each other. …
ISABEL:… [In] What Countrey?
BONAVIDA: *England.*
ISABEL: What place there?
BONAVIDA: Of their chiefe Cities, the Metropolis, *London.*

– Thomas Heywood, *A Challenge for Beauty* (1636)

Early modern English dramatist, pamphleteer, and pageant writer Thomas Heywood consistently and enthusiastically dubbed London a *metropolis*. In *An Apology for Actors* (1612) Heywood argues that playhouses and "the Citty Actors" are as essential to London's metropolitan status as they were to the ancient "*Metropolis*" of Rome, "a place whither all the nations knowne vnder the Sunne, resorted."[1] Heywood's mayoral pageants celebrate London as a "*Metropolis*" whose distinctions in culture, history, commerce, and religion render it superior to both ancient and contemporary cities.[2] In *A Challenge for Beauty* (1636) comparison remains Heywood's strategy of choice for praising England's capital. Through the dramatization of a contest of womanly excellence, he portrays London's pre-eminence in a manner more subtle yet no less significant than in his prose and pageants.

As the play opens, the honest Lord Bonavida questions the superlative beauty and virtue of Isabella, the proud queen of Spain and Portugal. Isabella summarily banishes Bonavida for speaking truth to power and pronounces that on pain of death he may not return "Till hee can find, produce, and set before vs, / Our match in Face and bosome."[3] In search of Isabella's "match," as Bonavida later explains, he "travell'd Kingdomes through, / Search'd Courts, examin'd Cities, nay even Villages" (sig. C2v). In England's "chiefe [of] Cities," he discovers Hellena, "the chiefe Paragon / Of Beautie match't with Vertue" (sig. D3v). By repeating the word "chiefe," Heywood highlights that the play's eponymous challenge is not simply between characters or even nations but also between metropolises. Just as Hellena challenges Isabella as the paragon of womanhood, so, too, London rivals "*Civill*," or Seville, "the chiefe [city] of *Spaine*," as the metropolitan ideal (sig. H2r). And just as Hellena ultimately trumps Isabella in beauty and virtue, London outshines Seville in civility, meaning the governance of a city in accordance with the code of law and in pursuit of its citizens' well-being.[4] Isabella proves herself anything but a civil ruler when Bonavida returns to announce his discovery and offers to bring Hellena to Spain. Rather than abide by her original sentence, Isabella condemns Bonavida, then arranges for the denouncement of her English rival as a whore. Only Hellena's arrival from London prevents these incivilities from taking place and establishes justice in Seville.

The staging of judicial place and procedure highlights the specifically metropolitan implications of Hellena's triumph. Entering "with Officers, and executioner" (sig. I3v sd), Bonavida frames his punishment as a performance:

> The Queene playes with my death,
> And bids me act a bold Tragedians part,
> To which, such moving action I will give,
> That it shall glaze this Theater round with teares,
> And all that shall behold me on this stage,
> Pittying my fate: shall taxe her cruelty ... (sig. I3v)

Bonavida's references to spaces of performance juxtapose the play's fictional and actual urban settings. "*[T]his* Theater" and "*this* stage" are at once Seville's place of capital punishment and London's places of theatrical performance – specifically, Blackfriars and the Globe where, according to the title page, the play "hath beene sundry times acted." What it means to "act a bold Tragedians part" in both venues, moreover, appears identical. Bonavida theatrically narrates the condemned's "Prepar[ation] for death" (sig. I4r sd): "My forfeit head thus stoopes,"

"Now [I] bow to th' Axe of Iustice," "Thus I fall" (sigs. I4r–I4v). This "moving action," Bonavida insists, will elicit "teares" and pity from spectators, regardless of citizenship. The enactment of place, procedure, and response thus collapses "play[ing] with ... death" in Seville and playing at death in London. Yet the ending of *A Challenge for Beauty* frustrates this dual tragedy. After Hellena arrives in Seville from London and "interupts" Isabella's "Iustice" (sig. I4v), the play ends with the restoration of Bonavida's life and Hellena's honour, that is, as a conventional comedy. Ultimately, Heywood's play celebrates England's "chiefe [of] Cities, the Metropolis, *London*" as a locus of both civility and performance.

Metropolitan Tragedy captures the unique confluence of genre, justice, and the city that shaped the composition and reception of theatrical tragedy in early modern England. It argues that tragedy as an urban genre emerged within the bifold context of London's burgeoning metropolitan status and the city's established procedures for enforcing justice. London's demographic and topographical expansion, its growing international importance, heightened tensions between the city and the Crown, and the shifting responsibilities of God-fearing citizens – each of these aspects of life in England's capital shapes early modern tragedy. Recent scholarship explores the impact of these historical imperatives on various forms of London literature, but it has focused primarily on city comedy, perhaps as a result of the limited number of plays that might properly qualify as "London tragedy."[5] Yet early modern English tragedy – a broad discursive field that encompasses both practice and theory, both dramatic and non-dramatic texts – holds a crucial place in an extended tradition that strongly identifies tragedy with the metropolis in transition. Ancient myth links the rupture in humanity's relations with one another and with the gods to the move from the wilderness to cities, and in the Bible, the first act of murder coincides with the first urban settlement, when Cain, "cursed from the earth" for killing Abel, "build[s] a city ... Enoch."[6] Early modern English writers drew on these classical and biblical narratives to represent the metropolis as a locus of social upheaval, personal injury, collective suffering, and infrastructural ruin, even as they remade tragedy in accordance with the sources of injustice in their own age.[7] *Metropolitan Tragedy* puts early modern English tragedy back in its rightful place as an urban genre central to this longer tradition.

Throughout this book, I use my eponymous terms in all their intricacy, ambivalence, and contradiction. *Metropolitan* is not simply a synonym for urban or city, and as Raymond Williams observes, *tragedy* is simultaneously "an immediate experience, a body of literature, a conflict of theory, [and] an academic problem."[8] The task of parsing this semantic profusion, which has its origins in classical usage and persists in current popular and academic discourses, frustrates any clear-cut determination of causes and effects. Yet this same multiplicity of meaning is crucial to tragedy as an urban genre, in particular as it develops in early modern England. The overdetermination of both *tragedy* and *metropolitan* poses challenges to scholars interested in the dynamics between dramatic genre and lived experience. Real-world tragedies affect a metropolis's institutional and cultural circumstances as well as its political and social practices, including the performance and publication of theatrical tragedy. At the same time, theatrical tragedy is productive of the metropolis, shaping perceptions of civic spaces, communities, and events, often in collaboration with other modes of urban representation. These multiple and mutual interactions preclude a singular or simple understanding of my eponymous terms and the relationship between them. The polysemy of *metropolitan* (and) *tragedy* frustrates one-to-one correlation between text and context and discloses the diverse and unpredictable crossings of form and history.

For scholars of urban geography, history, and literature, *metropolitan* and its cognate *metropolis* refer to the physical *metre*, or measurement, of the *polis* as a built environment and a human community. Between the late-sixteenth and mid-seventeenth centuries, London's population exploded as a result of unabated and rapid immigration from elsewhere in England and from the Continent. To keep pace with this swelling populace, construction within the urban centre but especially in the suburbs occurred at a precipitous rate. One result of this surge in population and infrastructure was heavy congestion in the City of London, the twenty-six districts or wards located within and immediately adjacent to its engirdling ancient walls, and in the surrounding conurbation, especially in the direction of the City of Westminster, defined initially by the presence of the court but later associated with the fashionable West End. Another result was that, despite jurisdictional tensions, the City of London and the City of Westminster became increasingly bound together topographically, economically, and socially.[9] A principal reason I use the term *metropolitan*, then, is the way it reflects the imbrication of these two cities.

At the same time as *metropolitan* registers London's compound composition, it also denotes London's singularity. Within a few decades of the construction of London's first purpose-built playhouses, *metropolitan* became a descriptor of all things London and *metropolis* an epithet for the city itself.[10] Also dubbed *chief, capital,* and *primate* city, London figures increasingly as a hub of religious, political, economic, and imperial activities both at home and abroad. By the mid-seventeenth century, English writers asserted with confidence the superiority of the city on the Thames to other cities in the commonwealth and on the Continent. Thomas Fuller's *The History of the Worthies of England* (1662), for example, mocks "those who hope it [York] shall be the *English Metropolis*," responding that "they must wait untill the *River of Thames* run under the great Arch of *Ouse-bridge*," and James Howell's *Londinopolis* (1657), in a section entitled "A parallel, By way of corollary, Betwixt London, and Other great Cities of the World," compares London favourably to three major early modern urban centres: Paris, Antwerp, and Amsterdam.[11]

London's burgeoning metropolitan status inspired some writers to panegyric, others to jeremiad. The rise in illicit activity, both actual and perceived, that attended London's mounting size and importance led to unfavourable descriptions of the metropolis as a Duessa-like monster, part woman, part beast, and in some instances, wholly whorish.[12] London is a "general nuisance to the whole kingdom," King James I chafed, "like the spleen in the body, which in measure as it overgrows, the body wastes."[13] Grown out of measure, a *polis* without *metre*, the metropolis was in jeopardy of undermining its responsibilities as England's *mētēr polis*, or mother city. According to this definition, which appears in dictionaries and other writings throughout the period, London played the part of a protective and nurturing parent to daughter cities throughout England and its nascent empire.[14] It also gestures to the city's role as wife or consort to the monarch, with whom it shared a historically ambivalent and often tense relationship. Heywood offers a blunt rejoinder to unfavourable views of a feminized London in *A Challenge for Beauty* when Hellena proves neither a "faire false" nor a whore but an agent of Justice, "that Virgin, sent from heaven, / That beares the sword and ballance" (sigs. I3v, I1v). The establishment of justice occurs when the English maid instructs the Iberian queen in true beauty and virtue, thus giving birth to a civil Seville in a moment of immaculate urban conception. As mother city, London also wields the instruments of judgment and punishment to measure – that is, to appraise and correct – her civic offspring.

Heywood's *A Challenge for Beauty* also perpetuates an alternative sense of metropolis: the *polis* as subject of poetic *metre*, or literary representation. Although usage in this sense is rare, this definition bears significantly on perceptions and expressions of England's capital.[15] Like the concrete metrologies of demography and geography, literature measures the lived experiences of London's built environment and human communities according to culturally defined units of scale and value: metrical feet, rhythms of speech, and, of particular interest to my purposes, literary genres. Yet like London's conflicting epithets, measurements of the extent, quality, value, and effect of the metropolis were necessarily subjective and relational.[16] In early modern England multiple and diverse genres, both established and emergent, provided a range of ways to measure the metropolis. Tragedy was a principal yardstick for writers and audiences who perceived historical changes in London as sources of suffering and loss and thus reasons for lamentation and trepidation.

As a formal measure of the metropolis, *tragedy* is a genre with its own fraught history, one that stretches back to the ancient world and continues today. One source of protracted vigorous debate is that tragedy refers to both a *theory* and a *practice*, terms that bear their own critical burdens. For my current purposes, theory indicates the description, codification, and regulation of tragedy as a formal concept or abstraction; it is almost exclusively textual. In the early modern period it includes both defences and denunciations of tragedy, such as Thomas Heywood's *An Apology for Actors* and I.G.'s *A Refutation of the Apology for Actors.* By contrast, practice shows the execution of tragedy as an aesthetic experience; practice literally acts out tragedy. Early modern English tragedy frequently includes metatheatrical moments – dumb shows, plays-within-the-plays, and paratheatrical spectacles, as well as references to staging conventions – that bluntly call attention to its own enactment. The enactment of tragedy does not preclude imagined performances that are the result of reading, but usually it signals embodied performances. This point is significant because practice-as-performance reveals, constructs, and occludes meaning in ways unavailable to practice-as-script.[17] Although pitted against one another in competition over the meaning of tragedy, theory and practice frequently converge.[18] Theoretical explications of systematic order routinely include references to particular practices. Sophocles's *Oedipus Tyrannus* in Aristotle's *Poetics,* Buchanan's *Gorbaduc* in Sidney's *An Apology for Poetry*, Euripides's *The Bacchae* in Nietzsche's *The Birth of Tragedy* – these sorts of allusions serve as examples that demonstrate "proper" tragedy. This is not to suggest that theory is a servile complement to, or an unadulterated distillation of, practice. On the contrary, theorists cull their examples from a larger corpus of tragedy in practice and then hew and expound them to create a seemingly organic display of a predetermined principle. Practice evinces a similarly aggressive tendency: the practice of tragedy does not simply enact theories of tragedy but actually presents a critical exegesis of those theories.[19]

Just as tragedy-as-genre refers to and traffics between theory and practice, so, too, does tragedy-as-experience demarcate and traverse the difference between idiom and event. In the sixteenth and seventeenth centuries, no less than today, all sorts of very sad occurrences, both quotidian and extraordinary, prompted the colloquial use of *tragedy* and its cognates *tragic* and *tragical*. Early modern English writers did not reserve these terms for the murder of innocents and instances of blatant injustice; they also described petty offences, deserved execution, and divine retribution as tragedies. In Ben Jonson's *Every Man Out of His Humour* (1599) Carlo warns Sogliardo to "commerce not with bankrupts, or poor needy Ludgathians," because "They care not what violent tragedies they stir."[20] In the anonymous *A Warning for Fair Women*, published the same year as Jonson's portrait of the "tragedies" of debt and incarceration, an allegorical Tragedy plays chorus to the dramatization of historical acts of adultery, murder, and execution. Turning from stage to scaffold, a similar pattern of usage emerges. Accounts of the Gunpowder Plot of 1605 – also dubbed "the Powder Tragedy" – describe both the plotters' treason and their execution as tragedies.[21] The language of tragedy also pervades accounts of the Great Fire of 1666, even though popular opinion held that the destruction of four-fifths of medieval London was God's just punishment for the city's manifold sins.[22] Poet Simon Ford refers to the baker's house on Pudding Lane where the conflagration began as "Thou Source of Londons Tragedies"; Samuel Wiseman likens the fire's sparks to "Apt Actors for a purpos'd Tragedy"; and, elegizing the city's ruins, Elkanah Settle calls the Great Fire a "deep Tragedy" to which a personified Sun was "spectator."[23] What emerges from even these few examples is a sense of the way the idiomatic use of *tragedy* did not privilege one kind of suffering over any other but denoted a range of real-world events, both individual and collective, from loss of livelihood to the murder of citizens and kings to city-wide devastation.

The language of tragedy in early modern England assigns this shared sense of lived experience through affiliation with dramatic genre. A generalized terminology of performance (*actors, scene, act, spectator, stage, part*) compounds the linkage of historical conditions to formal modes of representation. Recalling the title pages of early modern tragic plays, accounts of the Great Fire – including images of the ruined cityscape, official acts and petitions, financial records, popular prose tracts, as well as letters, poems, and sermons – present the city's destruction as "sad," "dreadfull," "deplorable," "dismal," and "lamentable."[24] Accounts of not only actual events but also fictional ones reflect this connection between experience and genre. For instance, Jonson's dramatized warning against debtors "stir[ring]" "violent tragedies" evokes English defences of the stage that laud tragedy's capacity to discourage vice. The point is not that dramatic genre defines lived experience or vice versa; rather, that the language of tragedy renders form always already bound up with history.

Of course, not everyone perceived the metropolis in terms of tragedy: one citizen's pain meant another's profit, and one subject's rebellion was another's lawful opposition. The lived experience of early modern London, then, might be figured as comedy, tragicomedy, or homily, among other genres.[25] Yet the explicit or dominant frame of reference is often tragedy, not least, I argue, because justice is enforced in the metropolis. London's emergence as a national and international hub of commerce, culture, political debate, and religious reformation meant that changes in the metropolis had an impact well beyond its shifting borders. Conflict and deprivation in England's capital threatened the common wealth of the commonwealth. At the same time, London persisted as a judicial locus, where agents of God and the state disseminated the law and disciplined its violators. Consequently, the city led the charge against sin and disorder and towards the restoration of justice. Tragedy-as-genre provided recognizable frameworks by which writers, readers, and playgoers might register and respond to tragedy-as-experience, in particular the experiences of crime and punishment, in the metropolis.

This emphasis on the city as the space in which genre and justice overlap marks a point of continuity and rupture between ancient and early modern tragedy. In Plato's *Republic* the Guardians eject tragedians from the *polis*, citing the deleterious effects that tragic representations have on citizens. Plato proposes that by undermining citizens' capacity to respond judiciously to real-world tragedy, literary tragedy forestalls the actualization of a metropolitan ideal. By contrast, Aristotle's *Poetics* offers an exclusively formalistic definition of tragedy that elides the role of the *polis* in literary tragedy. This elision extends to the introduction of κάθαρσις, or catharsis, as the salutary if ambiguous effect of tragic representations. Debate about the precise operations of Aristotelian catharsis has a long history, of course. John Milton registers two prominent sides of this debate in the early modern period. On the title page of *Samson Agonistes*, Milton joins Daniel Heinsius and Gerardus Joannes Vossius when he translates catharsis as *lustratio*, a Latin word meaning spiritual and moral purification. Then, in the preface to his tragedy, Milton translates catharsis as purgation, thus echoing Sir Philip Sidney and others who argue for tragedy as a violent physical and emotional cleansing.[26] These divergent interpretations tend to divide early modern commentaries on the operations of catharsis; but most English writers agree that the object of tragedy's effects is the audience, and in particular, the metropolitan audience.

How early modern English audiences *actually* responded to literary tragedy necessarily remains a subject of speculation. Susan Bennett puts the matter mildly when she writes that "[k]notty problems emerge in any attempt to talk about historical audiences."[27] The individuals who paid their pennies to purchase theatrical and printed wares at London's playhouses and bookstalls were a subset of the metropolis's heterogeneous populace: they were native and foreign, urbane and provincial, educated and unlettered, gentry and citizenry. Age and sex also shaped how audience members responded to tragedy, even as common bodily features – eyes, ears, hearts, stomachs, skin – contributed to collective responses.[28] Institutional conditions could also turn individuals into an audience only partially and at best imperfectly, as Paul Menzer's discussion of crowd control and Matthew Steggle's of applause demonstrate.[29] I do not presume to undo these knotty problems. We possess little suggestive and subjective evidence, and no conclusive and unmediated proof, of individual reactions to early modern English tragedy. But if who responded how remains inaccessible, what responses were *historically available* is within our grasp.

To trace these historically available responses to tragedy, I draw on a rich archive of dramatic and non-dramatic representations of the metropolis. Printed images of early modern London serve a crucial role in this project.[30] These city portraits do not simply consolidate the experience of justice in specific sites, entities, or occasions; instead, they reveal pervasive if competing ideas about London and contribute to the formal production of ways of seeing the city that also inhabit the historical forms of tragedy. In addition to London's printed image, I discuss crime reports, religious tracts, political pamphlets, and accounts of the

Great Fire to demonstrate the diverse ways in which the lived experience of England's capital mediated responses to theatrical tragedy, even as theatrical tragedy provided alternative perceptions of urban life. As I begin to show in this introduction, and as we shall see throughout this book, the metropolis is a significant and previously unacknowledged connective tissue in early modern English tragedy. Rather than use *metropolitan* and *tragedy* as shorthand for a prefabricated set of texts and stable context, then, I work steadily to reveal the diverse and dense crossings of tragedy-as-genre and tragedy-as-experience.

This critical investment puts *Metropolitan Tragedy* in conversation with a growing body of scholarship known as historical formalism, new historical poetics, New Formalism, even "the revenge of the aesthetic."[31] In particular, in taking the metropolis and tragedy as its dual axes, this book builds on existing historicist scholarship on the forms of London literature. Written in the midst of the so-called spatial turn, Lawrence Manley's monumental *Literature and Culture in Early Modern London* (1995) takes a bird's eye view of England's capital and its representation. Resisting local and topical analyses in favour of complex spatial and historical networks, Manley argues for "a collective experience" of the city that "is not simply 'reflected' in the works [of early modern English writers] but inhabits their very forms."[32] More recently, the trend has been to view London and its literature from the bird's nest. This approach, especially prevalent in studies of city comedy, reveals the conjunction of various energies – commercial, erotic, religious, social, political – in specific London sites, such as the Royal Exchange, the Counters, Bartholomew Fair, and St Paul's Cathedral. In *Theater of a City* (2007) Jean E. Howard, citing Jean-Christophe Agnew's account of the *placelessness* of London's market economy, ascribes the sense of an elusive and unstable cityscape to the proliferation of anonymous financial transactions, improvised trading venues, and women and foreigners in commercial activities.[33] Adam Zucker in *The Places of Wit* (2011) makes a case for London's *"over-placedness,"* pointing to the efforts of authorities to enforce singularity and stability on an expanding and unruly marketplace.[34] And Mary Bly, in her important ongoing work on cultural geography, argues that the contested uses and meanings of official sites rendered urban place, in humanist geographer Ronald Davidson's phrase, *"recalcitrant space."*[35] Placelessness, over-placedness, and recalcitrance also inhabit early modern English metropolitan tragedy, specifically its representations of places of justice.

Tower Hill, arguably England's most iconic site of law and order, demonstrates the range of associations with London's judicial sites and procedures. A survey of Tower Hill's institutional and cultural functions as well as political and social histories thus provides a significant frame of reference for representations of justice in early modern English metropolitan tragedy. John Stow writes in *A Survey of London* (1598, 1603), "Vpon this Hill is alwayes readily prepared at the charges of the cittie a large Scaffolde and Gallowes of Timber, for the execution of such Traytors or Transgressors."[36] By "alwayes" Stow means continuously as opposed to occasionally, yet the term also implies for all time.[37] Like a pair of unflagging sentinels, the scaffold and gallows on Tower Hill signify how, even when London's places of justice stood vacant, they were not idle. This sense of vigilance is evident, as well, in accounts of executions on Tower Hill. According to James Howell's *Londinopolis* (1657), "In King *James*'s time, for 22 years, there was no blood spilt ... upon Tower-hill, only Sir *Gervase Elwayes*, [Lieutenant of the Tower of London, condemned for his role in the conspiracy to murder Sir Thomas Overbury,] was hanged there."[38] Helwys's dying speech offers some insight into the legal authority of Tower Hill:

> It may be some will say that most fittest was this place of execution appoynted for me, to terefie and daunt me so much the more: but alas I feare not death, place, nor any such like thinge: but I acounte it the kinge and councell especiall favor to me that I dye hear, first for that I requesting the same it was grannted: wherin now see this toiwer late wherin I should, being called to state busines, have performed better, and more loyall service to kinge and country then I did: next, that I was not appoynted to Tiburne, a place of publick reproach, now that I came hether brought being worthy of death, by due and lawfull Justice.[39]

Helwys's final words drive home that to die on Tower Hill is a dubious distinction but a distinction nonetheless. The "especiall favor" of dying on Tower Hill is largely due to the physical proximity and symbolic connection of "this place of execution" to "this toiwer," that is, the Tower of London. The Tower of London occupied a crucial place in London's status as *camera regia*, or royal chamber: in addition to functioning literally as a royal residence, the Tower of London operated as a state archive, armoury, treasury, and mint, and as evidence of the city's ancient foundation, it authorized England's monarchy through affiliation with classical Rome.[40] The Tower of London was also the state's chief place of "due and lawfull Justice." Inside its walls, traitors and other capital offenders might endure torture on England's purportedly "only ... *Brake* or Rack" before their execution.[41] A select few, usually nobles, clergy, and state officials, walked the short distance to Tower Hill, where they suffered beheading or hanging. The scaffold and gallows on Tower Hill thus made visible the operations of royal justice within the Tower of London, even as they exemplified a legal authority that knew no jurisdictional bounds. The permanent structures atop Tower Hill simultaneously gathered together and emanated the monarch's power to enforce justice in and beyond the metropolis.

A profusion of places of punishment in early modern London challenged the concentration of legal authority on Tower Hill. In a printed version of Helwys's dying speech, the condemned juxtaposes Tower Hill to "the place of common Execution where euery base Malefactor dyeth."[42] In fact, numerous places of common execution punctuated London and its environs. Scaffolds for the punishment of capital offenders stood in Tyburn, Cheapside, Newgate, Wapping, and Smithfield, to name only a few, and at the directive of city officials, each of London's twenty-six wards maintained structures for the disciplining of petty offenders.[43] For example, in November 1604, the Court of Common Council required the erection of "a payre of stockes" in every "parish w*it*hin this Cyttye and liberties thereof."[44] Less than a decade later, the Court of Aldermen ordered: "to eve*ry* Alderman w*it*hin this citty [of London] that they take spe*cia*ll care that stock*e*s cages and whipping postes be p*re*sently provided and sett vpp in their seve*ra*ll wardes in places convenient."[45] By 1623, John Taylor, the Water-Poet, could credibly claim that "In *London* and within a mile, I weene, / There are ... sixty Whipping-Posts, and Stocks and Cages, / Where sin with shame and sorrow hath due wages."[46] The abundance of disciplinary sites, Paul Griffiths argues, was part of an "optic order" designed to imbue city officials with seemingly providential powers.[47] Not only the placeless justice of royal authority, then, but also the overplaced justice of civic authority infused the early modern cityscape.

Although at times royal and civic authority worked in tandem, historically they were at odds. The erection of the scaffold and gallows on Tower Hill during the reign of Edward IV prompted complaints from "the Mayor and his Brethren," who feared these structures would lead to the "derogation and preiudice of the liberties and franchises of this cittie," and throughout the period, London's leaders continued to rankle at the Crown's presence on the City's edge.[48] Tensions came to a head when London hosted the execution of Charles I. George Cartwright's *The British Rebellion* (1661) – "an epic poem (of very little merit)," according to the British Library catalogue – laments the location of the king's death:

> To murther him, and take his life away:
> As how, and where, the most convenient place,
> That would contribute most to his disgrace.
> The place appointed for the Kingdoms fall,
> And Londons shame, was iust before White Hall.
> Ah Heav'ns! would no place serue but 'fore his door,
> As if he were a common Murtherer?
> There where in state he vs'd to Audience giue
> To all the world, must there disgrace receaue?
> This aggravates their malice to the hight,
> To put on Maiesty so great a sleight.[49]

Whatever its failings poetically, Cartwright's poem offers insight into the significance of the places of justice in early modern London. Whereas the scaffold and gallows on Tower Hill afforded a degree of respect and dignity befitting the condemned's status, common offenders were punished at what Helwys calls "place[s] of publick reproach," which included permanent sites of punishment as well as temporary ones, such as the crime scene and the offender's home. When members of Parliament ordered Charles I's beheading "iust before White Hall," they treated him as a "common Murtherer," no different than any other "base Malefactor," rather than England's supreme judge and anointed ruler. In terms of the associations of judicial place in the early modern metropolis, the location of Charles I's scaffold denied his claims to God-given prerogative and subjected him to the public's reproach.

For Charles I's supporters, of course, the king's scaffold was not a site of justice at all. Royalists flagrantly opposed the spatial associations that so vexed Cartwright, and they used image and text (as we will see in chapter 3) to encode the scaffold with rival meanings. Charles I's execution is thus an extraordinary example of oppositional interests frustrating the official purposes of judicial sites and procedures. Even on Tower Hill, London's locus of "due and lawfull Justice," Foucauldian paradigms of power sometimes fell short.[50] For example, the execution of Thomas Wentworth, Earl of Strafford, in 1641 upended associations of Tower Hill with absolute justice. Set against a broader backdrop

Figure 1: Wencelaus Hollar, *The true maner [sic] of the execution of Thomas Earle of Strafford* (1641). Prints & Photographs Division, Courtesy of the Library of Congress, LC-USZ62–95956.

of national crisis and impending war, the earl's condemnation shows royal power bowing to partisan agendas and popular outrage. Wentworth died not because he offended the monarch but because members of Parliament and an overwhelming number of English subjects passionately despised him. Wencelaus Hollar's *The True Maner [sic] of the Execution of Thomas Earle of Strafford* (1641) pictorially registers the tension and turmoil surrounding Wentworth's execution (Figure 1). In this topical print, a huge crowd envelops the scaffold on Tower Hill. These spectators, who cover the ground, purpose-built stands, and nearby buildings, were anything but passive witnesses to the administration of justice. Hollar's print shows soldiers surrounding the condemned, a customary preventive against resistance to official procedure. It also depicts the moment during Wentworth's execution when one of the stands collapsed, sending members of the crowd tumbling to the ground. This portrait of Tower Hill thus offers testimony of the fugitive history of the scaffold, to appropriate Ellen MacKay's turn of phrase, in which judicial process could "[careen] off the course of its expected event and headlong into disaster."[51]

The contents and organization of this book enact its larger claim about the imbrication of genre and experience in early modern English metropolitan tragedy. Each of the four chapters uses close readings of representative plays to examine the metropolitan imperatives of a particular tragic subgenre: domestic tragedy and infrastructural upheaval, revenge tragedy and imperial ambition, tyrant tragedy and political debate, and Christian tragedy and apocalyptic fervor – all of which took place in the shadow of London's places of justice. The order of these chapters is roughly chronological so as to trace the development of early modern English tragedy as an urban genre, while charting its origins, innovations, and implications. *Metropolitan Tragedy* thus demonstrates both cohesion among different kinds of tragedy and the dynamism of tragic form as coextensive with the historical city in transition.

The book opens with a period of upheaval in London's cityscape and innovation in tragic convention. Early modern English domestic tragedy, which breaks from classical tragedy in featuring citizen protagonists and contemporary events, emerged at the end of the sixteenth century in response to London's rapid demographic and topographical growth. The proliferation of strange faces, overcrowded tenements, and shady corners led to anxieties about law and order – anxieties seemingly confirmed by sensationalist accounts of historical crimes. In chapter 1, "Topography, Murder, and Early Modern Domestic Tragedy," I examine the way spatial specificity counters these anxieties in the anonymous *A Warning for Fair Women* and Robert Yarington's *Two Lamentable Tragedies*. These plays locate murder and execution in a recognizable cityscape, thereby constructing a fantasy of London as chartable, exposed to view, and hence resistant to crime. This myth of England's capital as self-policing is evident in other cultural modes, including pictorial images; yet the brief heyday of domestic tragedy suggests that this vision of the metropolis fell short of reconciling formal innovation to ongoing urban change.

The next chapter shifts focus from an emergent subgenre to an ancient one, from situated place to physical movement, and from London's seedy underbelly to a grand imperial setting. In chapter 2, "*Translatio Metropolitae* and Early Revenge Tragedy," I argue that Elizabethan and Jacobean revenge tragedy complicates the project of *translatio imperii*, or translation of empire, the literary tradition of using the classical past to authorize the early modern present. My analysis centres on the ways *Titus Andronicus* challenges this project through its representation of the city as the setting for movement. In Shakespeare's early revenge tragedy, enactments of triumphal return, disciplinary procession, and emotional testimony fail to move audiences to tears, let alone restore justice to the *polis*, in the manner expected of tragedy. Instead, the play reveals how revenge tragedy invites scrutiny of the implications of London's rise to national and international prominence. These oppositional energies appear, as well, in city portraits that juxtapose the geographies of pageantry and punishment. At the turn of the seventeenth century, both in the playhouse and at the bookstall, representations of urban movement challenged the teleology of imperial inheritance.

Later Stuart England metropolitan tragedies turn their gaze inward from the empire to the court where avengers execute judgment on corrupt and willful rulers in the name of the common good. These shifts in the setting and motive for revenge occasion more explicit engagement with early modern political debates about the respective authority of kings and the people. In doing so, these plays, more so than the revenge tragedies of earlier decades, disclose rising concerns about England's *camera regia* as the locus of royal prerogative and popular resistance. In chapter 3, "Tyrant Tragedy and the Tyranny of Tragedy in Stuart London," I argue that these concerns pervade both dramatic representations of abusive monarchs and literary theories that assert tragedy's capacity to reform unjust rulers. I begin with the overlapping lexicons of tragic and political discourses to show that the uniquely English interpretation of Aristotelian catharsis as a judicial prophylactic requires spiritual compulsion and physical brutality – that is, the very sort of violence associated with tyranny. Philip Massinger critiques this overlap in *The Roman Actor*, a play that straddles ancient Rome and early modern London, dramatic theory and practice, and "actual" and theatrical tragedy. I conclude with the legacy of Massinger's critique in the history, politics, and pictorial representation of the place of Charles I's execution.

This legacy includes *Samson Agonistes*, in which John Milton explores the metropolitan function of tragedy in relation to the Great Fire of 1666. Chapter 4, "Noise, the Great Fire, and Milton's *Samson Agonistes*," begins with the prefatory epistle to Milton's dramatic poem, in which he ascribes to tragedy the "power by raising pity and fear … to temper and reduce them to just measure."[52] I historicize the acoustic meaning of "just measure" in terms of Milton's other writings and early modern understandings of sound, then show how the Great Fire put the measuring effects of tragedy to the test. According to sermons, proclamations, and poems, when London burned, its denizens failed to hear correctly the sounds of devastation and despondency. Milton reproduces this urban soundscape in *Samson Agonistes* as part of his representation of an analogous moment when infrastructural ruin and collective suffering fall short of leading the human *polis* to proper *metre*. In this way, I argue, Milton's tragedy alerts readers to the call to salvation amidst the "harsh din" of the fallen metropolis, sounds that continue to be heard in printed plans for London's reconstruction.[53]

Samson Agonistes, although bound up with local events in Restoration London, represents the earthly city's structural and ethical undoing within a universal, theological context. Milton's dramatic poem thus exceeds the specific subgenres of closet drama and Christian tragedy as well as its immediate time and place. It serves an analogous function within the structure of this book, reflecting many of the crossings with which I engage: practice and theory, neo-classicism and innovation, protracted conflict and sudden upheaval. Ultimately, by illuminating an understanding of form and history that frustrates traditional disciplinary boundaries, *Samson Agonistes* expands what counts as early modern English metropolitan tragedy.

Pursuing this expansive understanding of early modern English metropolitan tragedy to its logical limit, in a brief postscript I consider its place in relation to modern-day performance. I focus on a 2002–3 Royal Shakespeare Company production of *The Roman Actor* that reflects the persistent imbrication of genre and experience in current understandings of tragedy. Produced in the aftermath of 11 September 2001, the RSC's *Roman Actor* engaged audiences in an extended history of spectacular violence while summoning them to action in the present. In doing so, the production not only resumed the political and aesthetic work that Massinger's play began almost four hundred years earlier, it also showcased the transhistoricity of metropolitan tragedy.

By concluding with the notion of transhistoricity, I do not mean to suggest that metropolitan tragedy is a timeless or universal genre. Instead, my purpose is to illustrate the chronological dialectic at work in the history of form.[54] Throughout *Metropolitan Tragedy*, I indicate how early modern English writers redeployed prior notions of tragedy and heralded new ones. Because classical writings did not map neatly onto early modern urban preoccupations, English writers self-consciously reworked their tragic inheritance, sometimes to celebrate, other times to challenge, the metropolis as a locus of justice. The mismatch between the classical and the early modern also inspired the pioneering of new kinds of tragedy. These plays and theories situate metropolitan concerns in contexts minute and vast, from London's street corners to the Christian cosmos. As they looked to the past and the present, early modern English writers also created a corpus of tragedy for the future to remake in its own urban image.

Chapter One

Topography, Murder, and Early Modern Domestic Tragedy

A Physition riding ouer Shooters hill in Kent was afraide of Theeues, and by chance he saw a farre off a troope of people afore him. Wherupon he bid his man ryde towards them, to discouer what they were: Mean time he hid himselfe close behind a bush: The fellow comming vnto them, vnderstood that they conducted a murtherer to execution.

– Anthony Copley, *Wits fittes and fancies* (1595)

Amidst the outpouring of scholarship on representations of early modern London in various genres, the city's importance to theatrical tragedy has gone largely overlooked.[1] This is striking not least because in the late sixteenth century, at the same time as city comedies and mayoral inaugurations registered commercial and political changes in England's capital, domestic tragedy and revenge tragedy explored the judicial implications of London's emergence as a metropolis. In the next chapter I examine how Elizabethan and Jacobean revenge tragedy, like civic pageantry, takes the ancient *polis* as a point of reference and organizes the relationship of the city to legal authority in terms of dynamic movement. In choosing to open with a chapter on domestic tragedy, I foreground a subgenre that breaks from classical models in its setting and plot and bears strong affinities to another early modern theatrical innovation: city comedy. Among the earliest dramatic expressions of London's burgeoning metropolitan status, domestic tragedies represent widespread anxieties about the upheaval of the city's human community and built environment in terms of actual crimes and punishments in England's capital. These plays tend to originate, as the nineteenth-century critic John Payne Collier put it, in "recent tragical incident[s]" of adultery, murder, and execution; yet Collier misses the mark when he writes that domestic tragedy represents these "known occurrence[s], without embellishing, or aiding [them] with the ornaments of invention."[2] Domestic tragedy brings representations of real-world tragedy into the service of urban *fantasy* – what Wendy Wall defines as "the cultural setting or syntax for desire."[3] In so doing, this subgenre of metropolitan tragedy set the stage for generations of London drama to come.

In this chapter I argue that domestic tragedy transforms London's discomfiting conditions and infamous crimes into sources of theatrical pleasure. Specifically, in response to perceptions of the cityscape as unknown, impenetrable, and thus fertile ground for the proliferation of crime, domestic tragedy projects a fantasy of a secure metropolis. Through close readings of the anonymous *A Warning for Fair Women* (1599) and Robert Yarington's *Two Lamentable Tragedies* (1601), I reveal domestic tragedy's counterfactual spatial semiotics, a system of urban signification that belied actual experiences in England's capital. Sprawled out and turned in on itself, early modern London was anything but a well-designed city. Without the aid of schematic or descriptive guides, both inhabitants and tourists (often one and the same) depended on particular spatial features to cognitively map the city.[4] London's byways, boundaries, and landmarks – these spatial features appear routinely in domestic tragedy's representation of the law's violation and enforcement. By naming the places of historical crimes and punishments, domestic tragedy transforms London's perceived (if no less actual) incomprehensibility into urban legibility.

Domestic tragedy takes London as a principal location, dramatizes everyday urban life, and features the city's heterogeneous populace, including women and foreigners. These aspects mark points of similarity with city comedy, the genre that has received the lion's share of attention from scholars interested in literary London. As Henry Turner argues, in both domestic tragedy and city comedy, "specific, identifiable" locations in London "emerge as structuring principles for representational action … because these were the very sites in which the conflicts and fantasies of everyday urban life were taking place."[5] Domestic tragedy and city comedy differ, however, in the exact purposes to which these representations of urban life are put. City comedy resolves the concomitant conflicts of London's transformation into a global marketplace in terms of easy profit and civic incorporation, to take just two recent readings of the fantasy of city comedy.[6] Domestic tragedy privileges fatal conflicts that a self-policing metropolis resolves by preventing and punishing crime.

Significantly, these unique emphases are not mutually exclusive. Both kinds of London drama bring radical changes in the city's topography and population into the service of fantasies of normalcy and stability. More important, city comedy's placeless exchange is predicated upon domestic tragedy's placeless justice. Civic and economic prosperity may occur if and only if the metropolis is understood as a safe place in which to live and conduct business.

In scholarship on domestic tragedy the plays' metropolitan imperatives tend to take a backseat to their religious, social, and political investments.[7] Critical reception of the realistic representation of England's capital emphasizes domestic tragedy as a kind of didactic literature, an expression of early modern identity politics, and a reflection of dynamics in and between households and their analogical macrocosm, the state.[8] These emphases result in no small part from the identification of Thomas Heywood's *A Woman Killed with Kindness* (1607) as *the* definitive domestic tragedy. *A Woman Killed with Kindness* takes place exclusively in rural Yorkshire, a setting that, as Richard Rowland recently pointed out, was "geographically remote" and "topographically and culturally foreign" to Heywood's original (i.e., London) audiences.[9] For the original audiences of *A Warning for Fair Women* and *Two Lamentable Tragedies*, London was more geographically proximate than Yorkshire, yet quite likely many of these playgoers perceived England's capital as topographically and culturally foreign as the northern city. By setting domestic tragedy in and in relation to London, Heywood's fellow playwrights offered audiences a vision of the metropolis as still familiar and knowable.

This vision stood at odds with widespread perceptions of London as foreign terrain. These perceptions were the product of rapid changes in the metropolis's demography and topography in the sixteenth and seventeenth centuries. During this period, London's population grew three times as quickly as the rest of the nation's as immigrants moved to the capital from elsewhere in England and from the Continent. This demographic explosion and diversification, Keith Wrightson argues, put "considerable strain upon inherited social structures, values and social relations."[10] It also put pressure on London's medieval infrastructure. Within the City of London, new construction led to a multiplication of alleys, or "closes," and renovations to existing structures, in particular adding floors and dividing rooms, produced a proliferation of tenements, or "rents."[11] London's conurbation also expanded further into the northern and southern suburbs. In *A Survey of London* (1598, 1603)

John Stow describes neighbourhoods, once filled with trees, fields, and a smattering of houses, "nowe ... made a continuall building throughout" and "pestered with diuerse Allyes."[12] Urban congestion and sprawl turned London's once-familiar network of streets and neighbourhoods into an alien labyrinth. The aids familiar to modern-day city dwellers and tourists did not yet exist: the first London Directory appeared in 1677, and street signs and numbering became mandatory only in the 1760s. Consequently, England's capital became increasingly resistant to navigation, even among long-time inhabitants. A century before Reverend Robert Kirk described London as "a great vast wilderness" in which "[f]ew ... know the fourth of its streets," the metropolis could turn both denizens and visitors into strangers in a strange land.[13]

London's transformation provoked alarm from many quarters. Residents and city leaders expressed concerns about the impact of crowding and sprawl on law and order in the metropolis.[14] As Vanessa Harding shows, many Londoners feared that as the metropolis grew "relatively unchecked," so, too, would crime.[15] Paul Griffiths explains that civic authorities apprehended that "light, regulation, and citizens' routes" did not permeate London's nooks and crannies, which "appeared to turn off to all points of the compass, giving shelter to threatening 'sorts.'"[16] The records of London's Common Council and Bridewell Hospital anxiously note, for example, the growing number of "private" spaces, "secret corners," "close" passages, and "unknown places" where activity could be concealed from view.[17] For many Londoners, the metropolis was quickly becoming hostile territory.

Domestic tragedy, city comedy, London-based history plays, and urban chorography – all of which developed at the turn of the seventeenth century – offered London's heterogeneous audiences various ways to make sense of the changing cityscape. Indeed, the multiplicity and popularity of London genres points out a widespread perception of the metropolis as alien and threatening. Not only citizens and leaders but also immigrants, women, and other members of London's diverse population desired representations of the metropolis less anonymous and more coherent than the one they experienced. Notably, this populace is largely absent from domestic tragedy. Appearing most conspicuously in execution scenes, Londoners function less as deliberate agents of justice than as unwitting deputies of a self-policing city. Time and again, they stumble across opportunities to discover offenders, but, just as frequently, they fail to do so. Instead, deterrence, exposure, and punishment result from dramatic acts of location.

Domestic tragedy takes the cityscape as the "tangible referent" of transgression and order.[18] These plays deprive London's shady locales of their anonymity: they name Stow's "diuerse Allyes," open to view the Common Council's "secret corners," and render knowable the "unknown places" noted by Bridewell authorities. With the flagging of every nook and cranny of the dramatized metropolis, fewer narrow alleys and dark corners remain to conceal transgression. By representing London as geographically known, domestic tragedy invites audiences to imagine, if only for the duration of the theatrical performance, that the metropolis is itself judicially secure. This sanguine city portrait proved strikingly short-lived, however. In its representations of a recognizable, navigable, and preternaturally lawful metropolis, domestic tragedy co-opts the scopic regime by which civic and state authorities attempted to recuperate London's places of crime and sin. Dramatically, urban overgrowth ceases to be a source of "tragical incidents," and the metropolis assumes the comprehensible geography of placeless justice. Historically, this fantasy of absolute security could not keep pace with the realities of relentless upheaval and ongoing lawlessness.

"[T]his true and home-borne Tragedy"

In the Introduction to *A Warning for Fair Women* a personified Tragedy announces her "subject [is] too well knowne" to the playgoers "now in this round."[19] Tragedy's well-known subject is twofold: a series of historical events and an urban setting. *A Warning for Fair Women* portrays the 1573 murder of London merchant George Sanders and the executions of the principal murderer, George Browne, and his accessories, including Sanders's wife. Although the play was probably written and performed ten to fifteen years after these events, playgoers could have known about them from any number of sources.[20] Up to sixty years later, a range of publications continued to broadcast Sanders's murder and the perpetrators' punishments – from Thomas Lodge's *Wits Misery* (1596) to T.E.'s *The Law's Resolutions of Women's Rights* (1632), Thomas Heywood's *Troia Britanica* (1609) to John Stow's *Annales* (printed numerous times between 1580 and 1632, including two expanded editions by Edward Howes).[21] As much as the crimes and punishments represented in the play, the metropolis in which they took place is the well-known subject of *A Warning for Fair Women*. "Our Sceane is London, native and your owne" (l. 95), Tragedy explains in the Induction, and immediately upon her exit, George Sanders enters with his wife and several others, and says, "Gentlemen, *here* we take our leave" (l. 103, emphasis added). The Sanderses do not exit immediately, and ensuing dialogue defines "here" as England's capital. When Sanders asks Browne about Ireland, Browne replies that he is "no better knowne in London *here* / Than [he is] *there* unto the better sort, / Chiefely in Dubline" (ll. 109–11, emphasis added). Browne's acknowledgment of his fame in two capital cities underscores the play's setting: although Browne's reputation extends elsewhere, the dramatized action occurs specifically in London. Furthermore, it emphasizes that London is "here," an immediate and familiar metropolis, and not "there," a distant and unknown locale.[22] The subject of *A Warning for Fair Women* is well known, then, because it is a "true and home-borne Tragedy" (l. 2729), a relation of tragic action based in actual occurrences and set where many playgoers, even those born elsewhere, made their homes.

In its persistent claims to topical and spatial familiarity, *A Warning for Fair Women* threatens to communicate the exact opposite. Rather than convince playgoers of their knowledge of events and setting, the play gives an inkling of protesting too much.[23] The disparity between what individual playgoers may or may not know and what the play represents becomes evident as the plot shifts to criminal affairs. When Browne seeks advice from Anne Sanders's confidant, Anne Drury, and Drury's servant, Roger, the play introduces the three characters that eventually become accessories to George Sanders's murder in terms of the play's urban setting: Roger describes Drury as "as curteous a gentlewoman, as any is in London" (ll. 178–9); Drury introduces her servant as "trustie … As anie fellow within London walles" (ll. 187–8); and she portrays Anne Sanders as "As kind a peate [i.e., pet] as London can affoord" (l. 209).[24] Through these comparisons, *A Warning for Fair Women* insists that its characters are as familiar as its "Sceane." Yet as Roger, Drury, and Anne Sanders conspire to commit and conceal murder, the play exposes these flattering descriptions as counterfactual portraits. So, too, London as it emerges in the opening scenes is not the overgrown and incomprehensible city that many playgoers experienced on a daily basis.

The insistence upon familiarity continues to break down as the play juxtaposes places in the metropolis. In plotting the seduction of the merchant's wife, Drury directs Browne to watch for an "oportunitie" to speak with Anne Sanders when "her husband goes to the Exchange" and she "sit[s] at [the] doore" of her home (ll. 286–93). The former location, "the Exchange," receives no geographical, historical, or cultural gloss. The play takes for granted that playgoers – whether long-time residents of London, recent immigrants, or first-time visitors – will understand this allusion to the Royal Exchange. The representational energies of *A Warning for Fair Women* focus instead on the Sanderses' residence, the whereabouts of which would have been wholly unknown and must be charted through reference to a particular neighbourhood, streets, and structures. The juxtaposition is telling, not least because the Royal Exchange features so prominently in city comedies contemporaneous with *A Warning for Fair Women*. In these plays, as Jean Howard shows, the Royal Exchange functions as a locus of London's financial, mercantile, and "symbolic and psychic economies."[25] For example, in William Haughton's *Englishmen for My Money* (1598), the representation of the Royal Exchange as a "[coordinate] on the 'map' of London," in Crystal Bartolovich's words, constructs "an experience of London as a culturally triumphant safe haven from economic disruptiveness."[26] In *A Warning for Fair Women* the Royal Exchange serves to highlight a different set of theatrical priorities. The initial anonymity of Anne Sanders's "doore," in sharp contrast to the presumptive familiarity of the Royal Exchange, draws on a perceived link between topography and criminality. At the same time, *A Warning for Fair Women*'s dramatic mapping of transgression begins the work of inscribing law and order upon the metropolis.

The play makes the site of adultery legible twice: first, discursively; then, theatrically. When Browne is told that the Sanderses live in "Billingsgate-ward" (l. 257), the play locates the attempted seduction in a ward in eastern London, inside the ancient city walls and near the River Thames. Greater topographical precision is necessary to pin down the Sanderses' residence. Each of London's twenty-six wards had specific "bounds," yet according to Vanessa Harding, these jurisdictional boundaries became "increasingly meaningless as experienced spaces" due to the surge of construction in the sixteenth and seventeenth centuries.[27] At first, topographical precision is not forthcoming. When Browne inquires, "But where's [Anne Sanders's] house?," he receives the ambiguous reply: "Against *Saint Dunstones* church" (ll. 301–2). Not one but two Saint Dunston's churches stood in sixteenth-century London: one outside the city's western wall near Fleet Street, and the other in the eastern part of the city within the ward of Billingsgate. Seemingly forgetting the reference to Billingsgate Ward less than fifty lines earlier, Browne seeks clarification: "*Saint Dunstones* in Fleetestreete?," he asks, to which Drury responds, "No, neere Billingsgate, / *Saint Dunstones* in the East, thats in the West" (ll. 303–5). Once Drury names these well-known churches, street, and ward, they become points on a dramatized urban network that effectively locates the attempted seduction. By "mapping" the Sanderses' residence, *A Warning for Fair Women* not only offers the alternative topographical pleasures of novelty and familiarity. It also fulfills a desire for a cityscape more legible and more secure than the one beyond the theatre walls.

In staging the Sanderses' residence, the play shows spatial legibility frustrating illicit activity. Anne is discovered "sit[ting] / at her doore" on an "obscure street," and her physical solitude and indeterminacy render her available to Browne's intimate address (ll. 321–2 sd, 343). "Sit ye to take the view of passengers?," Browne asks, to which Anne replies: "I giue smal regard / Who comes, or goes, my husband I attend, / Whose comming wil be speedie from th' Exchange" (ll. 354–8). Anne's response undermines both Browne's intents and the premise for his query (i.e., just because she sits alone on her threshold does not mean she is interested in anything other than domestic matters). By framing her questionable solitary and liminal position in terms of appropriate wifely duty, it also draws attention to her confident authority over access to her residence and person.[28] Anne reiterates this conjunction of place and propriety when she insists to her husband that she is able to discern and regulate her "company" (l. 402). This ability seems a product of repeated trials upon her virtue. Anne describes Browne as just one of those "arrand-making Gallants" who walk London's streets and find excuses to chat up the women sitting at their doors (l. 394). Punning on "arrand," or errant, as both wandering and mistaking, the play depicts the public street as a frequent site for questionable behaviour and figures the threshold of the Sanderses' home as a place of resistance against roving, lustful interlopers. Over the course of *A Warning for Fair Women*, this conjunction of emplacement, supervision, and security comes to characterize the metropolis as a whole.

By pinpointing the locations of offence, *A Warning for Fair Women* constructs a sense of placeless justice similar in design to the scopic regime of London's judicial authorities. Drury's interference leads Anne Sanders to return Browne's advances, but Browne, unsatisfied with their adulterous relationship, wishes to marry Anne and makes three attempts on her husband's life. Browne trusts that London's secret corners and close paths will conceal his offence, yet each of these spaces becomes an identifiable place that thwarts crime. Browne's first attempt occurs in the evening as George Sanders walks home. Browne waits at "a corner" along the path that he believes his victim "should come" (ll. 904

sd–904). This shrouded urban crevice threatens to facilitate Browne's design, and only after the play literally and figuratively sheds light on the spot is murder averted. Sanders takes the predicted route, but at the moment "Browne drawes to strike," a gentleman enters with his servant and a torch (l. 924 sd). After identifying the gentleman as a friend, Sanders explains that he was "here at a friends of [his] in Lumbard streete" (l. 933). The men exit together, leaving Browne onstage to rail against the "light" of the torch and the "companie" that bears it for foiling his attempt (ll. 930, 954). According to Peter Lake, these mundane causes for the crime's delay signal the continued role of providence in post-Reformation popular theology. In *A Warning for Fair Women* and other domestic tragedies, Lake argues, divine intervention forces murderers "to commit the crime on home turf, in a context where anonymity and secrecy are virtually impossible."[29] My point is that recourse to a Christianized *deus ex machina* is unnecessary to make sense of the representation of murder in domestic tragedy. As the plays locate sites of attempted offence in relation to identifiable streets, neighbourhoods, and landmarks, the entire cityscape becomes, in Lake's phrase, "home turf." In the scene of Browne's first attempt on Sanders's life, murder is prevented as much by the figurative light shed by the naming of Lombard Street as by the literal light of a torch.

Significantly, the author of *A Warning for Fair Women* chose to set Browne's first attempt, which is not detailed in any account of Sanders's murder, on a well-known street with a singular, historically established name. According to Stow, it was named "for the Marchants of Florence, which proueth that street to haue had the name Lombard street before the raigne of *Edward* the second."[30] In contrast, many of the city's pathways had multiple names, their appellations changing with householders' signs, dominant trades, and other immediate associations. For example, Stow describes a lane in Billingsgate "called Rother Lane, or Red Rose Lane, of such a signe there, now commonly called Pudding Lane, because the Butchers of Eastcheape haue their scalding House for Hogges there, and their puddings with other filth of Beastes, are voided downe that way to theyr dung boates on the Thames."[31] Whereas staging Browne's first attempt along Lombard Street offers a vision of London as a network of definitive locations, citing a path such as Rother (or Rose or Pudding) Lane would gesture to the city's historically unstable topography. The metropolitan investments of theatrical tragedy emerge in the transformation of London's labyrinthine cityscape into a fantasy of urban knowledge.

If London's incomprehensible topography threatens a crime wave, its legibility promises the enforcement of law. This inversion of the source of real-world tragedy to the purposes of theatrical tragedy is evident in Browne's second attempt on Sanders's life. Undaunted by his initial failure, Browne tries again after Roger tracks Sanders throughout the City of London and its environs. In a lengthy speech Roger describes lying in wait, then frenetically chasing Sanders "too and fro" (l. 1138). From the Sanderses' home in Billingsgate, Roger follows Sanders to "a marchants warehouse" in "Cornhil," "[f]rom thence … to the Burse," then back home to dine, and finally to "Lion Key," where Sanders hires a boat to take him to "the court" at "Greenewitch" (ll. 1123–37).[32] Roger's account of clandestine surveillance may arouse fears of being hunted within London's urban wilderness. The legibility of the characters' itinerary displaces this anxiety and ultimately renders it a source of pleasure. In relating his travels, Roger persistently names renowned places in and around London that many residents and visitors could cognitively map with ease. For those who could not, this catalogue of places extends the dual pleasures of edification and a sense of belonging. Readily identified and imagined, the locations where Roger observes Sanders unawares would thus appear incapable of concealing urban predators. London's topography no longer endangers citizens but ensures their safety.

The play enhances this vision of the metropolis when Browne's murderous intent is again forestalled. While following Sanders around Greenwich, Roger overhears Sanders arrange to land "at Lion key this evening," and so returns to London to advise Browne on how he "might dispatch [Sanders] and escape unseene" (ll. 1144–5). Roger even recommends at which "corner" he and Browne should lie in wait, a location Browne "like[s] … well" because "tis darke and somewhat close, / By reason that the houses stand so neare" (ll. 1164–6). As in Browne's first attempt, the reference to lying in wait, undetected in a shadowy and narrow corner between close-standing tenements, suggests a cityscape that encourages illicit activity. But once again the play opens London's murky hideaways to view and murder is prevented. Browne gives the coordinates of the corner where he awaits his victim: he approves the spot Roger recommends because it not only conceals him but also places them "betwixt [Sanders's] house and him" whether "he should land at Billingsgate" or at Lion's Quay (ll. 1167–8). Once the play locates this corner in relation to both docks and the Sanderses' residence, it ceases to be an obscure and obscuring space. Just as topographical references mark the intended murder site within the play's urban image, a seemingly providential event does so within the play's plot. Anne Sanders enters on her way to meet her husband, inspiring Browne to curse, "A plague upon't, now am I prevented, / She being by, how can I murther him?" (ll. 1191–2). As in Browne's first attempt, the unexpected entrance of company ostensibly prevents murder. The topographical details that also mark both attempts demand that we read the scene differently. As characters (unwittingly) survey their quotidian itineraries, the play turns London's nondescript nooks and crannies into distinct sites of deterrence.

In *A Warning for Fair Women* the citation of place-names turns London's convoluted topography into a revelatory cityscape. As Browne bemoans his second foiled attempt, he stumbles upon a third opportunity to murder Sanders, and as Roger predicts, "The third time payes for all" (l. 1231). Rogers follows Sanders once again and learns how he intends to return to London. Whereas the previous two attempts are made at night and company enters unexpectedly, Browne makes his third attempt during the daytime (approximately 7:30 in the morning, l. 1346) and with foreknowledge of a third party's presence (John Beane, the servant of Sanders's host in Mary Cray, ll. 1323–6). Browne seems aware of these disadvantages and improvises strategies to deal with them. Without the dark of night to hide him, Browne attempts to "shrowd [him]selfe" behind some "bushes" (ll. 1349, 1362). As for Beane, Browne dismisses him as "that stripling" and orders Roger "unto the hedge corner / At the hill foote" to look out for additional passersby (ll. 1327–8). So when Sanders and Beane enter en route through the "wood," Browne, confident that vegetation and solitude will permit him to get away with murder, "steps out" and stabs both men (ll. 1353, 1372 sd). At first blush, the scene of homicide juxtaposes rural space, where crime occurs, to urban place, where crime had been prevented. Quite literally, the wood and not the street becomes the murder scene; bushes rather than corners conceal offenders, and desolation occasions that which habitation forestalls. But in terms of the play's broader spatial semiotics, Browne's success cannot be credited to a dearth of topographical specificity. It results, instead, from the scope of domestic tragedy's urban fantasy.

Before the double-homicide occurs, Browne and Roger's location remains relatively indeterminate. The title page of *A Warning for Fair Women* notes that Sanders is killed "nigh Shooters Hill," but the dialogue reveals merely that the murderers are somewhere between Woolwich and London and within sight of both "Greenwich parke" and "black heath" (l. 1330).[33] Only in the crime's *aftermath* does the play locate the murder site with greater precision. Upon reading a letter that describes Browne's "very bloudy act," a Lord exclaims, "Ev'n at the edge of Shooters hill, so neare?" (ll. 1674, 1683). Shooter's Hill lies in the county of Kent, south of and jurisdictionally separate from London; yet the Lord's exclamation gestures to its actual and perceived proximity to the city. At first blush, the Lord's "so neare?" refers to Greenwich (another Lord expresses amazement that murder was "committed in eye of Court," l. 1675), suggesting that a citizen's murder is a state problem. Yet the pervasive references to urban places endorse a different reading: "at the edge of Shooters hill" functions as a euphemism for "at the edge of London." Whereas growth within London's walls produced nooks and crannies that promised to conceal offenders, London's expansion made extramural crime a metropolitan issue. In *A Warning for Fair Women* the fantasy of a legible and secure cityscape requires the conurbation be brought under the judicial gaze of the metropolis.

Whereas the return to the metropolis (which is the focus of chapter 2) might seem to expose the limits of London's placeless justice, in the transformation of the murder scene into the site of discovery and punishment, *A Warning for Fair Women* extends its urban fantasy to a swelling conurbation. After Browne fatally wounds Sanders and Beane, Sanders dies almost immediately, but Beane survives to identify his and Sanders's killer. Shooter's Hill then serves as the setting for Browne's postmortem suffering. Tried, sentenced, and executed onstage, Browne is condemned to have his "bodie be convaide to Shooters hill, / And there hung up in Chaines" (ll. 2482–3). The mortifying display of criminals' bodies was a penalty in and of itself, as the play emphasizes through Browne's repeated appeals for immediate burial. It served, as well, to publicize to passersby that a community would not allow transgression to go undetected or unpunished. Though at first an imprecise space that facilitates murder, Shooter's Hill is reclaimed as a place that relentlessly reveals crime.

In domestic tragedy, as in other modes of metropolitan tragedy, the conditions of life in England's capital become formal strategies for the representation of justice. Although murder among neighbours and family members was actually quite rare in early modern London, the popular perception was that domestic crime occurred frequently in the metropolis. The discrepancy between actual and perceived crime rates has been credited to representations of a few sensational crimes, including the dramatization of George Sanders's murder in *A Warning for Fair Women*.[34] This argument assumes that identifications of where crime happened before, and therefore may happen again, stir up only panic and paranoia. However, there is also the entertainment value of literature that, in Cynthia Marshall's words, "repackage[s] the inequities and horrors of everyday life."[35] On London's commercial stages, dramatizations of real-world violence elicited "the elements of anxiety- and pleasure-ridden fantasy" and "the ambivalent mixture of desire and fear," as Peter Lake and Margaret Owens explain.[36] I have argued that the pleasure afforded by domestic tragedy results from its imitation of theatrical transgression within a fantasy of urban space.[37] During the play's three-hours traffic upon the stage, London did not undergo a physical transformation, but perceptions of the cityscape may have. By constructing a *fantasy* of urban legibility, domestic tragedy makes it possible for playgoers to imagine the metropolis as *actually* more knowable and secure.

Revisiting the City and the Country

Like *A Warning for Fair Women*, Robert Yarington's *Two Lamentable Tragedies* repurposes early modern London's topography from the grounds for "actual" tragedy to a foundation of theatrical pleasure. As its title suggests, and its running title – *Two Tragedies in One* – makes clear, Yarington's play incorporates two plots. One plot is set in London, the other near Padua. The London plot would have been familiar to many in the play's original audiences. This plot dramatizes the 1594 murder of Robert Beech and his servant by tavern-owner Thomas Merry and the hangings of the principal murderer and his sister, who is condemned as an accessory. News of these events spread via a pamphlet account of infamous criminal events entitled *A World of Wonders, A Mass of Murders* (1595) as well as five ballads, a "booke," and a play by William Haughton and John Day (all now lost).[38] Once scholars determined the real-life events dramatized in the London plot, they began to search for the Paduan plot's source. In her critical edition of the play, Anne Patenaude appraises several possibilities, then concludes: "[U]ntil firm evidence appears to link the orphan plot to any source, all hypotheses remain pure conjecture."[39] I propose that this lack of an identifiable source may be precisely the point. *Two Lamentable Tragedies* strategically omits the topical and topographical specificity of its London plot from its Paduan plot.[40] Not only is there no source for the Paduan plot; audiences should recognize this indeterminacy. Through contrast to an unknown rural space, the familiar metropolis emerges in *Two Lamentable Tragedies* as a highly particularized locale with judicial efficacies of its own.

This contrast is already evident in the play's full title: *Tvvo lamentable tragedies. The one, of the murther of Maister Beech a chaundler in Thames-streete, and his boye, done by Thomas Merry. The other of a young childe murthered in a Wood by two Ruffins, with the consent of his Vnckle.* "Thames-streete" can be distinguished from other streets in a manner that "a Wood" cannot be from other dense growths of trees. So, too, proper names individualize the victim and offender in the London plot while the "young childe," "Vnckle," and "two Ruffins" of the Paduan plot remain anonymous. In due course audiences learn the names of the Paduan victim and principal offender: Fallerio hires assassins to murder his nephew, Pertillo, to secure Pertillo's inheritance for himself and his son, Allenso. Yet the play denies audiences the place-name of the crime scene. Without fail, throughout the Paduan plot, offenders, victim, and officials alike occupy unspecified spaces. The play's Induction establishes this vague Italian landscape when a personified Truth is incongruously circumspect about the location of Pertillo's murder. Truth reveals only that "the young childe['s]" murder occurs "Neere *Padua*," and then adds, in a mischievous tautology, that this setting is "further off" from audiences than is the site of Thomas Merry's offences, that is, London.[41] Even as the play stages Pertillo's murder, the setting remains uncertain. The only location-specific clue is Fallerio's command that the assassins kill the boy at "a thicket ten miles from this place" (sig. D1v). Audiences are left to wonder even the general direction of this thicket when Fallerio feigningly announces, "I haue deuisde to send the boye abroade, / With this excuse, to haue him fostred, / In better manners then this place affords" (sig. D1v). Subsequently, the play discloses that Fallerio purportedly sends his nephew "abroade" to Padua.[42] This information proves not particularly helpful, however, for the play continues to withhold the name of Pertillo's starting point ("this place"). These bits of information, like "a Wood" and "Neere *Padua*," leave the crime scene quite nebulous; it is somewhere between an obscure place of origin and a generalized Paduan destination. The site of Pertillo's murder could be any wood – near Padua or elsewhere, for that matter.

Of course, neither Yarington nor many in his original audiences had likely travelled to Italy, let alone Padua. However, they had access to information from which to construct a mental map of this foreign metropolis and its environs. In the late sixteenth and early seventeenth centuries scholars, statesmen, and entertainers brought information about Padua to England, where it spread through manuscript accounts, casual conversation, and popular literature.[43] Shakespeare's comedies, for example, illustrate a popular association of Padua with education and beauty.[44] Travelogues, such as Fynes Moryson's *An Itinerary* (1617) and Thomas Coryate's *Coryats Crudities* (1611), filled out readers' imagined cartographies with particularities of the cityscape, including Padua's "forme," landmarks, streets, gates, and suburbs.[45] Significantly, no such detail makes its way into Yarington's play, and his Italian characters inhabit a strikingly featureless landscape. This spatial indeterminacy is exactly the point, for the Paduan plot serves primarily as a foil to the place-specific London plot.

Yarington's comparative approach in *Two Lamentable Tragedies* parallels the spatial strategies of contemporary dramatists. Early modern playwrights routinely used Italian settings as a way to comment on English events, issues, and values.[46] When plays represent Italy as a fount of freedom and humanism, English restraint and provincialism are implicit targets of critique. England appears to greater advantage in plays that represent Italy's more unsavoury associations with Machiavellian stratagems, clandestine violence, and promiscuous vice. Printed the same year as *Two Lamentable Tragedies* (1601), the Quarto version of Ben Jonson's *Every Man In His Humour* takes place in Florence, a locale that "rendered 'safe'" for Elizabethan audiences the play's satirical representation of social behaviour.[47] The version of *Every Man In* that appears in Jonson's 1616 Folio is set in a highly particularized London. By this time, and in no small part due to Jonson's influence, England's metropolis had become a familiar setting for comic representations of how men and women conduct themselves in society.[48] In Yarington's domestic tragedy we find a transitional moment between Elizabethan and Jacobean sensibilities. The conjunction of Italian and English settings reveals that Italy does not hold a monopoly on deception and murder.[49] Descriptions of the Paduan crime scene even evoke contemporary accounts of London's alienating topography: Pertillo's murder takes place in a "woody sauadge labyrinth," an "erroneous winding wilderness," so full of "thickets" and "vnknowne pathes" that one "can finde no way to issue out" (sig. F1r). If *Two Lamentable Tragedies* portrays Italy and England as comparable dens of iniquity, it also shows the sylvan but not the urban setting frustrating the discovery of crime. By mapping judicial practice onto civic places that audiences would recognize – and by omitting place-realism from the representation of foreign, rural space – Yarington's play renders safe the representation of a "recent tragical incident."

Through the juxtaposition of the Italian countryside and the English metropolis, *Two Lamentable Tragedies* highlights domestic tragedy's particularly urban investments – investments also evident in plays that are set elsewhere in England but locate their tragic action in relation to London.[50] In the anonymous *Arden of Faversham* Arden's murder ultimately occurs in his home in Faversham, yet several attempts are made on his life in London, where he stays "in Aldergate street," eats at "the Nag's Head" tavern in Cheapside, and conducts his business at "Paul's."[51] The play also highlights the proximity between Faversham and London – between the sites of successful transgression and of truncated attempts – through references to several locations on the route from one to the other, including Rochester, Rainham Down, Sittingburgh, and Gadshill.[52] Through more indirect references, Rowley, Dekker, and Ford's *The Witch of Edmonton* relates its immediate setting to London. For instance, to defend Dog, the demonic familiar who facilitates the crimes represented in the play, the naive Young Banks cites well-known venues in London, including Paris Garden, Newgate, Temple Bar, and St Dunstan's Church in the East.[53] Not all domestic tragedies name specific sites in London, of course. The anonymous *A Yorkshire Tragedy*, for instance, refers simply to generalized "London" and only in its opening scene. Yet in this seventy-six-line introduction, the play's setting, referred to only as "here," is related to England's capital no less than nine times (less one reference in a stage direction).[54] This is particularly striking because the emphasis in the play's title is on the dramatic setting *there*, in the far north of England, and not *here*, in or near London where the play was performed. By topographically pinpointing the dual actions of crime and detection in or in relation to England's capital city, these plays also revise the anxieties of real-life violence into the pleasures of urban fantasy.

The juxtaposition of the city and the countryside works differently in city comedy. In Thomas Dekker's *The Shoemaker's Holiday*, for example, the representation of rural space is bound up with the competing temporalities of early modern London. Jonathan Gil Harris argues that Dekker's references to Ludgate disclose a "contradictory logic" of "antiquarian and mercantile sensibilities," and Erika Lin shows how allusions to the places of the play's performance expose tensions between the calendars of festive and commercial theatre.[55] These different kinds of time are also evident outside the city. At Old Ford, the Lord Mayor's extramural estate, his daughter weaves a flower garland for her aristocratic beloved and a well-to-do citizen hunts deer but stumbles upon a dear. In these scenes, the conventions of pastoral – idyllic setting, springtime activity, romantic love – put into relief the continuities and ruptures in civic identity and seasonal practice that elsewhere in the play emerge in terms of London locales, including the marketplace and the playhouse.

Printed about a year after Dekker's city comedy, Yarington's domestic tragedy uses urban and rural spaces to highlight a related set of concerns. In the Paduan plot, Fallerio's unnatural acts of greed and homicide – Pertillo is, after all, his ward and nephew – occur in an inverted pastoral setting. As Allenso "circl[es]" through a "winding wildernesse" in search of his cherished cousin, and the Duke's hunt concludes not with a dead "hare" but with a murdered heir (sig. F1r), the Italian woods seem to conform to human deviance. In the London plot, Thomas Beech commits an analogous offence when he kills his neighbour and customer for financial gain. London's competing temporalities, which are audible in references to specific weekdays, hours, even Bartholomew's Day, arguably call attention to the economic roots of uncivic behaviour. However, Yarington's representation of the places of crime and punishment activates another temporality in which opportunistic crime is inevitably followed by discovery and punishment. The cityscape refuses to aid and abet offences that put strain on traditional social dynamics and emerging commercial relations in England's metropolis.

With the juxtaposition of the city and the country, Yarington takes a different approach to the representation of crime than the writer of *A Warning for Fair Women*. Both plays introduce extra-urban crime scenes in terms of imprecise deictic references and without place-names. Likewise, both plays present the discovery of murder as accidental. Allenso stumbles upon the "murtherous spectacle" of the bloody bodies of Pertillo and the assassins, who turn on one another after stabbing the boy (sig. F1v). One assassin briefly survives his wounds – just long enough, in fact, to point the finger at his employer. The discovery of murder and its architect does little to quell anxieties evoked by the representation of violent crime, however. Whereas *A Warning for Fair Women* ultimately identifies the site of Sanders's murder, thus incorporating it into a dramatically preternatural cityscape, *Two Lamentable Tragedies* leaves the site of Pertillo's murder unknown. Unable to place the Paduan plot, audiences must remain doubtful that the detection of illicit activity is at all inevitable. Even condemnation provides insufficient relief, for the scaffold also eludes placement. The play neither identifies the location of "the place [of execution]" (sig. K1v) nor shows Allenso and Fallerio die or the latter "hang in chaines" (sig. I4v). The Paduan plot, which begins in a vague locale and unfolds amidst the confusion of an Italian wood, ends in a judicial no-place. Unlike *A Warning for Fair Women*, which recuperates Shooter's Hill within a network of identifiable urban places, Yarington's Italian landscape frustrates a desire for legibility and security.

In *Two Lamentable Tragedies* Padua's not-so-pristine wilderness shows to advantage London's charted corners and exposed alleyways. Whereas Italy's confused and confusing woods are conducive to crime, England's legible metropolis relentlessly exposes crime. When Thomas Merry plans to murder Robert Beech "in [his] garret," he gloats, "The night conceales all in her pitchie cloake, / And none can open what I meane to hide" (sig. B3r). Thomas's confidence is misplaced, and recalling Browne's foiled attempts on Sanders's life in *A Warning for Fair Women*, Yarington's play brings the crime scene to light. A literal light is shed on homicide when Thomas's sister, Rachel, brings a candle so he and Beech need not "tarry in the darke" (sig. B4r). Topographical details shed light of another sort on Beech's death. Truth explains that this "cursed deede" occurs "Within that streete whose side the riuer Thames / Doth striue to wash from all impuritie" (sig. A3r). Thames Street is a rather lengthy thoroughfare, running through seven of London's wards. By naming the Merrys' tavern-home, "the Bull" (sig. B4r), the play begins to pinpoint where along Thames Street Thomas's first crime takes place. Around the turn of the seventeenth century, at least nine establishments went by the name of the Bull, or the frequently interchangeable names Bull Head and Bull's Head. In fact, extant records indicate that about fifty years after Thomas Merry died for his crimes, a Bull Inn stood on Thames Street.[56] Whether or not this inn is the same Bull that Thomas Merry historically operated is less important than that by naming "the Bull," *Two Lamentable Tragedies* offers one critical piece of information needed to locate the scene of Beech's murder.

In dramatically locating this historical "tragical incident" Yarington takes the difficulties of urban navigation as a source of urban fantasy. In early modern London, an establishment by the name of the Bull would have had jutting out from its side a sign representing either a whole bull, a bull's head with or without horns, or only horns. Such images served, as one historian of London signage explains, "to indicate a location in streets without numbers, and as a means of identification of a residence or a tradesman when few people were capable of reading a name."[57]

However, because numerous establishments could use the same sign, additional information, such as a street name or an adjacent landmark, would have been necessary to find a particular business or household. An illustrative example of this chorographic means of location appears on the title page of Yarington's play: *Two Lamentable Tragedies* was "Printed for Mathew Lawe, and to be solde at his shop in Paules Church-yarde neere vnto S. Austines gate, at the signe of the Foxe." Three topographical markers – a famous churchyard, a particular gate, and a specific sign – help place Mathew Lawe's shop. In a similar fashion, Yarington's play locates the Merrys' tavern-home by situating it along Thames Street and naming its sign. In this way, even though the crime takes place in a dark garret, a space that pointedly evokes the disordered build-up of contemporary London, the play spotlights the site of murder.

Two Lamentable Tragedies creates a counterfactual image of England's metropolis by persistently linking place-names to the exposure of illicit activity. As Thomas Merry tries repeatedly to cover up Beech's murder, London proves a legible network of places that discovers transgression. Thomas worries that Beech's servant, Winchester, can identify the Bull as the last place where Beech would have been seen alive.[58] Thomas intends to seal this potential leak of incriminating evidence by killing Winchester, but his second murder becomes a veritable geyser. When Thomas attacks Winchester, the servant cries out, "rais[ing] the neighbours round about the street" and calling attention to their location "neere Lambert Hill," a well-known district located along Thames Street (sigs. C4v, G1r; see also I2v, I4r). Thomas's next step is to dismember Beech's body and dispose of the parts in "*Paris-garden* ditch" and "some darke place nere to Bainardes castle" (sigs. E2r, F3v). Yet both places discover their bloody contents to passersby. Two watermen walking along the "narrow lane / Neere Bainardes Castle" literally stumble upon Beech's legs and head, and a gentleman, inspired by his dog's barking and fawning, "make[s] the ditch be dragd, / Where then was found" Beech's trunk and arms (sigs. G1v–G2v). As the city disgorges this gruesome evidence, place-names associated with the concealment of murder become coupled with its detection, as well.

Despite these revelations, the murderer escapes detection, due largely to human ineptitude. Literally, London's denizens fail to see what the cityscape brings to light. A neighbour who witnesses Winchester's murderer leaving the crime scene cannot identify him, claiming "twas so darke [she] could see no bodie" (sig. C3v). The other neighbours prove wholly ineffective detectives: they conduct a supposedly thorough search of the neighbourhood but find no evidence of the murderer (sigs. D3r, D4r). When Beech's trunk is found in a bag still bearing the "marke" of its seller, the neighbours track down "the Salters man that solde the bag" and convince him to "Go round about to euery neighbors house" (sigs. G2v, G3r). When the Salter comes to the Merrys' tavern-home, he fails to recognize Rachel as the woman to whom he sold the bag, and despite a search of the Bull, the neighbours unearth no new clues. The inability of Londoners to discover the murderer highlights the play's specifically topographical fantasy. Whereas human efforts fall short of exposing Thomas's guilt, the cityscape persistently divulges incriminating evidence.

Against the lived experience of London's growing size and complexity, domestic tragedy presents a metropolis that will not permit transgression to remain hidden. Both *A Warning for Fair Women* and *Two Lamentable Tragedies* redeploy the familiar maxim of "murder will out" to the purposes of urban fantasy. Proverbial in England since the fifteenth century, this maxim frequently yoked place and providence. As Alexandra Walsham explains, "topographical legends current in the Elizabethan and early Stuart period … embodied a belief that God literally inscribed His judgements on the landscape."[59] In domestic tragedy the cityscape does not simply disclose God's judgments but actually executes them by bringing offenders to justice. In *A Warning for Fair Women*, after he stabs George Sanders, Browne worries that "the very bushes will discover [him]," and upon learning of Browne's bloody deed, Anne Sanders exclaims that "the very stones / That lie within the streetes cry out vengeance, / And point at us to be the murderers" (*Warning* ll. 1401, 1668–70). Despite Browne's apprehensions of an accusatory cityscape, neither shrubs nor cobblestones reveal his guilt; instead, Beane's bleeding wounds and dying words point to the murderer. Yet the play implicitly shifts back responsibility to urban place through a comparison of Browne's exposure to another instance in which London refused to conceal a murderer (ll. 2027–35).[60] Similarly, in the London plot of *Two Lamentable Tragedies*, the discovery of Beech's remains promises but fails to lead to the murderer's arrest. Instead, it is a discussion of urban place that ultimately brings Thomas Merry to justice. After Beech's murder, Harry Williams, Thomas's servant, flees the Bull and takes up residence at the Three Cranes (sigs. C1r, D3v). When asked why he does not return "vnto [his] maisters house," Williams lets slip Thomas's guilt (sig. H3r). In both plays the exposure of guilt hinges upon Londoners' physical and discursive negotiation of a legible cityscape. The dramatic fictions of domestic tragedy reorganize the metropolis's concomitant human and environmental energies to a fantasy of urban security.

The representation of punishment reinforces London's preternatural justice. At the end of *Two Lamentable Tragedies*, Truth introduces the scenes of execution with a couplet that conjoins the Paduan and London plots in terms of judicial procedure: "Heere comes the Duke that doomes them both [Allenso and Fallerio] to die, / Next *Merries* death shall end this Tragedie" (sig. K2r). As we have seen, in the Paduan plot, "Heere" continues to resist placement; like the "woody" site of murder, the "tree of infamie" (sig. I2v) on which father and son die remains elusive. By contrast, Smithfield, the historical place of the Merrys' execution, although not identified in the dialogue, is represented onstage: "*Enter* Merry *and* Rachel *to execution with Officers with Halberdes, the Hangman with a lather, &c.*" (sig. K1v).[61] After brother and sister mount the ladder and hang, the Officer pronounces the siblings' ultimate doom:

> Cut down their bodies, giue hers funerall,
> But let his body be conueyed hence,
> To Mile-end greene, and there be hang'd in chaines. (sig. K2v)

First visually, then verbally, the play makes London's scaffolds theatrically present onstage. Unlike the explicit Italian "Heere," in which justice is confined to the dramatic representation, an implicit English "here" is constructed in performance. The place of theatrical tragedy becomes momentarily legible *as* a place of judicial procedure. Genre and geography come together in a theatrical vision of a secure metropolis.

The dynamics of form and space take on new meaning in the play's final scene. After she dismisses Covetousness and Homicide from "heare," Truth boasts:

> My selfe will bring your close designes to light,
> And ouerthrow your vilde conspiracies,
> No hart shall intertaine a murthrous thought,
> Within the sea imbracing continent,
> Where faire *Eliza* Prince of pietie,
> Doth weare the peace adorned Diadem. (sig. K3r)

These lines narrow the geographical scope of Yarington's representation: "heare" is no longer two locales – one Italian, the other English – but exclusively London. At the same time, England's metropolis assumes greater legal responsibility. The *camera regia* is associated with the monarch as source of "pietie" and "peace," or as enforcer of virtuous and lawful behaviour. Other modes of metropolitan tragedy figure the city as the locus of imperial ruin, tyrannical violence, and cosmic catastrophe. Domestic tragedy stands out, then, not simply for its formal innovations and its London-specific setting. It is unique, as well, in its fantasy of the metropolis as an effective force for justice. London ensures law and order within and beyond its walls by bringing to light adultery, theft, murder, treason – any offence that threatens England's peace and prosperity.

The View from Shooter's Hill

By the second decade of the seventeenth century, domestic tragedy had largely disappeared from the commercial stage, and the energy of dramatizing London passed to city comedy. The brief heyday of domestic tragedy could be ascribed to the way it packages and sells the metropolis. In her analysis of cultural tourism in London's liberties, Mary Bly uses city comedy to show how site-specific theatre commodifies geographical knowledge. By "rework[ing] the place myth of the district in an attempt to fasten onto the symbolic economy that drew people to the liberty," Bly argues, "plays create a dreamscape ..., a staged inauthenticity that celebrates as it sells."[62] The metropolitan tragedies examined in this chapter offer both support for and a caveat to Bly's argument. On the one hand, *A Warning for Fair Women* and *Two Lamentable Tragedies* activate "urban memory" in relation to "London's contemporary preoccupations," specifically concerns related to crime in an increasingly alien cityscape.[63] These plays thus point up metropolitan tragedy's "inculcat[ion of] a kind of city knowledge" that is not necessarily available in other forms, including city comedy.[64] On the other hand, the city knowledge that domestic tragedy inculcates is not exactly cultural tourism. The plays were not performed in the same neighbourhoods as the crimes and punishments that they represent.[65] Moreover, for all its emphasis on locality, domestic tragedy brings London's particular places of crime and punishment into the service a more expansive fantasy of the self-policing cityscape. What domestic tragedy sells is not so much "place myth" as a broader myth of the early modern metropolis.

Figure 2: Shooter's Hill. *The View of the Cittye of London from the North towards the South*, anonymous engraving (circa 1600–13), detail. Utrecht University Library, Gr. form. 12. Reproduced with permission from Utrecht University Library.

This metropolitan myth is evident, as well, in London's established judicial procedures. *The View of the Cittye of London from the North towards the South* (circa 1600–13), a rare profile of early modern London's northern suburbs, offers a telling portrait of London's legal geography (Figure 2). In the foreground of *The View of the Cittye* is an amphitheatre playhouse that may be the Curtain or the Theatre.[66] Both theatres were used by the Lord Chamberlain's Men in the mid- and late-1590s and therefore are possible locations for performances of *A Warning for Fair Women*. In the background of *The View of the Cittye,* Shooter's Hill is visible. At first blush, the inclusion of Shooter's Hill conforms to Henry Peacham's instructions on portraying landscapes in *The art of drawing* (1606):

> for example [if] I should Draw the citty of *London,* I would beside the citty it selfe, shew in vacant places (as far as my table or Horizon would giue me leaue) the Country round about, as Shooters hill, ... which [places] are beside my purpose, because I was tied to nothing but the city itselfe: [yet inclusion of] this kind of all other is most pleasing, because it feedeth the eie with varietie.[67]

Like Peacham's hypothetical city portrait, *The View of the Cittye* includes "places ... round about" London, both its suburbs and neighbouring counties. In so doing, *The View of the Cittye* (contra Peacham) illustrates the extent to which "the Country" was increasingly "tied to ... the cittye itself."[68] In the case of Shooter's Hill, *The View of the Cittye* produces an illusion of geographical proximity between possible places of *A Warning for Fair Women*'s performance and the place of crime and punishment represented in the play. Of course, Shooter's Hill, which stood southeast of London in the county of Kent, was nowhere near either the Curtain or the Theatre. In fact, the Globe, which stood eight miles from Shooter's Hill and is a third possible location for the play's performance, was closer to the historical scene of homicide and post-mortem display than either of the northern suburban theatres. *The View of the Cittye* occludes these distances and visually evokes the same immediacy as the Lord's "so near" in *A Warning for Fair Women*.

This sense of proximity signals the compass of official scopic regimes. Shooter's Hill, although part of an aesthetically "pleasing" prospect, was also a principal place from which to take in the view of the city and the country. In 1522 John Fitzherbert wrote that from "Shotershyll" one could "ouer loke the cytie," albeit at a distance that would prevent a precise survey of London's "goodly stretes" and "fayre buyldings."[69] In the section of Holinshed's *Chronicles* (1577) titled "Of the ayre and soyle of Britaine," we read that "[t]he whole Isle ... is full of hilles, ... as wée may sée by Shooters hill," which rolling landscape extends "from the Thames ... along the south side of the Island westward" and "into the borders of Scotlande."[70] This outlook presumably informed Elizabeth's habit of greeting visiting ambassadors atop Shooter's Hill. From here they could take in London's splendour and industry as well as England's geographical scope and natural resources. Shooter's Hill provided a vantage point for authoritative oversight of both "the cytie" and "the whole Isle."

Shooter's Hill also had less celebrated associations. In a letter contemporaneous with the crimes represented *A Warning for Fair Women*, William Burleigh writes, "Here hath been a murther committed about Shooters-hill, somewhat to the reproof of this place."[71] Indeed, George Browne's offence contributed to perceptions of Shooter's Hill not as a locus of official scopic regimes but as a setting for robbery and murder. Shooter's Hill is not unique in its notoriety: Gadd's Hill, Salisbury Plain, and Hyde Park Corner also became known as places where the unwary traveller might lose his purse and even his life. Yet Shooter's Hill arguably becomes the most infamous. A range of early modern texts identifies Shooter's Hill as *the* place where desperate lovers, down-and-out soldiers, and former servants lie in wait for potential victims.[72] Within a few years of George Sanders's murder, William Whetstone, best known as the writer of *A Mirour for Magestrates of Cyties* (1584), poetically described a wanton prodigal who, to appease "Cupides brands," risks "death ... hanging on a tree [i.e., a gallows]" by "purchas[ing] pence, on top of Shooters hill."[73] Around the same time as the possible first performance of *A Warning for Fair Women*, Thomas Harman illustrated his definition of "A Ruffer," which comes down to "he [who] hath serued in the warres, or els ... ben a seruing man" and turns to "robb[ing] and steal[ing]," with a tale of theft on Shooter's Hill.[74] State officials also cited the crimes perpetrated atop Shooter's Hill. During Henry VIII's reign, when the clergy defended their spiritual autonomy on the basis of custom, Sir Thomas Aubrey purportedly asked: "The vsage hath euer beene of théeues to rob on Shooters hill, ergo is it lawfull?"[75] Amidst the heightened political tensions of the mid-seventeenth century, opponents of ecclesiastical and monarchical privilege cited Aubrey's question in defence of the law over "tyrant custom."[76] By the time London played host to royal execution, Shooter's Hill was a geographical and discursive *topos* for impassioned violations of law rather than its circumspect enforcement.

A Warning for Fair Women attempts to recuperate Shooter's Hill as a space of judicial oversight. Historically, officials pursued this project through established procedures of justice in early modern London. By converting the crime scene into a site of post-mortem punishment, state and civic authorities framed the prospect from Shooter's Hill in terms of their own scopic regime. Within the dramatization of one such "tragical incident," recuperation hinges upon a different set of formal practices and effects. The play uses the innovative idioms of place-realism to redistribute the preternatural powers of surveillance and enforcement. A self-policing metropolis, rather than urban denizens and leaders, ensures peace and prosperity through "the cytie" and the "whole Isle." In its fantasy of urban space, domestic tragedy apprehends a principal concept in the modern discipline of urban semiotics. According to Michel de Certeau and Kevin Lynch, among others, the city becomes safe for human activity when it is available to textual representation and mental comprehension. If in city comedy, as Adam Zucker argues, "juridical fantasies" of "stasis and orderly arrangement" hinder commercial and civic pursuits, in domestic tragedy a complementary judicial fantasy makes possible the hustle and bustle of urban life.[77] Domestic tragedy imaginatively constructs the lawful, secure metropolis in which the characters of city comedy may pursue profit and pleasure.

However complementary these theatrical visions of early modern London, domestic tragedy enjoyed a considerably briefer heyday than city comedy. One explanation for this disparity is domestic tragedy's conjunction of a "new" mode of dramatic representation and "old" theatrical efficacies.[78] In particular, the place-realism of domestic tragedy resists reconciliation with the plays' allegorical landscapes. In *A Warning for Fair Women,* with its emphasis on the concealing bushes at the site of Sanders's murder, the defeat of error coincides with the transformation of this rural space into the known and knowable urban place of Shooter's Hill. *Two Lamentable Tragedies* concludes with a similar effect, when not an errant knight but the metropolis itself champions England's fair queen in the inevitable triumph of peace and piety. In these plays the contest between virtue and vice unfolds in realistic cityscapes imbued with judicial authority and moral force. This fantasy of a legible and self-policing cityscape simply could not keep pace with urban change as the presumptive source of "actual" tragedy. Throughout the period, rates of demographic and topographic growth did not slow down, rendering implausible any holistic vision of the metropolis. The dramatization of London's alien terrain thus fell to comedy, which proved more commercially successful in its conjunction of innovative and conventional modes of representation.[79]

Tragedy did not secede its investments in the metropolis, of course. In the 1590s, at the same time as London's physical growth gave rise to new dramatic forms, its emergence as an imperial centre occasioned the revival of the classical genre of revenge tragedy. Early modern London showed all the signs of realizing the ancient promise of *translatio imperii,* or translation of empire, according to which England was rightful inheritor of the great empires of the past. This same promise of cultural, political, and literary eminence also brought with it a possible return of metropolitan catastrophe – civic upheaval, foreign invasion, and infrastructural ruin.[80] In the next chapter I show that English revenge tragedy links this recursive history to the repetitive violence of revenge. Often set in thinly veiled versions of London, these plays enact the historical and formal returns of *translatio imperii* and revenge as embodied returns to the metropolis. This fraught urban vision endured long after domestic tragedy's counterfactual portrait faded from view, due in part to a similar reason for London comedy's success. Revenge tragedy reconciles form and history, even as it threatens more, not fewer, "tragical incidents" in the metropolis.

Chapter Two

Translatio Metropolitae and Early English Revenge Tragedy

For now me thinkes I once againe behold
That famous Troy in flaming fier burne,
...
Nay more, the funerall and buriall day
Of countrey, citie, London, now the seate
Of English Kings that Brittish Scepter sway.

– Francis Herring, *Popish pietie, or The first part of the historie of that horrible and barbarous conspiracie, commonly called the powder-treason* (1610)

Ancient tragedy, according to classicist Simon Goldhill, functions as "a machine to turn epic myth into the myths of the *polis*."[1] Goldhill's myth-making machine found an outlet in the revival of ancient tragedy on the early modern English stage. The resurgence of revenge tragedy in England coincided with the heyday of domestic tragedy. As we saw in the previous chapter, although domestic tragedy deploys allegory in a manner reminiscent of epic romance, it privileges the innovative theatrical idioms in its London fantasy. By contrast, revenge tragedy brings epic myth into the service of England's imperial ambitions. In particular, it reflects perceptions of London's emergence as a hub of international politics, commerce, and culture as confirmation of the classical project of *translatio imperii*, or translation of empire, according to which the achievements of ancient empires – whether Troy or Rome or Jerusalem – became England's rightful inheritance. Alongside this bluntly teleological movement, revenge tragedy enacts the recursive violence that historically attends the translation of empire. London's rise to international prominence promised not simply achievement; it also threatened rebellion and ruin. Early modern English revenge tragedy enacts this alternative trajectory of *translatio metropolitae*, or translation of the metropolis, in which the return of imperial eminence coincides with the return of metropolitan tragedy.

Historically and theatrically, empire and metropolis are bound up with one another. In the ancient world the metropolis functioned, in Emrys Jones's words, "like the hub of a wheel," creating "an interdependence of the centre and the territory it control[s]."[2] Early modern London and a budding British empire shared such a relationship.[3] An illustration of this interdependence appears in Francis Herring's verse (if not exactly poetic) account of the Gunpowder Plot. If the plotters had succeeded in blowing up the Parliament building, Herring explains, they would have brought about "The cities ruines, and the Realmes decay" – that is, the toppling of not only an eminent urban edifice but also the larger political and geographical entity that it represents.[4] In the stanzas that serve as an epigraph to this chapter, Herring states more bluntly the far-reaching consequences of tragic events in England's capital. After comparing "London the Empires seat" to "famous Troy," Herring writes that the Gunpowder Plot threatened to inter metropolis and empire in a single tomb: "the funerall and buriall day / Of countrey, citie, London, now the seate / Of English Kings that Brittish Scepter sway."[5]

Titus Andronicus (1592) portrays a similar menace to the *polis* and thus to the empire. As Heather James demonstrates, Shakespeare's early revenge tragedy participates in the tradition of *translatio imperii* through repeated evocations of ancient history, politics, and literature.[6] James's focus on *Titus Andronicus*'s engagement with this tradition results directly from critically privileging Shakespeare's use of classical texts. When we shift the object of study from textual citation to embodied performance, this play invites a consideration of not so much the translation of empire as the translation of metropolis. In this chapter *Titus Andronicus* serves to illustrate how early modern English revenge tragedy takes the movement of *translatio imperii* as an opportunity to disclose the dynamics of *translatio metropolitae*. This historical and spatial conjunction becomes evident in the play's enactment of embodied movement. Titus's triumphal return to Rome, his sons' procession to the scaffold, his daughter's emotionally "moving" testimony, and the concluding executions of revenge – through these scenes, Shakespeare's play demonstrates the extent to which the metropolitan investments of revenge tragedy emerge in performance.

Titus Andronicus also exemplifies that the formal structure of revenge tragedy *is* the movement of return. As its nomenclature highlights, revenge tragedy represents a cycle of violence that ends in suffering and death. In his discussion of Renaissance English tragedy, Michael Neill explicates revenge as an "attempt to revive and atone for the violated past, [which] finishes by re-enacting the crime of violation."[7] As avengers return injustice upon their violators, they are invariably caught up in the repetitive momentum of their own violence, which returns boomerang-like upon them. These looping itineraries are not simply narrative and thematic but also physical and spatial.[8] In *Titus Andronicus* the movements of Revenge through the metropolis exceed allusion and allegory. She enters Rome on the heels of Titus's triumphal entrance, follows Lavinia to the woods and processes to the scaffold with Martius and Quintus, then reenters the city alongside Lucius and his foreign army. These movements chart the recursive trajectory of revenge tragedy as embodied movements in urban space. Other plays, which are often set in or in relation to cities, also link the physical return to the metropolis to the retributive violence characteristic of revenge tragedy. The language and performance of return shows the importance of movement within a metropolitan setting for the formal structure of this subgenre.[9]

Many of the movements that revenge tragedy represents, including judicial procedure and civic pageantry, worked historically to "spatialize" England's capital.[10] Popular images of these movements confirm the troubling effects of *translatio metropolitae*. Portraits of early modern London routinely depict the heads of traitors atop London Bridge, and several of these same images explicitly or implicitly evoke royal entries. This conjunction of body parts and triumphal procession illustrates a cityscape haunted by a history of violent unrest. Like revenge tragedy, these images show that tragic returns may not remain confined to London's past but extend to the future metropolis.

Returning to Rome

Titus Andronicus opens emphatically on the subject of return. In the first 225 lines of Shakespeare's early revenge tragedy, the word "return" appears no less than eight times.[11] In each instance, "return" refers to Titus's physical activity of coming back to Rome. Having left his place of origin to fight in distant lands, Titus, now victorious in Rome's foreign wars, retraces his steps. The play stages this return as a formal triumph: Titus's "passage to the Capitol" is accompanied by the "Sound [of] drums and trumpets" and prisoners "as many as can be" (1.1.12, 1.1.69 sd). Neither the 1594 Quarto nor the 1623 Folio version of *Titus Andronicus* calls for a chariot, such as rolled onto the theatrical stage in many contemporaneous scenes of triumphal procession.[12] A case could be made for its inclusion as a visual index of return as physical movement across long distances. An actual chariot would also make palpable one of several troubling correspondences between the movements of theatrical tragedy and civic pageantry, which took classical triumphs as its organizing principal.[13] Evoking perhaps the most pervasive performance of London's connection to ancient Rome, *Titus Andronicus* exposes *translatio imperii* as the foundation for metropolitan tragedy.

Stately and solemn, Titus's "return to Rome" (1.1.76, 1.1.221) corresponds, ostensibly at least, to a return to peace. After years of violence, barbarity, and death in foreign lands, Titus heads back to that apparent beacon of civilization, Rome. This associative counterpart to Titus's physical homecoming appears in the slew of "*re-*" words in the play's opening scene.[14] Titus asks that "Rome *re*ward" his surviving sons (1.1.82), and he buries his dead sons with the hope that in the family tomb they will finally find "*re*pose" (1.1.151). In anticipation of his own well-earned rest, Titus refuses the empery (1.1.187–200), and promising to "*re*store" to Saturninus "The people's hearts" (1.1.210–11), he advances the emperor's elder son in the hope that Saturninus's "virtues will ... *Re*flect on Rome" (1.1.225–6). Then, "in the sight of Rome," Titus asks Saturninus to "*Re*ceive" his sword and prisoners as rightful "tribute" (1.1.246, 1.1.251). With this final gesture, Titus attempts to complete his re-turn to Rome: having repeated and reversed his movement away from the city, he seeks to resolve once and for all his role in political and military affairs.

The competing movements of revenge and rebellion soon trouble Titus's peaceful return. Revenge enters by way of the funeral procession that is a solemn counterpart to Titus's triumph. Along with prisoners of war, the conquering hero bears back to Rome "a coffin covered with black" (1.1.69 sd), by which he returns his sons' remains "unto their latest home" (1.1.84). Titus condones Alarbus's sacrifice to the spirits of the dead, thus inadvertently setting in motion the revenge plot. After Titus refuses Tamora's appeal for mercy, Demetrius advises his mother to "stand resolved" in anticipation of "revenge," when she may "quit the bloody wrongs upon her foes" (1.1.135–41). The opening scene of *Titus* thus implies the figurative entrance of revenge, although it is not until the penultimate scene that the play directly evokes the physical movements of an allegorical Revenge. When Tamora enters disguised as Revenge, Titus offers to ride with her as she circles the earth in pursuit of vengeance. "I'll come and be thy wagoner / And whirl along with thee about the globe," he says,

> To hale thy vengeful wagon swift away
> And find out murderers in their guilty caves.
> And when thy car is loaden with their heads
> I will dismount, and by thy wagon wheel
> Trot, like a servile footman, all day long. (5.2.48–9, 5.2.51–5)

John Dover Wilson's comparison of *Titus* to "some broken-down cart, laden with bleeding corpses from an Elizabethan scaffold" bears a striking resemblance to Titus's description of Revenge's "vengeful wagon," which "whirl[s] ... about the globe," "loaden with ... heads."[15] This echo, while probably unwitting, is nonetheless revealing. It would have been theatrically possible for Tamora to enter on a wagon or "car."[16] Yet like Titus's triumphal entry, Tamora's entrance as Revenge does not require a stage property vehicle to enact return as literal movement both within fictional Rome and across the actual stage.

In the language and performance of return with which *Titus Andronicus* opens, we not only hear the conquering hero's triumphal entry and anticipate the approach of Revenge's fatal wagon but also see stately ceremony devolve into civic rebellion. After agreeing to Saturninus's "motion" to wed Lavinia (1.1.243), Titus confronts what appear to be treacherous motions. In order to "restore Lavinia to the emperor" (1.1.292), he kills one of his few remaining sons and threatens to kill another. For his fanatical efforts on the emperor's behalf, Titus is not "Receive[d] ... to favour" (1.1.418) but rewarded with "reproachful words" (1.1.305). Indeed, it is only through the disingenuous intervention of Tamora that Saturninus, pretending to "remit" their rebellion (1.1.481), is seemingly "reconciled" to Titus and his family (1.1.464).[17] Shakespeare stages this chaotic turn of events as a frenetic series of physical returns. Every named character, with the exception of Titus, exits and enters the stage multiple times over the course of the scene. For example, Lucius exits with his sister and Bassianus, returns when Titus kills Mutius, then exits again after condemning his father's act. At some point after Lavinia's seizure, Saturninus exits, then "Enters aloft" with Tamora (1.1.294 sd), and re-exits after swearing to "not re-salute the streets of Rome" until he and the Goth queen "consummate [their] spousal rites" (1.1.323, 1.1.334). In their final entrances in the scene, Lucius and Saturninus come onstage simultaneously from opposite doors, the former to plead for pardon, the latter to heed his bride's advice to "Yield at entreats" (1.1.446). This sequence of exits and entrances physically enacts not only the conventional helix-like plot of early English revenge tragedy but also the metropolis as the site and subject of this dramatic action.

Several early English revenge tragedies show return to or from the metropolis as the impetus for retributive violence. Even when urban settings are vague – often they lack names, or appear in just a few scenes or only as discursive points of reference – they contextualize the movements of physical return and violent revenge. In Thomas Kyd's *The Spanish Tragedy,* which represents the streets, walls, and scaffold of an unnamed Spanish city-state, the cycle of vengeance is set in motion, first, by Andrea's failure to return to Spain from the war with Portugal and, then, by Horatio's murder after his honourable return. The play enacts both kinds of return to the metropolis through the formal procession of "men of war ... all, except three hundred or few more ... safe returned."[18] Recalling the opening scenes of both *Spanish Tragedy* and *Titus Andronicus,* Beaumont and Fletcher's *The Maid's Tragedy* begins with Melantius's return "home to Rhodes," a locus of imperial designs in both the ancient and early modern worlds, having "with blood abroad buyest us our peace."[19] The plot then unfolds in palace halls and bedrooms seemingly cut off from the city, although a pivotal scene occurs "on the walls" of the urban fort.[20] The procession that "passes over the stage" at the beginning of Thomas Middleton's *The Revenger's Tragedy* is a part of decadent courtly revels rather than a public triumph; yet this physical movement sets in motion the revenge plot by inspiring Vindice, first, to feign "speedy travel" from the (presumably Italian) city-state, as represented in various urban domestic and judicial locales, and then to "turn into another" (i.e., assume a disguise) in order to return to the court, where he avenges the murder of his beloved.[21] Shakespeare's *Hamlet* is set in a city-less court that nonetheless is repeatedly and unfavourably compared with European metropolises.[22] Hamlet's return to Elsinore from Wittenberg coincides with the return of his father's spirit, disproving the notion that "No traveller returns" from death (*Hamlet* 3.1.82). Like the processions that open Kyd's and Middleton's plays, the repeated returns of King Hamlet's ghost – it "comes again" and again and again (*Hamlet* 1.1.38, 107; see also 1.4.19 and 3.4.97) – are staged as literal movement over and under the stage.[23] The ghost's account of the place from which he comes is as vague as Hamlet's account (in Quarto 2 of the play) of the unnamed metropolis from which the players come to Elsinore, although editors identify it with London.[24] Yet as we will see in chapter 3, it is the arrival of the "tragedians of the city" (*Hamlet* 2.2.316) that facilitates Hamlet's project of avenging his father's death and bringing an end to the ghost's nightly returns.

In *Titus Andronicus* the intersection of the form of revenge tragedy and the performance dynamics generated onstage takes place in an explicitly and insistently urban setting. Repeated expressions of appeal trace the topography of a dramatized Rome.[25] After failing to convince Titus to pardon her son's life (1.1.104–20), Tamora threatens to "make [the Andronici] know what 'tis to ... Kneel in the streets and beg for grace in vain" (1.1.451–2). Her suppliant words and kneeling posture reappear, first, in this same scene in front of the Capital, when Titus's sons and Marcus seek forgiveness for defying Saturninus (1.1.469–82); next, in the wood, when Lavinia begs Tamora to show pity rather than to allow her defilement (2.3.161–78); on the road to the scaffold, when Titus appeals to the tribunes to pardon his sons' lives (3.1.0 sd–15); and last, at the Andronici residence outside the city, when Titus kills Chiron and Demetrius (5.2.156–78).[26] Revenge follows an identical itinerary through the metropolis. She enters the *polis* along the same processional route to the Capital as Titus's triumphal entrance, and from this locus of political, civic, and religious authority, she moves to the "vast ... woods" and "sandy plot[s]" (4.1.53, 4.1.68) of greater Rome, then along its "wicked streets" (5.2.98) and to its residences ("old Titus' ... house," 5.3.141). As Revenge's car rumbles between Rome's centre and its periphery, retracing the path of the play's non-allegorical characters, it accumulates a gruesome pile: first, Alarbus's hewed limbs; then, Lavinia's maidenhead, tongue, and hands; then, Quintus and Martius's heads and Titus's hand; and eventually Chiron and Demetrius's heads, as well.

At the structural centre of the play, the staging of Roman space and body parts provides a clear demonstration of the intersection of literal and figurative movements of return. Act 3 opens with Titus appealing to Rome's tribunes to show mercy towards Martius and Quintus, who have been convicted and condemned for the murder of Bassianus. In legal terms, Titus seeks his sons' pardon, and in practical terms, their lively return. When Aaron enters and announces the emperor's offer to "send thee hither both thy sons alive" in exchange for an Andronici hand (3.1.155), an opportunity for this dual return emerges. Of course, the opportunity to "redeem" Titus's sons is a ruse (3.1.180). The hand that Titus sends as "ransom" (3.1.156, 3.1.172) is returned, is "sent back" (3.1.236) along with his sons' heads, thereby compounding the suffering that attends the returns of his "mangled daughter" and "banished son" (3.1.254–5). When Titus's sacrifice is "repaid" with this further loss (3.1.233), and his "resolution mocked" by the emperor and his court (3.1.237), the play embeds his suffering in the circulation of body parts through Rome and thereby enacts the same dynamics of return as the performance of repetitive speech and gesture.

Here, too, at the structural centre of the play, Titus realizes that he has not returned to the Rome of his imaginings – a luminous beacon of civility. The *polis* has moved on, as it were, along a path of lawless violence, and Titus dismisses the delusion that he can restore Rome to its former glory.[27] Whereas in the opening scenes Titus engages in a fanatical pursuit of a lost metropolitan ideal, in act 3 he charts an alternative movement through an emergent unjust Rome. Titus's new trajectory is marked by his first reference to vengeance. With his severed hand and dead sons' heads, his violated daughter and exiled son, onstage with him, Titus asks: "Then which way shall I find Revenge's cave?" (3.1.269). The conception of forward movement in search of Revenge coincides with the recursive movement of revenge: for Titus to appease his and his family's suffering, he must seek out a figure previously unknown in Rome and return with her to the city where she may return pain and loss upon his tormenters. The tragedy of *Titus Andronicus* is, then, a tragedy of movement: the return to the metropolis sets in motion a turn to lawlessness.

The oath to revenge that follows Titus's invocation of Revenge underscores the intersection of narrative and performative returns. The sequence of stage action is significant. First, referring to the disembodied remains of his sons Quintus and Martius, Titus describes the compulsion to vengeance: "these two heads do seem to speak to me / And threat me I shall never come to bliss / Till all these mischiefs be returned again / Even in their throats that hath committed them" (3.1.270–3). Next, Titus asserts that he will "swear" to avenge his family (3.1.277). Then, without any indication of the manner or duration of intervening stage business, he says, "The vow is made" (3.2.278).[28] Contrary to widespread associations of swearing with speech, Titus's vow is silent. It is staged exclusively as embodied movement, specifically a three-hundred-and-sixty-degree turn. "You heavy people, circle me about," Titus directs his brother and two surviving children, "That

I may turn me to each one of you / And swear unto my soul to right your wrongs" (3.1.275–7). This circular movement performs the exactitude with which Titus brings the Andronici's suffering full circle in the play's final act when Titus literally returns Tamora's mischiefs even in her throat. This conjunction of dramatic narrative and theatrical performance is implicit in other early English revenge tragedies. In *Hamlet,* for example, at Hamlet's "request" and the ghost's insistence, Horatio and Marcellus repeatedly, and at various places around the stage, "swear" "Upon [Hamlet's] sword" to "Never make known what [they] have seen" (*Hamlet* 1.5.146–82). Hamlet's subsequent pursuit of vengeance is as tentative, reactive, and haphazard as the fulfilment of this vow.[29] In *Titus Andronicus* the staging of narrative return as bodily turning makes explicit the way theatrical enactment bears on the structural and thematic elements of revenge tragedy. Like Titus's return to the metropolis, Revenge's return to Rome actualizes in *and as* performance.

The intersection of narrative and performative returns has implications, as well, for the audience. Whereas playgoers are "in" on Hamlet's, Hieronimo's, and Vindice's plans for vengeance, they are arguably not bound by the same vow as the revengers and their compatriots or co-conspirators. Playgoers remain, like Andrea's ghost, physically separate from if nonetheless emotionally invested in the action. The staging of *Titus Andronicus* challenges this arrangement by activating the spatial organization of the early modern public playhouse, which modern theatre practitioners might analogize to theatre in the round. As Titus turns to vow vengeance to each family member standing in a small circle around him, he would also be turning to the larger circle of playgoers standing and sitting around the stage. Whether or not Titus's gaze remains fixed on his brother and children or spans the yard, galleries, and Lords' rooms, his embodied movement would have the effect of including the audience in the ritual.

Why should the motions enacted onstage in *Titus Andronicus* bear on the play's narrative structure and thematic elements of return? The answer to this question is ultimately about geography and genre. In Shakespeare's play the representation of repetitive violence that is conventional to revenge tragedy becomes indistinguishable from the movements of urban life, both formal ceremony and improvised activity. The performance dynamics generated onstage thus render literal the pursuit of vengeance within the action as well as complicate ideas about how revenge tragedy works as a representation of the restoration of law and order. As we turn our attention to *Titus Andronicus*'s reproduction of the execution procession, we begin to see that the representation of judicial procedure engages the audience's participation in the processes of law and order inside *and outside* the playhouse. Revenge tragedy, conventionally defined by an elusiveness of justice, makes possible law and order's return to the metropolis through the experience of performance.

Processing to the Scaffold

Whereas the assignment of judicial efficacy to the stage creates problems that are the subject of the next chapter, in revenge tragedy it highlights the over-placedness of justice in England's metropolis. More so than triumphal chariots, let alone Revenge's wagon, early modern Londoners were familiar with a variety of disciplinary vehicles that moved through the metropolis on a regular basis. Both petty criminals and capital offenders were routinely transported publically between places of trial, incarceration, and punishment. These disciplinary processions have received less critical attention than the places among which they travelled. This disparity does not indicate relative irrelevance, of course; disciplinary processions were as essential to London's scopic regime as the city's numerous prisons, pillories, and gallows.

To begin to understand the efficacies of disciplinary processions such as the one represented in *Titus Andronicus*, we must turn not to the legal archive but to the repertoire of pedestrian and ceremonial performance.[30] Claes Jansz. Visscher's 1606 portrait of the Gunpowder Plotters' executions, although it postdates *Titus* by more than a decade, is useful for its striking depiction of the over-placedness of justice in early modern London (Figure 3). Visscher's portrait does not attempt a historically accurate rendering of the plotters' executions. The inscription at the top of the print explains that the eight conspirators were executed in two groups of four on two separate days ("De octo coniuratis sumium in Britannia, diebus 30 et 31 Jan. ... sumium quidem separatim de quaternis"), which events the artist intentionally conjoins ("hac tabellum conjunctim expressum"). So, too, Visscher's portrait conjoins the locations of the executions.[31] As T.W.'s *The arraignement and execution of the late traytors* (1606) relates, the first group of conspirators was "vpon sleddes and hurdles ... drawne into Powles Churchyearde," an established site of punishment, and the second group was drawn into the Old Palace Yard "ouer against the *Parliament house*," the site of the plotters' intended treason.[32] In Visscher's portrait the place of

Figure 3: The execution of the Gunpowder Plotters. Claes Jansz. Visscher, *Supplicium de octo coniuratis sumtum in Britannia* (1606). British Museum, Reg. No. 1848, 0911.452 © The Trustees of the British Museum.

execution is both places and neither place: curatorial descriptions of Visscher's initial drawing, early-seventeenth-century Dutch and German prints, and later English reprints identify the location variously as St Paul's Churchyard, Old Palace Yard, and a generic urban square.[33] The conjunction of times and places reflects not simply an earlier aesthetic mode but also the ubiquity of judicial places and activities in early modern London.

Accumulation and profusion also characterize the depiction of movement. Visscher seems intent on portraying all of the kinesthetic possibilities of this punitive event. The portrait shows one executioner poised atop the gallows, about to cut down one plotter, and two more executioners disemboweling and dismembering another plotter, whose leg a fourth executioner tosses into a boiling caldron. It also depicts the remaining six conspirators being dragged into the yard on horse-drawn sleds. Visscher sets these sanctioned acts of execution, torture, and transportation amidst the unscripted frenzy of a diverse group of spectators. Children, dogs, and grown men run amok in the yard, and many in the crowd extend their arms as if in the midst of gestures. Visscher's portrait thus offers a graphic if not necessarily reliable representation of the movements of offenders, officials, and spectators in the places of justice in England's metropolis.

To understand the meaning of these movements, it is helpful to consider a contemporary narrative account of the Gunpowder Plotters' trial and execution: *A true and perfect relation of the whole proceedings against the late most barbarous traitors* (1606). In the prefatory epistle to this anonymous pamphlet, the writer explains that, although the events he relates are well known, the progress of law and order is so significant and pleasurable that it warrants repetition. "Publique Justice passing," he writes, "doeth of it selfe import and giue the greatest satisfaction that can be to all men."[34] Here, "Justice" is introduced in terms of space ("Publique") and motion ("passing"). The space and motion of justice are not simply figurative but simultaneously physical and affective. As offenders pass publically through the streets of the metropolis, their crimes against city, realm, and empire (to paraphrase Herring) are put on display. Simultaneously, the condemned's physical movement to the scaffold enacts the restoration of law and order, a palpable return of justice.[35] The passage to the scaffold was also an affective experience. In addition to "satisfaction," disciplinary processions elicited a range of other emotions. Of the Gunpowder Plotters, T.W. writes: "Men that saw them goe to their Execution; did in a sorte grieue, to see such proper men in shape, goe to so shamefull an end, but the end was proper to men of so vnproper minds."[36] The movement to the scaffold was crucial to the re-establishment of justice and propriety in the metropolis.

These motions and emotions are not unlike those associated with theatrical tragedy. As I discuss in chapter 3, in early modern England, the widespread understanding of theatrical tragedy involved a representation of tears, trembling, and tribulation that also provoked these psychobiological responses. Early revenge tragedies provide an index of tragic efficacy in scenes orchestrated to move playgoers to impassioned responses.[37] In *The Spanish Tragedy* playgoers witness Horatio dishonorably hanged and stabbed, then Bel-Imperia dragged offstage crying for help, followed by Hieronimo's discovery of the body of his "sweet son" (*ST* 2.4.76). The entire "murd'rous spectacle" is designed to grieve, horrify, and, as the Ghost of Andrea says, "pain" audiences (*ST* 2.4.71, 2.5.1). Similar instances appear in *The Revenger's Tragedy* and *Hamlet*,[38] and *Titus Andronicus* itself is not void of overt attempts to elicit conventionally tragic responses. Visually and acoustically echoing the scene from *The Spanish Tragedy*, act 2 of *Titus Andronicus* portrays Bassianus's vicious murder, Lavinia's harrowing violation, and the discovery of these characters' respectively dead and mutilated bodies. Of course, by marking a uniform, collective effect, these scenes register the possibility of a range of other historically available responses. Through the urban movements enacted onstage, revenge tragedy activates associations above and beyond formal tragedy.

Titus Andronicus glosses Martius and Quintus's passage to the scaffold as a source of horror and lamentation from onstage and offstage audiences alike, even as it acknowledges other affective trajectories. Act 3 opens with the enactment of judicial movement: "Enter the Judges and Senators, with Titus' sons bound, passing on the stage to the place of execution, and Titus going before pleading" (3.1.0 sd). As the tribunes and the condemned pass over the stage to the place of execution, Titus attempts to halt their physical movement by moving them affectively. Still unaware of his sons' innocence, Titus petitions the tribunes to "stay" and "Be pitiful" (3.1.1, 3.1.8). More so than the youth, blood, and comfort that he lost in Rome's defence, Titus claims, the tribunes should show pity for the sake of the "bitter tears" that they "now ... see" on his face (3.1.6), his "soul's sad tears" (3.1.13) that fall to the ground even as he speaks. In fact, against the former rational arguments, Titus presents the latter emotional demonstrations as his "prevailing orators" (3.1.26). Meanwhile, Titus "lieth down" (3.1.11 sd), thereby enacting his intent of bringing the procession to a standstill. Yet neither Titus's words, nor his tears, nor his prostrate body prevail upon the tribunes, who, affectively *un*moved, "pass by him" (ibid.). Within the dramatic fiction, the representation of judicial procedure simultaneously enacts and forestalls responses associated with theatrical tragedy.

This juxtaposition finds a correspondence in the depiction of the metropolis as a built environment and a human community. When Lucius enters to find his father alone yet still pleading for Martius and Quintus's lives, he insists that it is pointless for Titus to continue to articulate his pain. "O noble father, you lament in vain," he says, "The tribunes hear you not, no man is by, / And you recount your sorrows to a stone" (3.1.27–9). Titus's response shows that although he fails to move the tribunes physically or affectively, his appeal is not wholly inefficacious:[39]

> Why, 'tis no matter, man: if they did hear,
> They would not mark me, or if they did mark,
> They would not pity me; yet plead I must,
> And bootless unto them.
> Therefore I tell my sorrows to the stones,
> Who, though they cannot answer my distress,
> Yet in some sort they are better than the tribunes
> For that they will not intercept my tale.
> When I do weep, they humbly at my feet
> Receive my tears and seem to weep with me,
> And were they but attired in grave weeds
> Rome could afford no tribune like to these.
> A stone is soft as wax, tribunes more hard than stones;
> A stone is silent and offendeth not,
> And tribunes with their tongues doom men to death.[40]

In this speech Titus deploys the trope of stony hearts that would persist throughout the early modern period in a range of discourses, including writings on tragedy (as I discuss in chapter 3) and on punishment. It appears, for instance, in a contemporary account of the execution of Thomas Wentworth, the Earl of Strafford, a pictorial print of which I examine in the introduction. Standing on the scaffold atop Tower Hill, Wentworth turned to the purportedly thousands in attendance and asked each of them to "lay his hand upon his heart" and "consider seriously whither the beginning of the happinesse of a people should be written in Letters of bloud."[41] Although Wentworth had been condemned in an "unofficial public trial" as well as by Parliament, his appeal "did even mollifie the most stony hearts there present, and many that before reioyced at the newes of his sentence, did not testifie their compassion by their teares."[42] Here, the softening of stony hearts is not simply a figure of speech; it implies actual movements, as well. The act of putting hand to heart brings about a shift in emotional response, specifically from joy to compassion, which is demonstrated by a collective shedding of tears.[43] Whereas on the scaffold Wentworth's evocation of motion and emotion go together, on the stage Titus's reference to stony hearts creates a juxtaposition of movements. Through his affective appeal, Titus attempts to halt the physical passage of the judicial procession. However, the tribunes remain stonyhearted and thus pass by him. Only the stones, which lack bodily mobility and therefore cannot abandon him, respond with tears.

This image of compassionate stones, however compelling within the dramatic fiction, breaks down in performance. According to all five early editions of *Titus Andronicus*, Titus enters in motion, "going before" the procession and "pleading," and at the eleventh line of his appeal, he assumes a prostrate position. During this stage business, Titus directs his words to the tribunes, asking them to "Let [his] tears," and not his "sons' sweet blood," "stanch the earth's dry appetite" (3.1.14–15). At or around this reference to the earth at line 15, where the First and Second Folios include the stage direction "Exeunt," the final tribunes exit. At this moment, as well, Titus shifts the audience of his appeal from the tribunes to the ground over which the procession has passed and on which he currently lies. Rather than address the now-absent tribunes, he apostrophizes the earth: "O earth, I will befriend thee" (3.1.16). Titus also anthropomorphizes the earth by giving it a "face" that he imagines as hardened by the seasons yet transformed to "eternal springtime" by his rain-like tears (3.1.21; 3.1.16–22). By giving the earth metaphorical flesh, Titus not only highlights the tribunes' figurative petrification but also points to the actual faces around him. Here, theatrical practice challenges a powerful poetic image, for the "face" onto which Titus's tears and words would have fallen was not earthen but human.

In Shakespeare's playhouse, no "stones" lay "at [the] feet" of the actor playing Titus. When the actor prostrated himself, he did so upon a stage composed of wood, not rock. Moreover, the actor would no more speak his lines into the boards of the stage than he would find stones there. He would deliver his character's sorrowful tale to the audience, perhaps particularly to the playgoers standing at the level of the actor's feet. Even if the actor playing Titus lay on his back, such that he directed his words upward in the direction of the galleries and Lords' rooms, his tears would run downward in the direction of the yard. Titus's reference to the "grave weeds" that the tribunes don and which the stones lack also supports the association of the "stones" and the humblest playgoers. Unlike the more moneyed playgoers seated in the galleries and Lords' rooms, the playgoers standing in the yard were unlikely to be "attired" in a manner comparable to Roman senators. When the actor soliloquized Titus's tearful appeal, then, he spoke not to the ground but most likely to the groundlings who stood at the foot of the stage and immediately around the prostrate actor.[44]

Titus's half-line – "And bootless unto them" – further corroborates the apposition of stones and groundlings in performance. Whereas some editors cut this half-line as a false start, others retain it on grammatical and metrical terms. The disruption of meaning and metre, the argument goes, reflects a collapse of cognitive and emotional control in the face of overwhelming grief.[45] The specific choice of the word "bootless" is also revealing. In the context of this scene, "bootless" means "to no purpose, without success; unavailing, useless, unprofitable." At the same time, the word resonates with the more literal meaning of "[w]ithout boots."[46] In *I Henry IV* Shakespeare plays on these two senses of the word when, in response to Glyndwr's boast of sending Henry "Bootless home," Hotspur says: "Home without boots, and in foul weather too!" (*1H4* 3.1.64–5). In Shakespeare's history play the pun on "bootless" is a self-conscious reference to the performance of linguistic difference, in particular Hotspur's mockery of the incomprehensibility of the Welsh. In his revenge tragedy the pun functions similarly to the extent that it appears as part of Titus's futile attempt to articulate his suffering. Despite the outpouring of Titus's sorrows, both his tears and his words are seemingly lost on the stony hearts of the tribunes. At the same time, the word "bootless" indicates the spatial and affective dynamics of the play in performance by drawing attention to the shift of Titus's audience from the tribunes, who walk around or over his prostrate body, to the playgoers, who stand at the level of the actor's feet.[47]

The implicit comparison of the dramatized stony ground and the "actual" audience concentrates the problem of movement in Shakespeare's revenge tragedy. *Titus Andronicus* attempts to move playgoers to tears and pity, and even implies that it succeeds; but these markers of audience response should not be taken at face value. Whether playgoers stood in the yard or sat in the galleries or Lords' rooms, they may, like the tribunes, remain *unmoved* by Titus's appeal. This response is not necessarily synonymous with indifference but may be a kind of self-control, such as Michael Schoenfeldt discerns in Shakespeare's representations of pain.[48] Or, repulsed by the hypocrisy of a man who seeks mercy when he shows none, playgoers may react to Titus's appeal with disgust.[49] Alternatively, they might laugh at Titus's histrionics.[50] His appeal to the tribunes is, at the very least, dramatically ironic; the audience knows, as Titus does not, that his sons are not guilty of Bassianus's murder. In this regard, *Titus Andronicus* evokes other scenes of judicial procedure – Pedringano's hanging in *The Spanish Tragedy*, Junior Brother's beheading in *The Revenger's Tragedy*, the Clown's summary condemnation in act 4 of

Titus Andronicus – that highlight the corruption of law and order to comic effect.[51] The system of participatory justice in Shakespeare's London contextualizes other possible trajectories of response. Lorna Hutson has shown that the English jury trial shaped forensic, rhetorical, and narrative habits of thought that taught people to rely on judgment and conscience in the determination of legal truth.[52] Yet opinion and passion routinely shaped responses to judicial procedures. Throughout the period, in both popular and official documents, we detect offenders' successful appeals for pity and tears, on the one hand, and the state's proscription of these emotions from legal proceedings, on the other.[53] In an effort to gain control over the emotions expressed at Wentworth's execution, for example, a more traditional dying speech was composed and published as his final words at the Tower of London.[54] The attempt to activate pity and fear in tragedy registers that scenes of suffering and injustice might elicit any number of other historically available responses – from revulsion to laughter to apathy.

Through its juxtaposition of motions and emotions, *Titus Andronicus* demonstrates how revenge tragedy revises understandings of *translatio imperii* and the conditions of urban life more broadly. When Titus enters the play, he is less a tragic protagonist than an epic hero. The political and affective force evident in Titus's opening speeches shows him to be like Neptune in Virgil's *Aeneid*, who compels auditors to "stand with attentive ears" and "rules their spirits with words and softens their hearts."[55] By act 3, however, Titus is no longer a leader of men but a subject of the corrupt authority of others, a victim of illicit violence, and eventually an outlaw himself. It is within the context of the unjust *polis* that Titus's words necessarily prove unable to make the tribunes stand still, let alone rule their spirits and soften their hearts. Shakespeare's revenge tragedy thus articulates how the motions and emotions generated within the theatre may elicit not tears but distinctly *un*tragic responses that are nonetheless appropriate to the pursuit of law and order in the metropolis. At the same time, because the play uses the representation of injustice to elicit this response, *Titus Andronicus* creates a problem around the movement of return in a metropolitan setting. At the end of the play, when Shakespeare's original audiences returned (so to speak) from Rome to London, they translated an understanding of imperial inheritance as tragic rather than triumphal.

Translation and *Translatio*

The translation of theatrical experience, like the phrase *translatio imperii* itself, has physical, judicial, and linguistic associations. In the strict etymological sense of a physical transfer from one place to another, translation signifies bodily movement across space. This meaning gave rise to the legal sense of translation as displacement, as Patricia Parker explains, both lawful (e.g., banishment) and unlawful (e.g., theft).[56] Translation also denotes, of course, the communication of language, ideas, and meaning. As literary scholars continue to explore, however, tragedy frequently enacts the failure to translate suffering.[57] This range of signification bears on the translations of Titus's surviving children, Lavinia and Lucius, and of revenge tragedy more broadly. Partial and ambivalent, these translations repeatedly fail to advance the project of *translatio imperii*. Instead, *Titus Andronicus* enacts empire as a source of "actual" tragedy – pain, injustice, invasion – in the metropolis.

The recursive movements of revenge tragedy replace translation of empire as a source of discursive, spatial, and legal authority. Despite Chiron and Demetrius's violent attempt to deprive Lavinia of the means of communication, she succeeds in revealing their names and crimes when "She takes [Marcus's] staff in her mouth, and guides it with her stumps, and writes" (4.1.75 sd).[58] Through this sequence of physical movements, Lavinia regains the power of translation as communication. Her tongue and hands are not literally returned, of course; nonetheless, she compensates for this loss when she uses her mouth and arms – the same body parts used for speech and embroidery – to convey the identity of her rapists. This revelation assumes the quality of legal testimony when Marcus urges Lavinia to "display" what she knows of "the traitors and the truth" (4.1.72, 4.1.75), albeit the legal testimony of "wilde Justice," in Sir Francis Bacon's well-known phrase.[59] After Lavinia names her assailants, Marcus refers repeatedly to revenge, and later in the play, Titus returns upon Chiron and Demetrius his daughter's loss of speech and bodily fragmentation.[60] The play aligns Lavinia's testimony with wild justice spatially, as well. She bears witness against Chiron and Demetrius not in a Roman courtroom, before the emperor, or even in a public street but on a "sandy plot [that] is plain" (4.1.68). It is "here" (4.1.67, 4.1.69, 4.1.72), in an indeterminate and seemingly rural space, that Lavinia "print[s] her sorrows plain" (4.1.74). By situating the restoration of communication in an extra-urban location, outside the spaces and conventions of judicial procedure, the scene highlights justice's persistent (if metaphorical) displacement.

When considered in terms of performance, the return of Lavinia's ability to communicate proves ambiguous in another way, as well. After Lavinia "writes" the names of her assailants and their crime, Marcus asks Titus, "O do ye read, my lord, what she hath writ?" (4.1.75 sd–76). This question was likely shared by Shakespeare's original audience – not because they did not know the names of Lavinia's violators and their offence (they did) but because they literally could not read what Lavinia writes. The audience's inability to read was a result not of widespread illiteracy or poor sightlines but of the simple fact that no visible impression would have been made when the actor who played Lavinia guided Marcus's staff over the stage. Here the reference to "plot" as a physical place and the repetition of "plain" work ironically. In early modern England "plot" could signify a geographical locale, a dramatic action, or the outline of a play that hung backstage.[61] The physical plot on which Lavinia writes is "plain" in the sense of a flat surface available to inscription only within the dramatic fiction. Within the theatrical performance, for which actors referred to the backstage plot, it was "plain" in another sense. London's unadorned stage would not be covered in sand for the scene of Lavinia's testimony, just as it is not lined with stones when Titus makes his appeal to the tribunes. In this regard, Lavinia cannot make "truth" "plain," in the sense of patently visible and readily understood, because there is nothing in which to inscribe it. Titus registers the limited efficacy of Lavinia's writing when he insists on transcribing it on "a leaf of brass," lest "The angry northern wind / Will blow these sands like Sibyl's leaves abroad" (4.1.101–4). Likewise, the penultimate scene of the play discovers Titus making a permanent record of his and his family's torment "in bloody lines," which, even if blown by the wind, "shall be executed" (5.2.14–15). Legal truth and personal suffering, the play suggests, must be recorded in brass or blood to be plain and thus efficacious.

The scene of Lavinia's testimony also revisits the possibility that no action performed onstage will have an effect outside the playhouse. Earlier in the play, when Titus makes his "bootless" appeal, he describes the stones on which his words and tears fall as "soft as wax" (3.1.44). The implicit comparison here is to a writing tablet made of wax, such as may be inscribed upon and wiped clean again and again.[62] Even if early modern playgoers proved soft and waxy, and not stonehearted like the tribunes, the impression of Titus's appeal might not endure. By the conclusion of the scene or the play, or some time after leaving the theatre, playgoers might find themselves wiped clean and ready for their next emotional experience. This suggestion of affective impermanence reappears in the scene of Lavinia's testimony. When Lavinia writes, supposedly inscribing in the sand but actually only miming the activity of inscription, the scene is moving in the sense of being physically in motion. Any impression that these motions make may not translate, or carry over, from the theatre to the metropolis. Instead, like sand blown by the wind, the experience of her words and gestures may disperse as playgoers reenter the "real" world.

These partial and ambivalent translations also develop in connection with Lucius's exile. For attempting to save Martius and Quintus from the execution block, Lucius is sentenced to the "doom of banishment" (3.1.50). This sentence is a translation in both the spatial and judicial senses of the word (as "an exile," Lucius "must not stay" in Rome, 3.1.283) that may or may not be permanent. In Shakespeare's *Richard II*, for example, Mowbray's "dear exile" has a "dateless limit," such that he may "'never ... return'" to his homeland (*RII* 1.3.145–6). By contrast, Bolingbroke's "banished years" have an expiration date, after which he may "Return with welcome home" (*RII* 1.3.203, 1.3.205). Lucius's banishment is, like Mowbray's, "everlasting" (*Titus* 3.1.50). Nonetheless, he intends to return and, like Bolingbroke, "Before the expiration of [his] time / In braving arms against [his] sovereign" (*RII* 2.3.110–11). After Titus, Marcus, and Lavinia exit the stage, the former two bearing Martius and Quintus's heads and the last Titus's hand, Lucius vows that he will "come again" to Rome (*Titus* 3.1.289) and bring down its rulers:

> If Lucius live, he will requite your wrongs
> And make proud Saturnine and his empress
> Beg at the gates like Tarquin and his queen. (*Titus* 3.1.295–7)

In these lines, the figure of return proliferates to include not only physical and retributive returns but also theatrical and historical ones. Lucius proposes to return to Rome (signified synecdochally by reference to the city's "gates")[63] to pursue revenge ("requit[al]") for the injustices done upon his family. In particular, he imagines making Saturninus and Tamora kneel in impotent supplication, an image that implicitly evokes Titus's and Lavinia's vain appeals earlier in the play.[64] Lucius also recalls an earlier moment in Roman history when he compares his public chastisement of the emperor and empress to the revolt led by his namesake Lucius Junius Brutus, which concluded in the expulsion of the tyrannical Tarquins and the establishment of the Roman Republic.

Lucius's translation-as-exile thus occasions a number of returns, the most revealing of which constitutes translation-as-*translatio*. At first blush, his physical return to the metropolis promises to bring about a return of Rome's glorious past. When Saturninus hears with trepidation of Lucius's imminent return, Tamora asks, "Is not your city strong?," to which Saturninus responds, "Ay, but the citizens favour Lucius / And will revolt from me to succour him" (4.4.77–9). The implication is that, at Lucius Andronicus's approach, the people will rise up and unseat Rome's tyrannical rulers just as they had at Lucius Junius Brutus's urging. However, Lucius Andronicus's "revolt" proves more ambiguous than that of his namesake. When Lucius concedes to Titus's request to "repair to Rome" (5.3.2), the play introduces two possible conclusions.[65] On the one hand, Lucius's return promises to mend a metropolis torn apart by tyranny; on the other, it threatens to destroy Rome. After all, he returns not to lead a civil revolution but at the head of a foreign army and former enemy, as the comparison of Lucius with Coriolanus drives home (4.4.67). Moreover, Lucius's stated purpose is not restoration but revenge. Titus's invitation to Lucius to "repair to Rome" follows hard upon Lucius's invitation to the Goths to exact "treble satisfaction" (5.1.8) upon the metropolis. The conjunction of physical return, moral rectification, and material reconstruction, specifically of a city, that the word "repair" implies thus emerges at the end of *Titus Andronicus* as something of a surprise.

The translation of metropolitan myths of ruin and repair occurs as a result of the complex urban space of revenge tragedy. Act 5 begins in an indeterminate setting outside of Rome but suggestively proximate to London.[66] Lucius's threat to hang Aaron and his child "on this tree" (5.1.47), although suggestive of an idyllic rural setting, also taps into a common word for gallows, perhaps especially the infamous "Tyburn tree" located only a few miles beyond London's walls. The allusion to "a ruinous monastery" (5.1.21) also drags the represented action from the ancient pagan world into a contemporary Christian one whose topography recalls the suburbs around post-Reformation London.[67] From this extra-urban locale, Lucius proceeds in the direction of Rome, specifically towards his father's house where he anticipates a parley with the emperor. As the familial banquet is exposed as a cannibalistic feast and political negotiations devolve into a bloodbath, *Titus Andronicus* shows disruption at home as parallel to disruption in the empire, thus evoking early modern political analogies between the household and the state. In the aftermath of this banquet-parley gone awry, it becomes clear that home and empire may be no more unhinged from one another than they may be from the metropolis.

Titus Andronicus enacts this spatial interdependence in performance and ultimately imbricates the space of theatrical tragedy itself. With the carnage around Titus's well-laid table still onstage, the final scene returns to earlier moments in the play through stage business and language. When Lucius goes aloft with his uncle Marcus to "teach you how to knit again ... These broken limbs again into one body" (5.3.69, 5.3.71), the repetition of "again" emphasizes how this movement creates a visual analogue to the opening scene on the Capital. *Titus Andronicus* begins in the symbolic heart of the *polis* with Rome's leadership likewise "aloft" (1.1.0 sd) and similarly intent on defusing civil conflict. At the end of the play, the stage does not suddenly represent the Capital, of course; the scene works more subtly to collapse "old Titus' sorrowful house" (5.3.141) and the heart of the metropolis, which was also the hub of the empire. In this complex space, Lucius elicits motions and emotions that his father and sister fail to elicit. Within the dramatic fiction Titus's appeal succeeds only in the sense that it does not lead to more capital sentences ("A stone is silent and offendeth not, / And tribunes with their tongues doom men to death," 3.1.45–6), and Lavinia's testimony makes an impression that nonetheless fails to restore justice. Lucius's tale of woe, by contrast, brings about a collective response that promises to return law and order to Rome. When a Roman lord asks Marcus to relate who is culpable for Rome's "civil wound" (5.3.86), Marcus yields the task to Lucius for fear that "floods of tears" will prevent his tale from "mov[ing] ye to attend" and "forc[ing] you to commiseration" (5.3.89–92). After Lucius tells the "wrongs unspeakable" that his family suffered (5.3.125), Emillius insists, "Lucius, our emperor – for well I know / The common voice do cry it shall be so" (5.3.138–9). Here, *Titus Andronicus* implies that Rome's citizenry responds unanimously with compassion for the Andronici's suffering. In performance, as this "cry" literally or figuratively resounds, the play translates "wrongs unspeakable" – rape, mutilation, murder, cannibalism, regicide – into the bases for metropolitan tragedy.

Moreover, by electing Lucius emperor of Rome, the "common voice" translates revenge as justice. The play denotes this translation spatially, as well, as the metropolis takes on distinctly judicial associations. "Now you have heard the truth. What say you, Romans?" Marcus asks and vows that if the Andronici have "done aught amiss," they will, "from the place where you behold us pleading,"

all headlong hurl ourselves
And on the ragged stones beat forth our souls
And make a mutual closure of our house. (5.3.127–33)

The explicit referent in these lines is Tarpeian rock, from which traitors to Rome were thrown. Of course, "the place" represented onstage is no more Tarpeian rock than it is the Roman Capital. However, through analogy to this well-known site of punishment, the setting of the final scene evokes earlier scenes that conjoin revenge and justice. Marcus's reference to "the truth" echoes his earlier urging of Lavinia to write "the traitors and the truth" (4.1.75) when she could not speak her violators' names; and his allusion to the "stones" on which the Andronici will "beat forth [their] souls" recalls the stones to which Titus turns when the tribunes ignore his suit (and, as it turns out, the legal truth). Just as Lucius succeeds where his father and sister fail, Marcus manages to bring together judicial procedure and affective response in a way that his brother and niece do not. At the end of *Titus Andronicus*, or so it would seem, *translatio* trumps translation, teleology displaces recursivity, and motion and emotion work in tandem.

A broader spatial convergence complicates this coordination, however. Marcus's references to "our house," used metonymically to mean the Andronici bloodline, and subsequently to "old Titus' sorrowful house" (5.3.141), which describes the setting in terms of genre, also evoke the play*house* in which *The Most Lamentable Roman Tragedy of Titus Andronicus* was performed. Moreover, the actor playing Marcus would presumably address his lines both to the fictional audience onstage and to the actual audience in the theatre. Early modern English men and women were trained to interpret classical imagery in local terms. Civic pageantry, in particular, invited Londoners to imagine themselves as the "people and sons of Rome" (5.3.66), the spiritual descendants of ancient Romans. Shakespeare's representations of the spaces and activities of the *polis* similarly render Rome a correlative to London. *Titus Andronicus* galvanizes this cultural trope through the production of a materially singular yet semiotically complex space. As a metropolitan space, "the place where you behold us" is at once not only household and empire, Tarpian rock and Roman Capital, but also ancient Rome and early modern London. The restoration of "proper" physical, affective, and judicial movements with which the play concludes, however ambivalent this restoration may be, may thus prove efficacious beyond the theatrically represented space. So, too, less desirable movements – revolt, regicide, invasion, ruin. The promise of glorious return brings with it the prospect of metropolitan tragedy.

The recursive movements enacted in *Titus Andronicus* are not unique to theatrical performance, let alone revenge tragedy. The pageantry of investiture and coronation, in particular, drew on the dynamics of the classical triumph to authorize the transfer of civic and royal power. Even as the physical translations, or acts of passage, of mayors and monarchs registered the bifold teleology of inheritance and progress, they were also troubled by threats of tragic return. London's history of rebellion haunted these ceremonial processions through the metropolis. Perhaps the best-known spectre of capital crime was also a principal point of entry to the capital city: London Bridge. Pedestrian and official processional movements across, beneath, and along London Bridge evince the paradox of *translatio*. England's neoclassical inheritance secured London's place among other European imperial centers, but it also communicated a legacy of catastrophic return that would eventually raze the metropolis.

Returning to London

In the diary of Frederic Gerschow, secretary to Philip Julius, Duke of Stettin-Pomerania, we find a description of the duke's return to London on 27 September 1602. Although the duke's entourage entered the city "[l]ate in the evening," they were able to see the display of post-mortem punishment on London Bridge: "Near the end of the bridge, on the suburb side, were stuck up the heads of 30 gentlemen of high standing who had been beheaded on account of treason and secret practices against the Queen."[68] Here, in the account of a foreign visitor to London near the end of Elizabeth's reign, the heads impaled on London Bridge evince an extended history of crime and punishment. The heads of condemned traitors had been mounted on London Bridge since 1405, when William Wallace's head was put on display at the bridge's centre. In 1577, not long after the construction of the Theatre, the heads were moved to the Southwark entrance of London Bridge, where Gerschow observed them upon his return to the city. When English monarchs returned to London, especially from coronation or victory abroad, they too encountered this spectacle.[69] These itineraries – the one of foreign visitors, the other of England's rulers – reveal the complex signification of pedestrian and official processional movement in early modern London. Entering the metropolis by way of London Bridge activated both an ancient inheritance of legal authority and a recursive history of "actual" tragedy.

Figure 4: The heads of traitors on London Bridge's southern entrance. *The view of London Bridge from East to West*, after John Norden (1597), detail. British Museum, Reg. No. 1880, 1113.1527 © The Trustees of the British Museum.

If London Bridge evoked topophobia from some English monarchs, as Karen Newman has argued, it elicited topophilia from many of their subjects.[70] John Norden's *The view of London Bridge from East to West* (1597) portrays its subject as a locus of civic pride and prosperity (Figure 4). The print features a stone structure, which, as the accompanying text explains, replaced the original wooden structure after recurrent damage by fire and ice.[71] This icon of resilience was also a hub of urban activity. "Passengers ... Carres, Cartes, and droues of Cattell" routinely passed over London Bridge, transporting people and goods between London and regions south. London Bridge was not only a thoroughfare between city and country but also "comparable in it selfe to a little Citie," on which stood "sumptuous Buildings, & statelie & beautiful Houses ... Inhabited by wealthy Citizens, and furnished with all manner Trades." In addition to accommodating travel, commerce, and residence, London Bridge functioned as a site of justice. Norden's image includes a detailed image of the heads of traitors on the Southwark entrance to the bridge – fourteen heads, to be precise, on poles of various heights and facing multiple directions; but they are not mentioned in the prose "*description of* London-*Bridge*." Whereas London Bridge's origins, economic functions, and unique architecture make it "one of the

Figure 5: John Norden, *Civitas Londini* (London, 1600). British Museum, Reg. No. 1880, 1113.1120 © The Trustees of the British Museum.

Wonders of the World," its judicial function appears literally not noteworthy. Presumably, the heads impaled on London Bridge do not provoke Norden's wonder because they were commonplace, an expected and mundane element of life in early modern London. Expected and mundane do not, however, mean neutral or irrelevant. To the extent that the heads became an intrinsic feature of the cityscape, they also naturalized law and order in the metropolis. Looming above the frenetic motions of life in the "little Cittie," the heads signified judicial stasis in greater London. In this sense, Norden's print constructs London Bridge in a manner that recalls domestic tragedy: London Bridge fixes lawlessness in place, making possible travel, commerce, recreation, and other quotidian pursuits throughout the metropolis.

A similar fantasy of London emerges from the depiction of civic pageantry in Norden's 1600 *Civitas Londini* (Figure 5).[72] This print portrays the Lord Mayor's Galley Foist travelling towards London Bridge. Part of a ceremonial performance of the city, the heads impaled on London Bridge bear sightless witness to the civic authorities who protect London's financial and political interests from rebellious assaults. As in *The view of London Bridge*, in which pedestrian performance appears protected by a preternatural cityscape, in *Civitas*

Londini the heads impaled on London Bridge endorse the portrait of "an autonomous ... civic space."[73] However, the metropolis was not a uniform, singular space but divided by competing claims to political, institutional, and jurisdictional authority.[74] This tenuous state of affairs is evident in the depictions of pageantry in *Civitas Londini* and the earlier views upon which Norden drew. Although all of these city portraits show the heads atop London Bridge, this spectacle signifies differently in each vis-à-vis the ritual celebrant who passes beneath it.

Whereas Norden's *Civitas Londini* depicts the Lord Mayor's Galley Foist, both the so-called copperplate map (circa 1560) and the view of London in Braun and Hogenberg's *Civitatis Orbis Terrarum* (1572) (Figure 6) feature Queen Elizabeth's barge. On 14 January 1559, the day before her coronation, Elizabeth entered London by water. Travelling along the Thames to the Tower of London, she passed beneath London Bridge and its display of heads, which Braun and Hogenberg's view depicts in detail.[75] Although topophobia may have contributed to the choice of a maritime royal entry, other explanations for this mode of transportation help to make sense of the fact that London Bridge remained on Elizabeth's itinerary. Susan Frye argues that, by design, the queen's entry by barge evoked the Lord Mayors' pageants and served as a gesture to city leaders of her intent to cooperate with their interests.[76] Whereas Norden occludes this conciliatory performance by replacing the queen's barge with the Lord Mayor's foist, Braun and Hogenberg call attention to it by juxtaposing Elizabeth's royal entry and other Tudor imagery, on the one hand, and the prominent depictions of citizen costume and activity, on the other. Rather than a consolidation of authority, Braun and Hogenberg "demonstrate a balance of power in the performance of the space of the city: royal and civic forces in mutual operation."[77]

On Braun and Hogenberg's city portrait, the image of Elizabeth's barge en route to pass beneath the heads impaled on London Bridge registers another source of the ambivalent translation of authority. Anne Boleyn's coronation also began with her passage by barge along the Thames, the first of numerous parallels between Elizabeth's and her mother's ceremonies.[78] Alice Hunt has shown how Boleyn's pageant procession constructed the king's pregnant consort as Imperial Virgin, a conjunction of classical and Christian imagery in a ceremony designed to elicit "the repetition and the restoration of the past, rather than the advent of the new."[79] To some extent, Elizabeth's 1559 royal entry served a similar purpose. By entering London in the same manner as her mother, Elizabeth began the project of commanding the

Figure 6: Georg Braun and Frans Hogenberg, *Londinum Feracissimi Angliae Regni Metropolis*, in *Civitatis Orbis Terrarum* (Cologne, 1572). British Museum, Reg. No. G, 2.3 © The Trustees of the British Museum.

meaning assigned to her gendered body that, as Frye demonstrates, characterized her almost forty-five-year reign. At the same time, by visually evoking Boleyn's procession, Braun and Hogenberg's city portrait, like the painting of Elizabeth's procession to Blackfriars, "participates in an isolable tradition of representing royal power which indeed draws upon triumphal motifs but is not in itself triumphal."[80] Only a few years after Boleyn travelled from the Tower to Westminster as Imperial Virgin en route to her coronation, she passed from Westminster to the Tower, having been found guilty of adultery, incest, and high treason and condemned to die by beheading. Boleyn's head was not displayed on London Bridge (nor was the head of her brother, George Boleyn, for that matter). Yet the spectacle of traitors' heads under which Elizabeth passed en route to her own coronation possibly elicited the fatal reversal that her mother experienced little more than two decades earlier. Braun and Hogenberg's city portrait thus conveys London's rich civic and royal inheritance as well as the strife that may revisit the metropolis.

More than a decade after Elizabeth's death, Claes Jansz. Visscher restored her barge to the city's portrait. Visscher's 1616 *London* invites interpretation in terms of the queen's relationship to the metropolis at the end of the sixteenth century. The dynamic between city and Crown was considerably different, for example, when Elizabeth entered London in 1592. Unlike in 1559 Elizabeth controlled her ceremonial representation, and both citizens and civic leaders accepted her as the sun of London's cosmos.[81] Visscher's depiction of the heads on London Bridge thus suggests Elizabeth's ultimate triumph over recursive history. When rebellion reared its hydra-like head, she cut it off. Whereas her mother was executed as a royal whore, Elizabeth died as she had reigned, the Virgin Queen. At the same time, Visscher's *London* may be read in terms of a desire for political return. Published during James I's reign, this city portrait registers nostalgia for an earlier metropolitan moment, for a period of amiability between city and Crown and a reign less dominated by neoclassical absolutism.

Beginning with his coronation procession into London, James's contests with local authorities over sovereignty played out repeatedly and variously in civic and royal ceremony.[82] They played out on the stage, as well, as writers of theatrical tragedy engaged in seventeenth-century political debate. As I examine in the next chapter, Jacobean and Caroline tragedies of tyrants routinely take place in London-like metropolises. These plays are not wholly distinct from revenge tragedy, of course; scholars discuss many of them, including *Hamlet* and *The Maid's Tragedy*, under both headings. Within the dramatic fictions of tyrant tragedies, however, avengers tend to act not simply in response to personal affronts but on behalf of an oppressed populace. More important, this shift from private to public justice is theorized as the work of theatrical tragedy itself. In chapter 3 I argue that metropolitan tragedy develops in tandem with London's central role in Stuart-era political contestation and debate. As tyrant tragedies enact the city's purgation through the punishment of unjust rulers, literary theory figures theatrical tragedy as an agent of disciplinary violence. However, the tragic stage is not a straightforward counterpart to London's disciplinary sites, one place within an extensive network of over-placed justice. Instead, it proves a kind of recalcitrant scaffold that forestalls, or even perpetuates, injustice.

Chapter Three

Tyrant Tragedy and the Tyranny of Tragedy in Stuart London

As a city ruled by tyranny commeth to destruction: so doth a man ouer whome perturbations haue sway.

– Francis Meres, *Palladis Tamia* (1598)

In the tragedies of tyrants of Stuart England, vengeance becomes increasingly a public rather than a private undertaking. As in the revenge tragedies of earlier decades, personal affront, rape, and murder continue to inspire retributive violence; but in tyrant tragedies, violators are often heads of state, and avengers claim to pursue justice on behalf of an injured populace. To the extent that these plays represent abuses of royal authority, it makes sense that their setting shifts largely to the court. In stately halls and palace bedrooms, tyrants rule by whim and will rather than by law and consent, producing the conditions in which courtiers become conspirators. At the same time, many tyrant tragedies locate these courtly spaces within broader urban networks of citizen homes, municipal fields, and public scaffolds.

Invariably, these metropolitan settings are thinly veiled versions of London.[1] Some Stuart tyrant tragedies take place in other early modern European metropolises, such as urban Sicily in Beaumont and Fletcher's *Philaster* (1609), Florence in Middleton's *Women, Beware Women* (circa 1613–21), and Verona in D'Avenant's *The Tragedy of Albouine* (1629).[2] More popular are ancient Roman settings. In the 1610s plays by Shakespeare (*Coriolanus*), Jonson (*Sejanus, Cataline*), and Fletcher (*Valentinian*) used ancient Roman settings to dramatize responses to James I's ideology of rule.[3] In the 1620s and 1630s this trend persisted in tyrant tragedies that offer not-so-subtle representations of tensions during Charles I's reign, including the anonymous *Tragedy of Nero* (1624), Thomas May's *Tragedy of Julia Agrippina* (1631), and several of Philip Massinger's plays.[4] The classical *polis* provided a suitable context for dramatized debates about tyranny, not simply for its association with humanist philosophy. Ancient Rome's historical connection to notoriously abusive, histrionic rulers – Nero, Domitian, and Caligula, among others – rendered it an apt setting for tyrant tragedies. At Blackfriars, where many of these plays were staged, and where audiences were likely familiar with early modern political discourse, the metropolitan setting of tyrant tragedy invited topical analysis.

In this chapter I argue that tragedy represents tyranny as a problem of the metropolis. In Stuart England contestation over royal prerogative had ramifications well beyond London, of course – not least the catastrophic civil wars that embroiled England, Scotland, and Ireland. In discussing tyranny as a problem of the metropolis, I follow Lawrence Manley by "examin[ing] larger historic changes from the standpoint of London, in order that the city's role *within* the process of change may be more fully appreciated."[5] Tyranny is a problem of the metropolis because London was where tyranny would originate but it was also where unjust monarchy could be prevented and, ultimately, where it would be punished. This notion is stated bluntly in the section of John Stow's *A Survey of London* entitled "An Apologie or defence of the Cittie of London": "euen as these societies and assemblies of men in Cities and great Townes, are a continuall bridle against tyranny, … So, being wel tempered, they are a strong forte and bulwarke not onely in the *Aristocritie* [*sic*], but also in the lawfull kingdome or iust royalty."[6] As elsewhere in his nostalgic chorography, Stow compares the urban population ("societies and assemblies of men") to the city's structures ("forte and bulwarke"). In its bifold meaning as human community and built environment, the metropolis is responsible for curbing tyranny.

Tragedy plays an important role in executing this charge. According to early modern English defences of the stage, tragedy does not simply represent abuses of royal authority but actually prevents and punishes them. In fact, tragedy purportedly enforces justice throughout the heterogeneous urban population that gathers around London's various stages. However, close scrutiny of early modern political discourse discloses a discomfiting relationship between tragedy and tyranny. In making the case for tragedy's enforcement of justice, defences of the stage present theatrical tragedy, like unjust monarchy and lawless citizens, as a source of "actual" tragedy in the metropolis.

In this chapter I examine the representation of this overlap of tragedy and tyranny in the metatheatrical action and melodramatic characters of Philip Massinger's *The Roman Actor.* Although not as well known as, say, Shakespeare's *Coriolanus*, Massinger's tyrant tragedy brings together several strains of Stuart drama in a scathing critique of the tyrannical means by which tragedy purportedly achieves its ameliorative ends. Performed in 1626 and published in 1629, *The Roman Actor* appeared during a period of acute political transition: James I died only a year before the play's first performance, and by the time of its publication, there could be no mistaking Charles I's particular brand of absolutism. Occupying a crucial moment in the history of England's monarchy, Massinger's play is profoundly topical, its portrait of Caesar Domitian employing conventional tropes of the tyrant to comment on the legacy of Stuart political ideology.[7] *The Roman Actor* also contributes to a small corpus of plays that dramatize early modern English defences of the stage.[8] Massinger has not composed a treatise on tragedy, and despite its representation of tragic inefficacy, *The Roman Actor* is not an anti-theatrical play, as some scholars have suggested.[9] The play serves, I argue, less as a condemnation of the practice of tragedy than an exposure of a fundamental flaw in the theory of tragedy in early modern England.

The Roman Actor locates its critique in a complex urban setting. At the beginning of act 3, scene 2, we learn that Caesar Domitian has summarily sentenced two senators to death and insists that they not be "Made away in private" but rather be "drawn / To the degrees in public."[10] "The degrees" alludes to the Gemonies, a site along the route to execution in ancient Rome.[11] By the late seventeenth century, the Gemonies signified figuratively to denote torture.[12] This semantic connection implies a historical conjunction between procedures of justice in ancient Rome and early modern London. This conjunction becomes explicit as the scene constructs an urban palimpsest in which English cities become visible beneath the dramatized Roman *polis*.

The stage direction in the 1629 printing of *The Roman Actor* specifies that the condemned senators enter "bound back to back" (3.2.46 sd). In doing so, the scene seems designed to evoke popular images of Christian martyrdom, in particular the illustrations in John Foxe's *Acts and Monuments*, or *Book of Martyrs*, one of the most influential texts in early modern England.[13] With this visual allusion, *The Roman Actor* draws political force from accounts of Marian tyranny as the subordination of divine and earthly justice to a monarch's personal desires. The play also taps into the "coherent pattern of illustration" established by Foxe and his printer, John Day, that included recognizable cityscapes.[14] Long before the senators' ghosts haunt the tyrant, the spectacle of their torment is ghosted by a history of tyranny in England's metropolises.

An implicit change of setting reveals another layer of urban signification. The senators' torture occupies only the first 124 lines of the scene; the subsequent 177 lines concern a courtly play-within-the-play. The transition from judicial procedure to royal performance takes less than thirty lines, and Domitian remains onstage as the action shifts location.[15] By forcing the continuation of the scene, Massinger frustrates efforts to determine precisely when the stage ceases to represent a scaffold and begins to represent the court. This conflation of public and royal spaces, combined with Domitian's enthusiasm for theatre, invites identification of ancient and Caroline urban courts. *The Roman Actor* thus points up what would have been obvious to Massinger's original audiences: tyranny is not simply the subject of theatrical tragedy on London's stages but the source of "actual" tragedy in the city's open streets and halls of power.

In its allusions to Stuart London, *The Roman Actor* participates in a general westward trajectory of seventeenth-century drama. Around the same time that city comedy began representing the ballrooms and parks of London's stylish West End, metropolitan tragedy turned its focus to Whitehall.[16] Recognizable in the regal architecture of many tyrant tragedies is this well-known structure, which, as we will see, was a popular subject of pictorial representation and political controversy in the first half of the seventeenth century.[17] In this context, *The Roman Actor* takes on new significance after 30 January 1649. For my purposes, Charles I's execution outside the Banqueting House at Whitehall functions not simply as a culmination of a generation of theatrical practice, as Franco Moretti famously argued.[18] The king's death on a public scaffold also demonstrates a logical if extreme outcome of the theory of tragedy in early modern England. In erecting a bulwark against tyranny's assault, tragedy exerts its own kind of tyranny over the metropolis.

Lexicons of Tragedy and Tyranny

A story rehearsed repeatedly and variously in early modern England prompts Hamlet's now famous assertion "The play's the thing / Wherein I'll catch the conscience of the King":

> I have heard that guilty creatures sitting at a play
> Have by the very cunning of the scene

Been struck so to the soul that presently
They have proclaimed their malefactions;
For murder, though it have no tongue, will speak
With most miraculous organ. (2.2.581–2, 2.2.566–71)

Inspired by these tales of tragedy eliciting confessions from murderous playgoers, Hamlet designs *The Mousetrap* to displace all doubt about Claudius's guilt and thus to legitimize retaliatory justice.[19] Yet when Hamlet returns from England he is intent less on avenging a past murder than on preventing "further evil" (5.2.71). The bifold function of tragedy as corrective and prophylactic also underlies Philip Sidney's definition of "high and excellent tragedy" in *An Apology for Poetry*. Tragedy, he contends, "maketh kings fear to be tyrants, and tyrants manifest their tyrannical humors" and "maketh us know, '*Qui sceptra saevus duro imperio regit, / Timet timentes, metus in auctorem redit*'" (The savage tyrant who wields his scepter with a heavy hand fears the timid, and fear returns to its author).[20] These accounts of tragedy catching guilty consciences and terrorizing unjust rulers exemplify a uniquely English interpretation of *catharsis*.

In book 6 of the *Poetics* Aristotle describes tragedy as a specific type of action – mimetic, complete, and weighty – that has a particular, if ambiguous, emotional impact upon audiences: "Tragedy, then, is an imitation of an action that is serious, complete, and of a certain magnitude ... through pity and fear effecting the proper purgation [*catharsis*] of these emotions."[21] Whereas medieval writers did not touch on the subject of catharsis, beginning in the sixteenth century writers focused considerable attention on this enigmatic element of Aristotle's theory of tragedy. Early in the period, writers produced more accurate translations of the *Poetics*, but continental and English commentators differed on how to reconcile Aristotelian catharsis with the Horatian maxim that poetry should teach and delight.[22] Continental writers tended to view catharsis in terms of medicinal cleansing or moral purification; tragedy, they posited, refines debilitating emotions such as sorrow and terror, so as to render the individual physically, mentally, and spiritually ready for civil service. By contrast, English writers privileged a more legalistic interpretation.[23] Catharsis stirs up admissions of guilt, they argued, rather than empties out harmful emotions; it leads to the exposure of vicious offenders, not the creation of virtuous citizens.

The "very special application of the Aristotelian doctrine" of catharsis in early modern England is not merely "an *expansion ad absurdum*" of the theory propagated on the Continent, as Stephen Orgel asserts.[24] Instead, it constitutes what Ellen MacKay has called a "persecutorial poetics," in which tragedy violates the very civil laws it claims to serve.[25] In early modern English defences of the stage and political discourse, a similar lexicon of physical and spiritual force describes both the ameliorative force of tragedy and the abusive violence of the tyrant. The uniquely English understanding of catharsis thus introduces a deeply troubling aspect of metropolitan tragedy. Rather than participate in London's response to injustice, theatrical tragedy becomes a source of "actual" tragedy in the metropolis.

As historians of early modern political thought have shown, the political vocabulary of sixteenth- and seventeenth-century Europe was both semantically ambiguous and historically specific. A duality of political discourse informed the struggle to define words such as "liberty," "absolute," and "common," as David Kelley explains: "Every term and value had a good and a bad, a spiritual and a carnal, face; and there was no way except personal conviction or submission to authority – inner light or outer direction – to tell them apart."[26] The same words, that is, might be used to support opposing theories of kingship. As Linda Levy Peck and Martin Dzelzainis show, writers with divergent political ideologies tapped into this duality to secure their respective positions.[27]

The word "tyranny" provides a case in point. Sixteenth- and seventeenth-century political writers inherited an ancient definition of "tyranny" as governance by a depraved, evil ruler in categorical opposition to a principled and righteous king.[28] Although these writers retained the notion that princes should be expected to adhere to a recognized standard, they radically revised the quality of this standard: in early modern political discourse, ethical principles – determined by classical philosophy, Christian doctrine, and Renaissance humanism – replaced legislative criteria, as characterized by an allocation of power among monarch, law, and people. This shift from morality to legality necessarily informed both of tyranny's faces: good and bad, spiritual and carnal.

The semantic ambiguity of "tyranny" appears in the writings of both uncompromising supporters of royal authority, such as Jean Bodin and James I of England, and "monarchomachs," William Barclay's name for George Buchanan and others who advocated popular resistance of tyrannical rulers.[29] For example, in *The six bookes of a common-weale* (1606; original French edition published in 1576), one of the most influential political texts of the period, Bodin introduces his discussion of "Tirannical Monarchie" by way of etymology.[30] "This word *Tyrant*," he explains, "in auncient time signified no other thing then [*sic*] a Prince, which without the consent of the people, had by force or fraud possessed himselfe of the state ... although he were a right wise and iust prince." Eventually the word came to signify an immoral and unjust ruler who "tread[s] vnder foot the lawes of God and nature." Although writing from the other side of the political aisle, the author of *Vindiciae contra tyrannos* (1648; first printed in 1579) also presents a dual definition of "tyranny": "he is reputed a tyrant" who "either gaines a kingdome by violence, or indirect meanes" or, "being invested therewith by lawfull election or succession, governes it not according to law and equitie."[31] Also like Bodin, the *Vindiciae* author asserts that these definitions are not mutually exclusive: tyranny by lack of lawful title and by unlawful governance "may very well occurre in one and the same person" (sig. O2r). Thus tyranny could indicate an illicit claim to power or an unwarranted use of power or both.

Writers across the political spectrum deployed the ambiguous definition of "tyranny" as usurpation and/or license to advance their respective political ideologies. But they no more agreed on the specific quality and features of tyranny (what does the tyrant usurp? what constitutes tyrannical excess?) than they did on the lawful response to tyranny. In *De jure regni apud Scotos, or, A dialogue, concerning the due priviledge of government in the kingdom of Scotland* (originally published in 1579), for example, George Buchanan contends that the people "conferre the Government on whom they please," with the understanding that kings "should obey the Lawes ... given them" and that kingly "power [is] not immense, but within certain limites bounded and limited."[32] Kings who exceed these limits not only "usurpe dominion" but also "[usurp] the name of King," such that they may, like "*Caligula, Nero, Domitian,* and such like Tyrants, ... be punished as breakers of divine and humane Law."[33] Tyrannical usurpation and license appear, as well, in James VI and I's political writings. In *Basilicon Doron* (1599) James distinguishes between "a lawfull good King, and an vsurping Tyran[t]": a king is lawful and good because he makes and executes "good Lawes," whereas the tyrant is a usurper because he "inuert[s] all good Lawes to serue onely for his vnrulie priuate affections."[34] Even though at first blush James appears to endorse Buchanan's account of tyranny, it becomes clear that the king redeploys his former tutor's language in the service of a competing theory of kingship. In his speech to Parliament on 21 March 1610, James explains that the people do not create, confer, or enforce the laws. Rather, "Lawes ... are properly made by the King onely," and although a king "leaues to be a King, and degenerates into a Tyrant, assoone as he leaues off to rule according to his Lawes," the people are not authorized to punish his transgression.[35]

The disagreement about precisely what constitutes tyrannical usurpation and license tends to engage two particular issues – one spiritual and the other carnal, to use David Kelley's terms. Political writers and their ecclesiastical contemporaries avidly debated a king's lawful authority over the souls and bodies of his subjects. Could a king legitimately compel hearts and minds, they asked, or impose his will through physical force? In response to this sort of question, the author of *Vindiciae contra tyrannos* derides the "many Princes in these days, calling themselves Christians," who "seeke to usurpe that sovereignty, which [God] hath reserved to himselfe over all men" (sig. A3r). The tyrant "assumes an unlimited power" specifically when he "assume[s] licence ... to inforce the Consciences, which appertaines cheifly to Jesus Christ" (sig. A4v). In essence, a king becomes a tyrant when he "assumes," in the dual sense of "takes on" and "takes for granted," a power over conscience that legitimately belongs to God alone. Many English writers agreed with the *Vindiciae* author that the king had no lawful authority over the souls of his subjects. In her study of treason in late Elizabethan and Jacobean literature, Rebecca Lemon demonstrates that many English writers understood tyranny as "a particular style of exercising power over the conscience and will of subjects: invoking discretionary power to rule over the law, even for the good of the state, spells tyranny."[36] Others took a more ambivalent position. Camille Wells Slights has shown that English casuists, or experts in case divinity, were often stumped by "the problem of a direct conflict between individual conscience and lawful authority."[37] Still others rejected outright the notion that the king who, in Ned Lukacher's colourful figuration, "[imposes his] will with a burning brand" upon the will of his subjects is guilty of tyranny, let alone sacrilege.[38] As Jonathan Goldberg demonstrates, James viewed the divinely ordained monarch to be lawful and just in placing conscience – everyone's conscience except his own, that is – under the jurisdiction of the state.[39]

The lack of consensus on a king's spiritual authority informed debates about his carnal authority. In his speech to Parliament on 19 March 1604, James warns English Catholics that as God's agent, he is authorized to claim dominion over their consciences. English Catholics' lack of conformity in religion renders them "but halfe my Subiects" – and the baser, corporeal half to boot, for James declares, "I want the best halfe of them, which is their soules."[40] To forfeit his authority over this "best halfe" and to allow English Catholics to practise and preach "their errors" would constitute a kind of tyranny: "Correction without instruction, is but a Tyrannie," he says, glossing "instruction" as the study and preaching of the true faith, with the implication that "correction" signifies corporeal discipline.[41] The limits of royal "correction" were routinely illustrated on early modern public scaffolds. Compulsion of conscience and physical suffering went hand in hand in what Michel Foucault calls "the scene of the confession," in which an offender's verbal testimony and tormented body made his or her guilt "legible for all."[42] Although the law confers on kings the "power of life and death over their subjects," as the *Vindiciae* author explains, the point at which lawful execution of justice became tyrannical excess varied across Europe (sig. K4v). On the Continent judicial torture was used systematically to elicit admissions of guilt. Not so in England, where continental interrogatory methods were roundly abhorred. In fact, in England not only was the authority to torture restricted to the monarch but this authority was also exercised, as Elizabeth Hanson puts it, "only in cases where the Crown had a special interest – a very small percentage of the total criminal investigations."[43] The infrequent application of judicial torture was both cause and symptom of English ambivalence about a king's authority to compel his subjects' souls and bodies.

When we look at early modern English explications of catharsis, we find a similar lexicon of presumptive violence in the name of spiritual instruction and corporeal correction. The operations of catharsis begin with affective manipulation. John Harington, in *A Brief Apology of Poetry* prefaced to his translation of *Orlando Furioso* (1591), asserts that "the Tragicall ... mou[es] nothing but pitie or detestation" and can also "terrifie."[44] Sidney also writes that tragedy "can move," though he ascribes this impact to slightly different affective causes: tragedy "maketh kings fear to be tyrants" by "stirring the affects of admiration and commiseration."[45] Sidney's "fear" and "commiseration" map onto Harington's terror and "pitie," respectively. "Admiration" is a translation of *admiratio,* which term continental writers used to denote various effects, especially their construal of Aristotle's doctrine of catharsis.[46] These emotional effects have explicitly spiritual consequences. In *Hamlet* the prospect of Claudius "but blench[ing]" becomes proof that tragedy's elicitation of fear and pity has "struck ... the soul" and "[caught] the conscience of the King" (2.2.574, 2.2.568, 2.2.582). And in *An Apology for Actors,* Thomas Heywood relates a purportedly true account of tragedy's "horrid and fearefull" representation of murder causing a playgoer guilty of that offence to "[find] her conscience (at this presen[t] ment) extremely troubled."[47] From the vantage point of defenders of tragedy, this process is eminently law-abiding and judicially beneficial: the elicitation of fear and pity in response to tragic representations causes a crisis of conscience that inspires confession and leads in turn to reformation or punishment.

From another perspective, catharsis constitutes an unlawful usurpation of divine and human authority. Even as English casuists remained ambivalent about the king's relationship to his subjects' souls and bodies, they were decided on the subject of tragedy's role. In their tracts and sermons, English experts in case divinity outlined a course of diligent self-assessment involving the believer, God, and, in some instances, the state – but never tragedy. In *The Whole Treatise of the Cases of Conscience* (1606), for example, celebrated preacher William Perkins juxtaposes judicial and theatrical presentments of crime. Citing Saint Paul's proscription against naming sin and offence, Perkins concedes that "Magistrates & Ministers" may name violations of divine and human law in order to "punish, and reforme them"; but he denounces "common plaies" as "nothing els, but representations of the vices & misdemeanours of men in the world ... for the causing of mirth and pastime."[48] In *A Refutation of the Apology for Actors* (1615) the author identified as I.G. mounts a similar argument through juxtaposition of divine and tragic efficacy. Responding directly to Heywood's contention that "these exercises" – that is, stagings of tragedy – "haue beene the discouerers of many notorious murders, long concealed from the eyes of the world," I.G. writes that the playhouse promises "much mirth from vanity," but God causes guilty spectators to "there ... bee prickt in conscience."[49] Providence, not catharsis, "bring[s] them to repentance, that God might saue their soules"; so, too, the "destruction" of "their bodies" evinces divine "iustice" rather than any legalistic by-product of tragic performance.[50]

The repudiation of catharsis is shaped in part by the Christianization of tragedy. Ancient tragic theory and practice outline two basic plotlines: tragedy represents the criminal behaviour of immoral kings and the arbitrary vicissitudes of fortune.[51] What links these plotlines is the way both immoral kings and fortune are tyrants in their willful, whimsical exercise of power over their subjects. Once God replaces fortune, any similitude must be denied. As John Milton, a later theorist and practitioner of tragedy, would illustrate in *Paradise Lost,* God legitimately wields the sort of absolute authority that in the hands of lesser beings constitutes tyranny.

The tyranny of tragedy appears not only as a usurpation of divine and secular authority but also as an unlawful use of corporeal violence. Early modern English explications of catharsis show that tragedy assaults the bodies of playgoers, often using the language of judicial torture to describe embodied emotion. In the anonymous *A Warning for Fair Women*, which I discuss in chapter 1, a personified Tragedy explains that to fulfill her "office," she "must have passions that must move the soule" (ll. 49, 44). As Bruce Smith writes, "[t]o 'move' ... is, for us, a figurative action," but in early modern England "it was a physical fact about how passions work in, on, and through the body."[52] As she proceeds to describe her "office," Tragedy boasts of "Mak[ing] the heart heave," "Extorting teares," and "rack[ing] a thought" (ll. 45–7). While Tragedy's nouns ("heart," "teares," "thought") put emphasis on her emotional and cognitive effects, her verbs ("heave," "extort," "rack") link these effects to the disciplined body. The goal of Tragedy's brutality is to "rap the sences from their course" (l. 48). "Rap," like "move," may mean to carry off or transport by force, as in its etymological and conceptual cognate "rapture." It may also signify violent assault, like its cognate "rape." These two meanings of "rap" clarify the "sences" that Tragedy claims to "move": both corporeal sensations, such as sight, and moral sensibility, as in "good sense." A similar conjunction of bodily and ethical senses characterizes "touch," another term used to denote tragedy's operation. In *An Apology for Actors* Heywood writes that tragedy works by "attaching the consciences of the spectators, finding themselues toucht in presenting the vices of others."[53] In early modern English usage, "attach" could denote arrest and indictment and "touch" a kind of trial, such that Heywood's language underscores the legalistic quality of early modern English catharsis.[54] As the common lexicon of tyranny and tragedy demonstrates, the difference between jurisprudence and catharsis is that between the necessary force of law and the gratuitous force of tyranny.

Significantly, both *A Warning for Fair Women* and Heywood's *An Apology for Actors* take London as the explicit or implicit venue for theatrical tragedy. When Tragedy addresses her audience as a collective – "All this faire circuite here" and "All you spectators" (ll. 92–3) – she implies not only a universal familiarity with the play's London setting and plot but also the metropolitan context in which she exercises her violent "office." In Heywood's *Apology* the examples of tragic efficacy take place at a distance from England's capital city: in Lynn, a provincial town in Norfolk; Amsterdam, a principal European trading centre; and ancient Rome, a locus of imperial and cultural authority. Yet London, both its commercial playhouses and courtly stages, remains the point of reference for Heywood's tribute to theatre as a definitive institution of the metropolis.

An urban context also characterizes court-based explications of tragedy. Hamlet's plan to catch Claudius's guilty conscience is inspired and carried out by "tragedians of the city" (*Hamlet* 2.2.316). Theatrical tragedy was all the rage "when [Hamlet] was in the city," but "now the fashion" in the metropolis is satirical drama, which is "most tyrannically clapped for" – an allusion to the Wars of the Theatres that shifts tyrannical behaviour from tragedian to playgoer (2.2.321–2, 327–8). Similarly, Sidney makes reference to the popular audiences of tragedy: "if evil men come to the stage, they ever go out (as the tragedy writer answered to one that misliked the show of such persons) so manacled, as they little animate folks to follow them."[55] "Folks" is scarcely a term for a royal audience, and Sidney's reference to entering and exiting the stage recalls his discussions of place-realism on the commercial stage.[56]

These plays and theories, while asserting tragedy's service to the metropolis, also disclose its shortcomings. The indiscriminate application of catharsis undermines its legitimacy. In *A Warning for Fair Women* Tragedy's use of "All" to refer to playgoers suggests that none of them can evade her violent effects, regardless of gender, class, affiliation, or, significantly, individual liability. Likewise, Hamlet, in response to the First Player's passionate representation of the weeping of Hecuba at the sight of Priam's slaughter, contends that the "tears" and "horrid speech" of an actor who shares "the motive and the cue for passion / That I have" would "Make mad the guilty and appal the free" (*Hamlet* 2.2.538–41).[57] In imagining the impact of tragic performance, Hamlet does not discriminate between tyrannical kings and loyal courtiers, queens and queans, "guilty" and "free."[58] In executing its purportedly ameliorative violence, then, tragedy persecutes rather than protects playgoers.

Even as catharsis works on the audience as a collective, it fails to affect some playgoers. In *Hamlet* and in defences of the stage, tyrants appear capable of evading the compulsion to confess and reform. Harington and Heywood attempt to illustrate the potency of tragedy by referring to a specific historical performance and playgoer. Each contends that the 1579 performance of Thomas Legge's Latin tragedy

Richard III could reform even the worst of tyrants – namely, Phalaris of Agrigentum, whose "cruelty," according to Cicero, "is notorious beyond all others."[59] These allusions are part of hypothetical rather than historical scenarios, however: Harington writes that the play "would moue (I thinke)" the infamous tyrant to terror, and Heywood supposes that "had" Phalaris seen *Richard III*, "it had mollified his heart."[60] When Sidney in his *Apology* relates a historical occasion on which a tyrant attended a tragedy, catharsis fails to actualize Harington's and Heywood's "what if?" scenarios. As proof of "how much it [tragedy] can move," Sidney cites the example of "the abominable tyrant Alexander Pheraeus," who wept during a performance of Euripides's *The Trojan Women*. The tyrant's affective response to tragedy did not result in a reformation of his vicious reign, however. Alexander "could not resist the sweet violence of a tragedy," but it "wrought no further good in him." For this failure Sidney blames neither Euripides nor the tragedians but the playgoer himself, for "he, in despite of himself, withdrew himself from hearkening to that which might mollify his hardened heart."[61] According to Plutarch's *Morals*, Sidney's likely source, the tyrant literally withdrew from tragedy: Alexander "was so moved" by Euripides's play that "he suddenly left the theater, made haste away, & went faster than an ordinary pace untill [*sic*] he was out of sight."[62] The "sweet violence of tragedy" moved the tyrant emotionally, but by removing himself physically from the theatre, Alexander appears to have prevented tragedy from moving his conscience.

In this anecdote, Sidney seems at pains to indicate that even though Alexander is responsible for interrupting the operations of catharsis ("he ... withdrew himself"), the tyrant is also a victim of this failure ("in despite of himself"). But Sidney omits the fact that Alexander is not the only victim. According to Plutarch, Alexander "went within a little of punishing that excellent actour most grievously" who led him to "shed teares, in compassion."[63] Rather than profit from tragedy's presumptive violence, that is, the tyrant comes near to wielding analogous brutality against another. By omitting this fact, Sidney occludes the troubling affinity between tyranny and tragedy that underlies his interpretation of catharsis.

In *The Roman Actor* Massinger taps into this common lexicon to reveal what Sidney occludes. In fact, Massinger's play raises the stakes of Sidney's anecdote. Caesar Domitian does not simply forestall catharsis but actually reverses its operations. When tragedy elicits his fear and pity, he punishes the actors "most grievously" by exacting the sorts of spiritual and corporeal torments that early modern English writers ascribed to catharsis. And when, like Alexander, Domitian falls victim to his own manipulations, he becomes an unwitting actor in his own tragedy. In *The Roman Actor* the tyrant becomes a tragedian of the city, and Massinger exposes metropolitan tragedy as a tyrant.

Gods of Theatre

Many early modern political writers point to the historical Caesar Domitian as an example of the usurping, excessive tyrant. For example, the author of *Vindiciae contra tyrannos* cites "that execrable *Domitian* who (as *Suetonius* recites) would be called God and Lord" to illustrate the limits of human authority (sig. B1r). It is not surprising, then, that Massinger's Domitian also claims "the style / Of lord and god" (1.4.35–6). What *is* startling is the extent to which Domitian assumes, in the sense used by the *Vindiciae* author to mean both "take on" and "take for granted," not only divine but also cathartic authority. Through the orchestration of both theatrical and "actual" tragedies, Domitian appropriates the presumptive violence of catharsis to his personal and political ends. In this sense, he becomes a figure for catharsis, not unlike the allegorical Tragedy in *A Warning for Fair Women*. Yet *The Roman Actor* makes clear that neither God nor the state confers on Domitian the power to command death and performance; rather, to the detriment of the metropolis, the tyrant *assumes* it.

Beginning with Domitian's "bloody entrance" at the end of act 1, Massinger sets the overlapping discourses of tyranny and tragedy emphatically in the metropolis (1.4.20). Recalling the processional entrance of Marlowe's Tamburlaine, Domitian comes onstage in triumph, atop a chariot and leading prisoners of war. Domitian pronounces that "this victorious arm hath made [his prisoners] / The scorn of Fortune" and condemns them to "Taste the extremes of misery" (1.4.16–18). By subordinating fortune's vicissitudes to his "victorious arm" syntactically and conceptually, Domitian denies the possibility that he too may fall from "the height of human glory" and suffer a miserable demise (1.4.14). Definitions of tyranny as usurpation and of tragedy as a representation of the vicissitudes of fortune conjoin in Rome's streets. The urban context in which political and theatrical discourses intersect is also evident in the tyrant's manipulation of tragic energies. Domitian commissions Rome's poets and players to "provide the people / Pleasures of all kinds" and warns, "'Tis death to him that wears a sullen brow"

(1.4.80–1, 1.4.83).[64] Theatrical pleasure, judicial death, and coercion of response – the tyrant's means of political control are also the means of Tragedy's "office." Massinger thus introduces the metropolis as a stage on which the tyrant executes tragic authority.

In the two inset performances that follow, the tyrant continues to act as a figure for tragedy. These performances take place in Caesar's palace, not a Roman street, and like Domitian's triumphant procession, neither performance is a theatrical tragedy. Once again, however, Massinger draws on early modern English explications of tragedy to frame each performance. Specifically, Domitian designs these performances to produce the physical and affective impact of catharsis. When performance fails to elicit the intended emotions, confessions, and punishments, Massinger's tyrant usurps tragedy and compels those effects that early modern English writers associated with catharsis. By turns horrific and absurd, tragedy's disciplinary function comes to fruition as Domitian dismisses spectators from the courtly stage to the block or gallows. The tyranny of tragedy may begin in a private gallery, but it concludes on the public scaffold.

The first inset performance is a vocal recital. Troubled by the thought that Senator Lamia retains a claim on the empress, whom Lamia is "forced" to divorce in act 1, Domitian requires his attendance at court with the expectation that the vocal recital will "Strik[e him], and with horror, dead" (2.1.130, 2.1.178).[65] The references to "Strik[ing]" and "horror," which call to mind the vocabulary of early modern English accounts of catharsis, frame this musical performance as a theatrical tragedy. In fact, the only time Aristotle uses the term "catharsis" outside the *Poetics* is in his discussion of singing in book 7 of the *Politics*.[66] Domitian's design is frustrated when Lamia hears the recital "without admiration" (2.1.231), meaning not only a lack of appreciative praise but also a dearth of the cathartic effects to which Sidney refers with the word "admiration." To elicit the desired response, Domitian summarily condemns Lamia: "I pronounce thee / Guilty of treason. – Off with his head! – Do you stare?" (2.1.234–5). The question "Do you stare?" registers Lamia's stricken horror in finding himself, in less than five lines, forcibly transported from Caesar's palace to the execution block.[67]

The second inset performance follows a similar pattern. In an attempt to reform the miserly Philargus, Domitian compels his attendance at a court performance of *The Cure of Avarice*. Although this play-within-a-play is a "comedy" (2.1.101), Paris, "the tragedian" and "chief of [his] profession" in Rome (1.3.31–2), boasts its reformatory potential in terms familiar to modern (and possibly early modern) audiences from Hamlet's description of tragedy as a conscience-catching thing. "I once observed," Paris recounts,

> In a tragedy of ours, in which a murder
> Was acted to the life, a guilty hearer,
> Forced by the terror of a wounded conscience,
> To make discovery of that which torture
> Could not wring from him. (2.1.90–5)

Though imitation may be the sincerest form of flattery, Paris's anecdote introduces not a tribute to but a parodic reproof of tragic theory. Evoking the concepts and language of early modern English accounts of catharsis, Paris offers himself as eyewitness to successful tragedy ("I once observed") and emphasizes its effects upon playgoers' emotions ("Forced by ... terror"), souls ("wounded conscience"), and bodies ("torture," specifically "wring[ing]" or pressing). Paris is convinced that *The Cure of Avarice* will reproduce his former success, but Domitian intimates that even though the play-within-a-play may fall short, he will not: "If the comedy fail / To cure him, I will minister something to him / That shall instruct him to forget his gold, / And think upon himself" (2.1.164–7). Although his language ("minister," "instruct," "think") calls to mind spiritual and cognitive effects associated with tragedy, it becomes clear that Domitian, like James I, views instruction as inseparable from correction. The tyrant redeploys tragic pleasure and profit as peremptory trial and punishment.

Upending the claim of tragedy's advocates, Massinger shows the stage operating in the service of *injustice* in the metropolis. At the conclusion of *The Cure of Avarice,* Domitian asks Philargus, "Dost thou in thyself / Feel true compunction, with a resolution / To be a new man?," to which the miser replies, "This crazed body's Caesar's, / But for my mind – " (2.1.427–30). This half-line is telling in several ways. First, it points up Domitian's own interruption of tragedy, not by cutting short the operations of catharsis but by literalizing them. When Philargus insists that he is "past cure," Domitian compels the "sudden change of life" that the play-within-a-play fails to inspire by summarily condemning Philargus: "thou shalt never more / Feel the least touch of avarice. – Take him hence / And hang him instantly" (2.1.436, 2.1.432, 2.1.437–9). Second, "But for my mind – " gestures to the limitations of plays as conscience-catching things. Performance may move playgoers' "bod[ies]," such as when it leads to weeping or punishment, but fail to move their consciences or "minds." Third, this half-line signals Domitian's failure to profit from tragedy precisely because he denies responsibility for judicially (if also syntactically) cutting off Philargus. Domitian turns Philargus's death into an example of "justice, / Since such as wilfully will hourly die / Must tax themselves, and not my cruelty" (2.1.445–7). The pun on "will" in these lines calls attention to the absurdity of Domitian's declaration. After all, Philargus is forced first to attend a theatrical quasi-tragedy at court and then to perform an "actual" tragedy at the gallows.

In the next two subsequent inset performances – the senators' torture and another play-within-a-play – *The Roman Actor* discloses the limits of the tyrant's tragic agency. Several scholars point to act 3, scene 2, as the moment when Domitian loses control of metatheatrical spectacle.[68] What has escaped critical attention is the extent to which this loss of control marks Domitian's transition from a figure for catharsis to its object. In this scene at the structural centre of Massinger's play, the spaces of theatre and punishment do not serve the tyrant's will, as they do in earlier scenes; but neither do they operate in the service of law and order. The metropolis becomes, instead, an expansive stage for performances of the tyranny of tragedy.

At the beginning of act 3, we learn that Domitian has "condemn'd" Senators Sura and Rusticus for "lamenting his cruel sentence / On ... Their patron and instructor" (3.1.104–6). The episode of judicial torture that follows presents an alternate version of Domitian's penchant for reversing the operations of catharsis. As in previous scenes of theatrical-cum-actual tragedy, this episode ends with literal purgation, as Domitian sends his enemies to their "death[s]" (3.2.121). In every other way, Domitian's attempt to reverse the operations of catharsis recoils upon him. Although Domitian designs the senators' torture to "remove / His doubts and fears," the horrifying spectacle initiates a painful crisis of conscience (3.1.31–2). The tyrant expects the senators to confess their treachery under the duress of bodily suffering, but they prove wholly uncooperative participants, drawing on Stoic philosophy which insists on the sovereignty of individual conscience and scripting of one's own death.[69] Even as Domitian directs their torture, the senators "grin" and accuse Domitian of "tyranny" (3.2.71, 3.2.96). Domitian raps the senators' bodies, but he cannot touch their hearts or minds; they remain, corporeally and spiritually, "unmoved" (3.2.90). But the tyrant *is* moved. Rather than free him of doubt and fear, the performance of punishment causes Domitian to suffer self-reproach and bodily pain: "I am tortured / In their want of feeling torments," he cries out and admits, "By my shaking / I am the guilty man, and not the judge" (3.2.88–9, 3.2.116–17). These cathartic effects do not lead to the tyrant's reformation but not because they are products of punitive rather than theatrical performance.

Domitian forestalls reformation when he sends the senators offstage to die, but like Alexander of Pherae, he becomes a victim of catharsis despite his physical withdrawal. The courtly play-within-a-play that immediately follows the senators' exit repeats the pattern of tragic agent turned tragic object and with considerably more dire consequences. Just as Domitian expects the senators' torture to alleviate doubt and fear, the empress Domitia asserts that a one-act version of *Iphis and Anaxarete* that she has "prepared" will "banish [Domitian's] melancholy" (3.2.129–30). The empress's principal motive in arranging this aristocratic performance is not to cheer her husband but to gratify her desire to see Paris impersonate a lover.[70] The empress's manipulation of tragedy backfires, just as her husband's does in the preceding punitive episode. When Paris, playing Iphis, threatens to hang himself rather than live without Anaxarete's love, the empress cries out for someone to "Restrain him" (3.2.282). Domitian wonders at his wife being "Transported thus" (3.2.283). Even she admits, "What I saw presented / Carried me beyond myself," and feels "upon the sudden ... indisposed" (3.2.288–9, 3.2.291–2). The next morning Domitia summons and seduces Paris, after she dismisses her husband by claiming to feel still "distracted" and "transported" (4.1.18, 4.1.87).[71] Subsequently, out of her inordinate lust for Paris, Domitia becomes complicit in a conspiracy to kill her husband.[72] In the play's final moments, the tyrant's "murder" is pronounced a capital offence, and Domitia is "drag[ged] ... to her sentence" (5.2.78, 85). This ending ventriloquizes the official position that an assault upon any anointed monarch, whether a tyrant or a just king, constitutes treason. More subtly, it presents an ironic rehearsal of Domitian's earlier assumption of cathartic authority. The tyrant condemns his enemies but at the cost of starring in his own tragedy.

Here, again, Massinger parodies early modern English explications of catharsis and in a manner that highlights the slippage between public scaffold and private stage. In *An Apology for Actors* Heywood relates a purportedly true story set in the town of Lynn. During the performance of a tragic play, a female playgoer emits "an out-cry, and loud shrike," then leaves the theatre "with a distracted & troubled braine."[73] "In this agony she some few dayes languished," Heywood explains, before she confessed "out of the trouble of her afflicted conscience" to adultery and murder. Like Heywood's playgoer, Domitia is moved to spontaneous exclamation, mental perturbation, and physical indisposition. But like Massinger's tyrant, the empress remains unreformed by catharsis; in fact, theatrical tragedy facilitates sexual and political offence. Moreover, although *The Roman Actor* concludes with the restoration of due process – Domitia is not executed summarily but "refer[red to] the hearing of the Senate, / Who may at their best leisure censure [her]" (5.2.86–7) – within the dramatic fiction, theatrical tragedy falls short of exposing criminal intent. Catharsis, ostensibly wielded in the city's defence, becomes a source of "actual" tragedy in the metropolis.

The metatheatrical and inset performances that punctuate *The Roman Actor* reverse the operations of tragedy. Instead of catharsis resulting from a representation of tyranny, tyranny literalizes the presumptive violence of catharsis. In this sense, the tyrant appoints himself a direct, not metaphoric, agent of tragedy. But at no point does Domitian profit from the tragedies that he orchestrates – neither "actual" tragedy in the form of torture in the city streets nor theatrical tragedy on the courtly stage. On the one hand, this failure of catharsis is due to the tyrant's refusal to remain a spectator and insistence on becoming an actor. On the other hand, by assuming the actor's position, Domitian condemns himself to the principal role in his own political drama. This turn of events situates *The Roman Actor* firmly within an extended tradition of tyrant tragedy as the dramatic representation of excessive bloodshed committed by *and against* unjust rulers. Through references to this tradition, Massinger glosses his critique of tragic theory as a problem of the metropolis, a problem that includes and exceeds Stuart London.

Tragic Allusions

The Roman Actor begins with an allusion to ancient tragedy:

AESOPUS: What do we act today?
LATINUS: Agave's frenzy
With Pentheus' bloody end. (1.1.1–2)

In seventeenth-century England, as today, Euripides's *The Bacchae* was the best-known, though not the only, dramatization of the "bloody end" of Pentheus, King of Thebes.[74] Scholars have considered Massinger's reference to *The Bacchae* in terms of *The Roman Actor*'s blurring of theatre and reality, but little has been said about how it bears on the play as metropolitan tragedy.

In Euripides's telling, Pentheus incites the god's ire when he opposes the *polis* cult of Dionysus. Disguised as a mere mortal worshipper, Dionysus convinces Pentheus to impersonate a woman so he may spy on the bacchantes' sumptuous rites. Pentheus's costume and rehearsal do not prepare him, however, for his role in the *sparagmos,* or ritual dismemberment of a sacrifice. At Dionysus's direction, Pentheus is torn apart by a group of female worshippers, including his mother, Agave. *The Bacchae* does not resolve the question of who is the (principal) tyrant: Pentheus for his challenge to divinity, or Dionysus for his excessive violence? This ambiguity informs *The Roman Actor* by alerting us to the continuity between Domitian's roles as agent, victim, and actor of tragedy.

At the beginning of act 4, as he watches his wife seduce Paris, Domitian likens himself to one of the "sad spectators" sitting in "the theatre of the gods" (4.2.115–16). Domitian's identification with divinity is of a piece with his earlier subordination of fortune and assumption of cathartic authority. Yet the tyrant does not remain separate from the action but participates in it. Domitian orders a court performance of a tragedy entitled *The False Servant,* with Paris in the title role and himself as the lord who discovers the infidelity of his wife and servant. Domitian's role, like Dionysus's, requires class cross-dressing.[75] It also affords Domitian an opportunity to violate "the trusted boundaries and safeguards of theatre," as if he, too, is a "god of theatre."[76] When the play calls for the lord to murder his false servant, Domitian actually kills his fellow actor: "Oh, I am slain in earnest!," Paris exclaims (4.2.283). As with the opening allusion to *The Bacchae,* when Domitian takes on a Dionysian authority to punish through performance, *The Roman Actor* registers the classical roots of early modern English metropolitan tragedy.

According to Richard Seaford, the violent Dionysian rituals in which tragedy originated served an important civic function. Although these rituals celebrated cruelty and lawlessness, they also created and strengthened social bonds. Pentheus's sacrificial death becomes a foundation myth for the Athenian *polis* by dissolving established boundaries between god and man, performance and actuality, "the community as a whole and autocratic rule."[77] In a similar fashion, Paris's "sudden death" brings together the metropolitan populace: the tyrant joins with poets, actors, and spectators in collective lamentation (4.2.307). Yet neither *The*

Bacchae nor *The Roman Actor* reconciles the tension between its representation of individual suffering and its production of civic unity.

This irresolution manifests in the decidedly *untragic* responses of those who violate the boundary between theatrical and actual tragedies. Rather than catharsis, the killings of Pentheus and Paris produce indifference. As Adrian Poole writes, "At the end of *Bacchae* it is hard to share Dionysus' indifference to the carnage he has wrought. It is more natural to protest with Cadmus that the gods *ought* to be better than this, better than *us*."[78] Domitian appears to know the appropriate response to Paris's death, describing the tragedian's killing as an act of "pity" that should move "spectators [to] weep" (4.2.293, 4.2.307). Yet Domitian remains coldly aloof to the "bloody ends" that he produces. Rather than join the communal expression of "ravishing sorrows," he offers the dying Paris only "applause ... By our imperial hand" (4.2.305, 4.2.299–300). It is fitting, then, that Domitian's death is met with similar indifference: a didactic aphorism pronounced by an unnamed tribune.[79]

In the cause and manner of his "unlamented fall," Domitian more closely resembles Pentheus than Dionysus (5.2.92). Indeed, the opening lines of *The Roman Actor* are usually glossed as a blunt analogue to the conclusion of the play, in which Domitian dies at the hands of a frenzied mob. Yet the performance of Domitian's demise recalls not only ancient but also early modern tragedy. The plot to kill Domitian begins with a validation of tyrannicide: "he deserves much more / That vindicates his country from a tyrant / Than he that saves a citizen" (3.1.76–8). The audience watches as the conspiracy swells to include several servants and women of the court, including the empress. In the final act, despite a trustworthy prophesy of doom, Domitian is lulled into a false sense of security. Then the conspirators fatally stab him, each blow accompanied by a melodramatic declaration of motive. Replace the name "Domitian" with "Julius," and the preceding sentences present a rather accurate synopsis of Shakespeare's *Julius Caesar*.[80] In this sense, *The Roman Actor* answers Cassius's question, "How many ages hence / Shall this our lofty scene be acted over, / In states unborn and accents yet unknown?": as Domitian Caesar is a simulacrum or type of Julius Caesar, *The Roman Actor* becomes an instance of "Caesar bleed[ing] in sport" (3.1.112–15).

The implicit references to *The Bacchae* and *Julius Caesar* underscore the cultural work of allusion throughout *The Roman Actor*. In his explication of allusion, Gregory Machacek argues, "Part of what cultures do is select from among the works that were valued in the past, assign contemporary significance to those works, and pass them on to the next generation."[81] *The Roman Actor* registers the value that early modern English defences of literature ascribe to classical tragedy, especially Aristotle's doctrine of catharsis, even as it critically assesses the significance that Massinger's contemporaries assigned to this legacy. In so doing, the play extends the work of allusion from practice to theory.

A formal defence of the stage in the opening act of *The Roman Actor* provides an overview of Massinger's critical assessment of early modern English tragic theory. When the Roman Senate summons Paris to respond to the charge that the actors "search into the secrets of the time ... and traduce / Persons of rank and quality," the tragedian delivers a speech that reads like a greatest hits of early modern English defences of literature, especially tragedy (1.3.37, 1.3.39–40). Paris presents a series of hypothetical scenarios in which plays inspire playgoers to confess or reform their offensive behaviour. Paris's legalistic description of tragic efficacy is undermined every time Domitian employs the language of catharsis to consolidate his tyrannical authority. The similarities between Paris's and Domitian's conceptual and semantic frameworks also point up the broader affinity between the discourses of tragedy and tyranny. Allusion thus underscores the local thrust of *The Roman Actor*. Massinger marshals an extended history of theory and practice to mount a potent critique of tragedy in early modern England.

Paris's formal defence of the stage brings into focus the specifically metropolitan imperatives of Massinger's critical tactics and strategy throughout *The Roman Actor*. As Paris describes the impact of tragedy on adulterous wives, grasping children, and corrupt judges, the line "we [the actors] cannot help it" becomes a choric refrain (1.3.114, 1.3.122, 1.3.130; see also 1.3.140). This rhetorical structure shifts responsibility from players to playgoers. Like the Renaissance defences of poetry that Margaret Ferguson examines, Paris's defence of the stage seems "aimed not so much [at] winning a verdict of innocent as at making prosecutors and judges see that they in some sense share the defendant's guilt."[82] In fact, Paris, who plays "an orator's part," presumably directs his defence to both onstage and offstage audiences (1.3.144). Within the dramatic fiction, his final exemplum of a corrupt judge is aimed at the senators ("this reverend assembly," 1.3.136) and his accuser in particular ("e'en yourself, my lord, that are the image / Of absent Caesar," 1.3.137–8). In performance, it arguably speaks to the members of the Inns of Court and other political insiders who attended Blackfriars. Indeed, Paris's other exempla, which implicate persons necessarily absent from Rome's senatorial jury, such as women and young heirs, point beyond the world of the play to the heterogeneous audiences at London's private theatres. The work of allusion in *The Roman Actor* thus extends into urban spaces where cultural discourses manifest in and as performance.

In the 1620s *The Roman Actor* registered the discomfiting intersection of England's political and theatrical legacies. Thirty years later, its critique would appear prescient of the outcome of this intersection. When the senators come onstage "bound back to back," Domitian likens them "to double-faced Janus," the Roman god of past and future (3.2.119). The generation after Massinger's would enact its own version of this scene of martyrdom – or tyrannicide, as the case may be – on the public scaffold outside the Banqueting House at Whitehall. Charles I's execution demonstrates the kind of future that Massinger could neither predict nor control, a point to which I return in the postscript. Yet *The Roman Actor* bears a relationship to this event through their shared discourses of tragedy and tyranny – a semantic overlay that, as we will see in the next and final section, materialized in the metropolitan setting of Charles I's death.

Double-Faced Janus

On 30 January 1649, Charles I was "executed in the open street before Whitehall," as his death warrant directed.[83] Specifically, he was beheaded on a scaffold draped in black erected outside the Banqueting House at Whitehall. Visible today as an imposing, early-seventeenth-century neoclassical stone building, the Banqueting House began in 1581 as a temporary wood structure erected to accommodate large state functions, in particular Elizabeth's marriage negotiations with the Duke of Anjou.[84] After Elizabeth refused the French match, the Banqueting House was not torn down; instead, it became a principal site for royal ceremony, festivity, and theatre and a crucial symbol of Tudor political authority and England's growing international influence.

Elizabeth's successor altered the physical structure and symbolic significance of the Banqueting House. Beginning the year after the Gunpowder Plotters' execution and continuing through 1609, James I initiated significant work on the building. Never pleased with the renovations, he had opportunity to build from scratch a decade later, when fire destroyed the Elizabethan edifice. In 1619 James commissioned Inigo Jones to design and oversee the construction of a new Banqueting House. Whereas the architecture of the Elizabethan Banqueting House was, like the rest of Henrician Whitehall, "highly conservative and ... familiar to Londoners," Jones's design was based on ancient architectural theory and neoclassical styles that were alien and illegible to most Londoners.[85] However, James's intended viewer was as much international as domestic: on the Continent, where print images popularized English architectural achievements, the Banqueting House was perceived as "the equal to any of the building projects in the capitals of Europe."[86]

The aesthetics of the Jacobean Banqueting House were of a piece with the king's political ideology. James framed himself as Europe's *Rex pacificus*, Britain's King Solomon, and England's Octavius Augustus – and he intended his Banqueting House to reflect this new Golden Age. Indeed, the transformation of the Banqueting House was just the beginning; James intended to rebuild all of London, his royal seat. In one of numerous proclamations related to urban building and infrastructure, James aligned himself with Augustus and London with the ancient *polis*:

> As it was said of the first Emperor of Rome that he had found the city of Rome of Brick and left it of marble, so Wee, whom God hath honoured to be the first of Britaine, might be able to say in some proportion, that we had found our Cities and suburbs of London of sticks, and left them of brick, being a material farre more durable, safe from fire and beautiful and magnificent.[87]

This proclamation declares various motives for James's intended renovation of London, beginning with the Banqueting House.[88] In the early seventeenth century many continental cities underwent restructuring along classical lines. If London did not update its medieval infrastructure, England might be left behind, unable to compete politically, culturally, or commercially.

To be modern in seventeenth-century Europe was to be classical, and the construction of the new Banqueting House was intended as the first step in updating England's metropolis. This architectural vision also marked James's dissociation from the previous reign, both aesthetically and ideologically. James perceived the Tudor style of affective rule, like their Gothic buildings and chivalric decorative idioms, to be unruly, violent, and effeminate. The Golden Age he intended to bring about was defined by individual reason, pan-European peace, and patriarchal order both in England's governance and in London's architecture. Lucy Gent's association of early modern English classicism with Julia Kristeva's concept of abjection is keenly appropriate here: "May not a charm of classicism be just that it promises the possibility of ridding oneself of the embarrassments that hover around identity by entering a realm of lucidity where all is ordered and expressed by proportion?"[89] The Banqueting House gave an internationally recognizable façade to a style and philosophy of rule unlike that of the preceding dynasty.

However successful James's international project proved, his domestic plan backfired. In contrast to Elizabeth's native aesthetics, which she deployed successfully to connect with her metropolitan subjects, James's classicism failed to foster a bond with most Londoners.[90] As the proclamation quoted above indicates, the king was keenly aware of the potential local benefits of renovating London. The intended changes to buildings and infrastructure would redress concerns about urban growth and congestion and the concomitant problems of disorder and disease.[91] However, many Londoners did not view the proposed changes as a boon to the city. Denizens remained largely unmoved by James's vogue for classicism and saw his plan to reshape the city exclusively as a display of royal power and prerogative. Moreover, civic leaders perceived the work of Inigo Jones, whom James named Surveyor of the King's Work, and of the Commission for Buildings, of which Jones was the head, as officious interference and an imposition upon London's sovereignty.[92] What James and his supporters at court understood as a means to prosperity and security, many Londoners interpreted as an attempt to privilege international over national concerns and to bolster the monarchy at the expense of the city. Contrary to its design, the Banqueting House thus became a visible symbol of tensions between the Crown and the metropolis around the limits of royal authority.

Similar tensions characterized the first decade of Charles I's reign, arguably contributing in the 1640s to London siding with Parliament. In the 1630s many civic leaders and citizens perceived the king's policies as impositions on London's ancient privileges. In 1642 Charles I fled London after a failed attempt to arrest several members of Parliament on charges of treason. His temporary court at Oxford could not command Whitehall's political, cultural, and economic authority, either at home or abroad. Charles intended to restore his royal seat in England's capital (from the Latin *caput* for head) and punish the rebel MPs; but when he returned to London, it was his head that was cut off. His execution on 30 January 1649 literalized a figurative beheading that had occurred years earlier. During this time, the Banqueting House at Whitehall remained largely unchanged.[93] When Charles I died, then, he died in front of the structure that looked exactly as his father had left it.

Figure 7: The execution of the Gunpowder Plotters, with the Banqueting House in the background. Michael Droeshout, *The powder treason ... founded in hell, confounded in heaven* (1620–5), detail. British Museum, Reg. No. 1852, 1009.248 © The Trustees of the British Museum.

The intersecting histories of politics and aesthetics in London constitute the background, both ideological context and visual backdrop, for this tragic event.

There are surprisingly few visual representations of Charles I's beheading in front of the Banqueting House. This dearth may be part of the general scarcity of topical print images in sixteenth- and seventeenth-century England that Antony Griffiths ascribes to official censorship and the uncertainties of the English market.[94] It is also, and more directly, I believe, a result of the event's specific metropolitan setting. The location of Charles I's execution made visible the crime for which the court condemned him. The area outside Whitehall, often referred to as Old Palace Yard, was associated with executions for high treason. In the lower-right-hand corner of Michael Droeshout's *The Powder Treason* (1610–25), labelled "The reward of Trechery," the walls and spires of the Banqueting House are clearly visible looming above the yard, in which one conspirator hangs from a gallows, another conspirator lies still bound to a hurdle, and a large crowd of spectators attends the spectacle of treason's punishment (Figure 7).[95] Unlike Visscher's depiction of the Gunpowder Plotters' executions (which I discuss in chapter 2), Droeshout's portrait attempts an identifiable representation of place. Not coincidentally, this place localized the abuses of authority with which London had long charged the king.

As the topographical seat and visual symbol of royal power, the Banqueting House illustrated Charles I's condemnation for high crimes against the state. More subtly, the building's neoclassical façade framed judicial regicide as reasonable and authorized. Reasonable because the king's death was necessary to the restoration of political order, as reflected in the adherence to aesthetic order in Jones's design for the Jacobean Banqueting House. And authorized because law and precedent, both ancient and contemporary, sanctioned the trial and execution of a tyrant, just as classical theory and contemporary construction authorized the building's architecture, idioms, and materials.[96] Built as a monument to monarchical power, the Banqueting House was brought into the service of legitimizing the execution of a king.

The few English prints of Charles I's execution in front the Banqueting House use the presence of a still-living monarch to resist the legitimacy implied by the building's façade. An anonymous late-seventeenth-century image exemplifies this trend (Figure 8). The upper panel, although labelled "A liuely Representation of the manner how his late Majesty was beheaded uppon the Scaffold Ian 30: 1648," does not show Charles I prostrate on the block or his head separated from his body; instead, it portrays him standing and addressing a crowd of spectators. In contrast, the lower panel, which bears the inscription "A representation of the execution of the Kings Judges," depicts the protracted punishments of the men who condemned Charles I: one hangs from a gallows, while executioners hold up the head and begin to dismember another. This juxtaposition of lively majesty and executed regicides is of a piece with the print's representation of place. Whereas in the upper panel Charles I stands in front of a single crudely drawn window that suggests the specific setting of his death, the lower panel lacks a background and thus frustrates viewers' ability to locate the site of execution. By showing Charles I calm and composed – "He nothing mean nor common did / Upon that memorable scene," in Andrew Marvell's now well-known phrase[97] – the print aligns the rational, orderly building with the king rather than with his judges. The backdrop that seems intended to highlight Charles I's crimes against England thus undermines the logic of condemnation and authorizes the condemned.

The inclusion of the Banqueting House could also overturn republican symbolism by producing an image of royal hagiography. Like Massinger's scene of the senators' torture, the small handful of English prints that

Figure 8: "A liuely Representation of the manner how his late Majesty was beheaded uppon the Scaffold Ian 30: 1648: / A representation of the execution of the Kings Judges." Anonymous etching. British Museum, Reg. No. 1863, 0418.672 © The Trustees of the British Museum.

depict Charles I's death before the Banqueting House appear to draw on the pattern of illustration established by Foxe's *Acts and Monuments.* The anonymous English print *The Death of the King*, for example, conjoins placeless apotheosis and the urban place of execution (Figure 9). The print is dominated by the image of Charles I rising amidst an angelic host towards a blazing light, and a smaller image in the lower right depicts the king

Figure 9: The execution and apotheosis of Charles I, with the Banqueting House in the background. Eighteenth-century engraving. *The Death of the King*, after an anonymous 1649 print. Private Collection © Look and Learn / Peter Jackson Collection / Bridgeman Images.

prostrate upon the scaffold. Behind and to the right of the scaffold stands the Banqueting House, rendered in striking if not wholly accurate architectural detail. A more precise portrait of the Banqueting House appears in an untitled 1649 print (Figure 10). The print includes five of seven lower-

Figure 10: The execution of King Charles I before the Banqueting House, Whitehall, 30 January 1649. Engraving, after Sir Godfrey Kneller (1646–1723) / Private Collection/ © Look and Learn / Peter Jackson Collection / Bridgeman Images.

level windows, which it renders accurately with alternating triangular and domed pediments and single intermediary Ionic columns. In addition, the print depicts somewhat meticulously the buildings that stood on one side of the Banqueting House and the King's Gate across the yard. These faithful portraits of the London setting of Charles I's death link the king with an earlier generation of English martyrs. Rather than a tyrant condemned for abusing authority under the title of divine anointment, Charles I becomes in these images another of God's servants who suffers for his beliefs.

The semiotic possibilities of the setting of Charles I's death brings us back to the relationship between tyranny and tragedy critiqued two decades earlier in *The Roman Actor.* Historian John Morrill points to the period between 1626 and 1629 – the exact years of *The Roman Actor*'s initial performance and printing – as crucial to Charles I's political and personal fate. According to Morrill, during this period Charles I's "arbitrariness of behaviour ... infected the means as well as corrupt[ed] the ends of government" and thus exposed the king to condemnation for "legal tyranny."[98] Yet for almost twenty years, the king's critics largely refrained from using "tyranny" and its cognates, a silence that Morrill explains as part of "a religious case for resistance, not the case from secular tyranny, [by which to mobilize] men against Charles I."[99] Martin Dzelzainis offers an alternative explanation for this silence: Charles I's "image as monarch – tyrant, defender of the ancient constitution, 'man of blood' – proved remarkably malleable in the hands of his supporters no less than those of his opponents."[100] Both the king's advocates and his critics exploited the duality of theatrical terminology no less than they did early modern political vocabulary. In the years surrounding Charles I's trial and execution, when the language of tyranny resurfaced with dire consequences for king and country, writers routinely employed metaphors of the stage to grapple with these unprecedented events.[101] Marvell's description of Charles I as a "royal actor" upon "The tragic scaffold" is simply the best-known instance of this metaphorical turn.[102] By figuring Charles I in terms of theatrical tragedy, his supporters sought to undermine accusations of political tyranny. Yet just as theatrical tragedy may not amend but perpetrate tyranny, the royal tragedian could as easily prove a tyrant as he could a martyr.

The slippage in political and theatrical discourses, like the instability of urban places of punishment, reappears in later metropolitan tragedy. When Charles I died, the commercial playhouses had been closed for seven years, and they would remain officially shut for another seventeen. During this period, writers repurposed the conventions of theatrical tragedy to other purposes, including political debate and satire. In this way, tragic form weathered the Interregnum, albeit not without alteration. When John Milton sat down to write *Samson Agonistes*, as I explore in the next chapter, he worked with a Janus-like vision of tragic form akin to the view of urban history presented in *The Roman Actor* in the scene of the senators' torture. On the one hand, Milton looked back on the legacy of tragic theory and practice that Massinger and his contemporaries had inherited, reworked, and transmitted onstage and in print. On the other, with the blind eyes of classical poet-seers, Milton looked to the future, to a time when theatrical tragedy might not only protect the earthly metropolis from tyranny but also inspire a pursuit of the heavenly city. Through this bifocal lens, Milton surveyed Restoration London. The Great Fire of 1666, frequently interpreted as divine punishment for London's complicity in regicide, deprived the metropolis of social and infrastructural cohesion. In *Samson Agonistes* Milton explores the extent to which tragedy may restore measure to England's *polis*.

Chapter Four

Noise, the Great Fire, and Milton's *Samson Agonistes*

So to heare then is to attend with the eare, to receiue with the heart, to conuert in the life and conuersation.

– Richard Crooke, "To the Christian and beneuolent *READER*," prefacing *The Boring of the Ear* by Stephen Egerton (1623)

I went againe to the ruines, for it was now no longer a Citty.

– John Evelyn, diary entry for Monday, 10 September 1666

In the epistle "Of that sort of Dramatic Poem which is call'd Tragedy," John Milton introduces *Samson Agonistes* in terms of "Tragedy, as it was antiently compos'd."[1] For Milton this means tragedy as theorized and practised by the ancient Greeks. He cites Aristotle's catharsis clause, albeit in an interpretive paraphrase informed by contemporary translations of the *Poetics*, and names Æschylus, Sophocles, and Euripides as "the best rule to all who endeavour to write Tragedy" (66, 68). What I find striking about this list of classical influences is its neat division along methodological and metropolitan lines. On the one hand, Milton's dramatic sources are self-consciously of and about the city. The tragedies of Æschylus, Sophocles, and Euripides take place in ancient *poleis* and handle urban issues. Written for performance in Athen's Theatre of Dionysus, they also served an explicitly civic function. On the other hand, Milton's critical source is conspicuously silent on the subject of the *polis*. Aristotle's *Poetics* gives no hint of the city either as the setting and subject of tragedy or as the venue of and reason for its performance.[2] Like Aristotle, Milton omits any reference to the metropolis from the definition of tragedy in *Samson Agonistes*'s prefatory epistle;

but like the Athenian dramatists he also cites, he saturates his tragedy with representations of urban place.

In this chapter I argue that *Samson Agonistes* appropriates its classical influences and biblical subject to a meditation on tragedy as an urban genre. Five years before the publication of Milton's dramatic poem, the Great Fire of London left four-fifths of the medieval city in ruin. Milton, who identified as a Londoner throughout his life, grew up in the parish where the fire began on 2 September 1666, and he was probably in London on that fateful Sunday morning, having fled the outbreak of plague the year before and returned in February or March of 1666. The lively experience of London's destruction is at the heart of Milton's tragic project in *Samson Agonistes*. In their examinations of *Samson Agonistes* in terms of the Great Fire, Laura Knoppers, Janel Mueller, and Mary Ann Radzinowicz emphasize the poem's temporal topicality, that is, its place in the history of English discourse, government, and religion as focused around a particular catastrophic event.[3] *Samson Agonistes* is also topical in the early modern sense of the word as "[o]f or pertaining to a place or locality."[4] The Great Fire occurred specifically in London, and *Samson Agonistes* is set emphatically in a metropolis. Milton's tragedy thus demands a spatially local reading.

Of course, the destruction of the metropolis has national implications both in Milton's England and in his dramatic poem. According to Thomas Vincent in *Gods Terrible Voice in the City* (1667), the Great Fire constituted "a National Judgment because *London* was the Metropolis of the Land, because the Beauty, Riches, Strength and Glory of the whole Kingdom lay in *London*; and it was not the Inhabitants of the City who alone did suffer by this fire, but the whole Land more or less, do and will feel the smart hereof."[5] Elkanah Settle's elegy on the Great Fire observes that London's suffering becomes England's: the city's "loss, imparts from hence / Through the whole Kingdome its sad *Influence*."[6] Likewise, in *Samson Agonistes*, suffering and loss extend beyond the play's immediate urban setting. When Samson pulls down the pillars that hold up the roof of the temple of Dagon in Gaza, he kills the "choice nobility and flower, not only / Of this but each *Philistian* City round" (*SA* 1644–5). Yet in accounts of London's burning and in Milton's tragedy, the emphasis is on the tragic undoing of the metropolis: the cacophony of structural ruin and the disharmony of the human community.

My language of cacophony and disharmony is not merely figurative. As I show in this chapter, sermons, proclamations, and poems often represent the Great Fire as an aural experience. So, too, *Samson Agonistes* registers sound's effects on audiences. In the prefatory epistle to his dramatic poem, Milton ascribes to tragedy the "power by raising pity and fear, or terror, to purge the mind of those and such like passions, that is to temper and reduce them to *just measure* with a kind of delight, stirr'd up by reading or seeing those passions well imitated" (66, emphasis added). "Just measure" – Milton's phrase, like the reference to purgation in the same sentence, draws on early modern commentaries on Aristotle's *Poetics* that present catharsis as a medicinal cleansing. This connection appears, as well, in *The Reason of Church-Government* (1642), where Milton invests poetry with the capacity "to imbreed and cherish in a great people the seeds of vertu, and publick civility, and to allay the perturbations of the mind, and set the affections in right tune."[7] A strict Aristotelian reading of these mission statements might imply a straightforwardly "homeopathic" operation, in which tragedy uses "savage music to cure savage interior rhythms."[8] The early modern meanings of "measure" trouble this reading, however, by directing attention to sound's diverse effects. The literature of sixteenth- and early-seventeenth-century England discloses a widely held belief that both representational sounds, like poetic metre, and presentational ones, including music, preaching, even cacophony, could set passions in right tune and thus produce virtuous citizens, or they could perpetuate the savagery of the urban wilderness. Milton evokes these oppositional qualities when justifying the choice of metre for his dramatic poem. The strict metrical forms of ancient tragedy were "fram'd only for Music," Milton explains, and are therefore "not essential to [his] Poem"; instead, "The measure of Verse" used in *Samson Agonistes* "is of all sorts" (68). Given Milton's identification with Orpheus, it is not especially surprising that he employs musical metaphors to describe the affective and civic effects of his tragedy.[9] In *Samson Agonistes* Milton uses various metres not as ends in themselves but to represent the acoustic measure – or, rather, *mis*measure – of the metropolis.

These sounds must be heard, of course, in the mind's ear. Printed in 1671, Milton's tragedy is a "Dramatic Poem" that "never was intended" for "the Stage" (68). Date and medium might appear to separate *Samson Agonistes* from the plays and theories examined elsewhere in this book. Part of what is at stake in this chapter, then, is what counts as early modern English metropolitan tragedy. In its confluence of genre, justice, and the city, *Samson Agonistes* marks continuities in English metropolitan tragedy across an extended early modern moment. When commercial performance in London fell silent in 1642, writers brought the strategies of the city's stages into the service of the printed page, including news plays, satirical pamphlets, and political polemic.[10] These texts provided readers with sensorial experiences on par with playgoing, although, as we will see, the notion that sounds move the passions was not an innovation of the Interregnum but a carryover from the Renaissance.[11] So, too, Milton's tragedy bears traces of earlier apocalyptic literature. Long before fire ripped through Restoration London, the metropolis resounded with the noise of doomsday. From bookstalls and pulpits, Londoners heard warnings of the clarion trumpet of judgment and were told to repent before it was too late.[12] Set in a polysemous city that resounds with the "harsh din" of the fallen world (to borrow a phrase from Milton's "At a Solemn Music"), *Samson Agonistes* challenges readers to hear the harmony of Revelation's New Jerusalem and Saint Augustine's City of God.[13] In Milton's hands, tragedy becomes the genre of not simply suffering in the here and now of the earthly metropolis; it also becomes the proper form in which to represent a divine history that culminates in salvation and a heavenly metropolis.

Rough Music

Almost four decades before the publication of his metropolitan tragedy, a youthful Milton explored early modern associations between sounds and the passions in his pastoral masque. Early in the printed text of *A Masque presented at Ludlow Castle*, a.k.a. *Comus* (1634; 1637, 1645), appears a stage direction for "*The Measure*" (*Masque* 144 sd). This stage direction may refer to the "light fantastic round" that Comus orders his "*rout of monsters*" to perform, the music to which they "beat the ground," or both the monsters' dancing and its instrumental accompaniment (143, 92 sd, 144).[14] Whereas its exact referent remains obscure, "*The Measure*" produces a specific acoustic and affective experience. According to the virtuous Lady, it makes "the sound / Of riot, and ill-managed merriment, / Such as the jocund flute, or gamesome pipe / Stirs up" (169–73). The sound of "*The Measure*," that is, reveals passions that lack proper measure or control. The Lady's allusion to the flute and pipe confirms this connection between unruly sounds and passions. Like his near contemporary Ben Jonson, whose *Pleasure Reconciled to Virtue* (1618) represents Comus's "wild music of cymbals, flutes and tabers," Milton follows Plato in correlating percussive and wind instruments with the body and irrationality.[15] The sound of "*The Measure*" takes the affective measure of Comus and his followers: their passions are riotous, unmanaged, unreasonable – in essence, *out of* tune.

Yet the relationship between sounds and the passions was not always so simple. In early modern England the same sound could produce opposite effects. Pipe music, for example, had a range of associations, not just Bacchic excess and abandon. A few years before the performance of Milton's *Masque* at Ludlow Castle, Richard Brathwait in his *Whimzies* (1631) described how the piper maintains order at country dances: "In Wakes and rush-bearings he turnes flat *rorer*. Yet the Youths without him can keep no true *measure*. His head, pipe, and leg hold one consort."[16] Whereas Milton's Lady charges the "gamesome pipe" with instigating disorderly movement, Brathwait credits it with directing collective choreography. The ordering effect of pipe music also appears in *Colin Clouts Come Home Againe* (1591), in which Edmund Spenser memorializes his relationship with Sir Walter Raleigh as bucolic duet: "He pip'd, I sung; and, when he sung, I pip'd."[17] This musical collaboration is part of Spenser's larger project to strip pastoral piping of its erotic associations and to invest it with a moral, nationalistic purpose.[18] A similar partnership and sense of mission, as well as Spenserian diction, characterize Milton's *Lycidas* (1637). The speaker recalls how he and Lycidas, "Together both," tended their flocks and sang "rural ditties … Tempered to the oaten flute" (*Lyc* 25, 32–3). But as "the uncouth swain … touche[s] the tender stops of various quills" (*Lyc* 186, 188) – that is, as he sounds *Lycidas* – he does not confine his song to rustic subjects. The poem's critique of the ecclesiastical establishment and self-conscious sense of mission render pastoral elegy more than an encomium by and for individuals. It becomes a protest of moral corruption and a proclamation of intent – not only to live virtuously, like Lycidas, but also to serve a purpose greater than oneself. If in *A Masque* the sound of the pipe reveals affections in discord, in *Lycidas* it has the capacity to set them in right tune.[19]

There is no simple one-to-one correlation, then, between acoustic and affective measure. If the same sound may produce opposite effects, so, too, opposite sounds may produce the same effects. In early modern England clergy often billed sermons as transmissions of the divine Word capable of moving auditors to virtue; however, this capacity was not absolute. Surveying sermons on the parable of the sower and the seed, Gina Bloom demonstrates that preachers presented salvation to be "contingent on parishioners' aural receptivity – the extent to which their ears can be penetrated and their hearts fertilized by the seed-Word."[20]

As the epigraph by Richard Crooke that prefaces this chapter points out, right hearing should produce right feeling and, consequently, right doing. Yet a number of physical and spiritual obstacles, including drunkenness, worldly thoughts, and ignorance, might impede these effects.[21] As a result, Crooke laments, despite "such faithfull preaching, such frequent hearing, so many should yet bee possest as it were with a dumb Deuill, and all our Sermons to the most of men but as sounding Brasse or a tinkling Cimball."[22] Here, "dumb" denotes "unheard, from the sound being drowned by a louder one"; but it also suggests physical and affective insensibility.[23] Whether deafened or deaf, auditors who hear Comus's winds and percussion in the celestial harmony of sermons are doomed to sin and incivility. In a different context, the sound of brass and cymbals does not impede but facilitates reformation. Throughout pre-modern Europe, as Martin Ingram explains, popular justice was executed to "the ringing of bells, the raucous playing of musical instruments, the beating of pots and pans and other household utensils, and the discharge of guns and fireworks."[24] According to E.P. Thompson, this "rough music," as it was called in England starting in the seventeenth century, "denote[d] a rude cacophony, with or without more elaborate ritual, which was usually directed mockery or hostility against individuals who offended community norms."[25] In one respect, the rough music of communal justice is like Brathwait's piper, whose wild playing controls unruly movement. In both scenarios, discordant noise operates as a restraint upon or a corrective to disorderly behaviour. At the same time, rough music is like Egerton's sermon, which seeks to compel auditors to hear the timbre of their souls. As social historians show, the practices of popular justice are often formal *and* functional counterparts to official procedures of state and church. Just as the popular practice of "riding" represents a satirical appropriation of the official punishment of "carting," for example, rough music inverts the aural modes of sermons and proclamations in pursuit of the same measuring result. Unscored, unsupervised, inarticulate noise – as much as scripted, authorized speech – could restore auditors to the order of commonwealth, communion, and community.

The overlap of preaching and rough music is not only affective but also spatial. Raymond Williams's *The City and the Country* (1973) inspired a generation of scholars to examine the division between urban and rural spaces, the former associated with capitalism and aristocratic culture, the latter with a feudal agrarian culture. More recently, early modern social historians and literary scholars have challenged this "analytical dichotomy" in favour of "a series of permeable boundaries," such as between London and its suburbs, each of which contributed to the development of a metropolitan mentality.[26] Although sonic experience could represent one such permeable boundary, as in the case of rough music, the seventeenth-century English countryside tended to sound distinctly different from the city. The rural soundscape remained largely unchanged from the previous century, albeit perhaps at diminished volume, as men and women left for urban centres. Meanwhile, London's soundscape had grown loud and sundry. The sedans and coaches that rumbled down city streets with greater frequency contributed to London's cacophony, at the same time as they secluded passengers from it.[27] A proliferation of separatist and dissenting congregations led to an increase in the number of pulpits from which preachers, claiming the cleansing fire of divine inspiration, loudly warned of impending apocalypse.[28] Add to these sounds those of a large, congested, international populace; of industrial production and political debate; of buying, selling, drinking, and playing – and what one hears is Londinium as pandemonium, in the sense used since the nineteenth century of "a noisy disorderly place."[29] As this etymology suggests, Milton may have drawn on the urban sounds around him when in *Paradise Lost* he figured Pandemonium as a "metropolis" and the city as hell on earth.[30]

Paradise Lost suggestively represents this experience of the early modern metropolis. In Book 9 Milton describes Paradise, and its difference from Hell, in terms of a city-dweller's excursion to the country. Satan "traverse[s]" the garden until he finds the "Spot" "delicious" where the solitary Eve prunes rosebushes:

> Much he the place admired, the person more.
> As one who, long in populous city pent,
> Where houses thick and sewers annoy the air,
> Forth issuing on a summer's morn to breathe
> Among the pleasant villages and farms
> Adjoined, from each thing met conceives delight,
> The smell of grain, or tedded grass, or kine,
> Or dairy, each rural sight, each rural sound[.]
>
> (*PL* 9.434, 425, 439, 444–51)

In this passage, which one scholar calls "some of the strangest lines in *Paradise Lost*," Milton represents Paradise and Hell in terms of the distinct sensorial experiences of the city and the country, paying particular attention to touch, smell, and sight.[31] The bodily, tactile experience of Hell is reminiscent of the city in that both are places of imprisonment. City-dwellers are "pent" "in," narrowly confined by "houses thick," and oppressed by noxious "air." This is solitary confinement: the city-dweller is "one," alone among the "populous city." The olfactory experience of this urban multitude, which lives and works in close quarters, is noisome. In fact, according to Ken Hiltner, this passage alludes to the "serious problem" of air pollution in seventeenth-century London.[32] The smoke and fumes emitted by sea coal produced a troubling visual experience as well. In addition to destroying the health of vegetation, livestock, game, and people in and around London, air pollution was blamed for degraded buildings and foreshortened vistas, which transformed the well-lit cityscape into "darkness visible" (*PL* 1.63). Milton juxtaposes this sensibly oppressive metropolis to an idyllic countryside full of sensorial pleasures. Having "Forth issu[ed]" from his urban prison, the city-dweller rambles "Among the pleasant villages and farms / Adjoined," where he "conceives delight" from each "smell," "each ... sight," and "each ... sound." The reference to sound is striking because, whereas the passage details what the city-dweller meets, smells, and sees in the country (e.g., villages, farms, fields, cattle, and their by-products), it leaves to inference what he *hears*. The implication is that the country offers soothing sounds, its quiet disturbed only by the gentle whishing of the breeze through the grass, the lowing of cows, or the clatter of a milkmaid's pail. By contrast, the city is understood to be a place of loud, offensive, and oppressive noises. Indeed, in the early modern metropolis, the sounds of human discourse, activity, and industry became increasingly inescapable.

The profusion of noise in seventeenth-century London informed broader cultural shifts in what it meant to hear rightly. Changes in the urban soundscape compounded what Lawrence Manley describes as an "ethical innovation ... of place," in which "a mobile inner paradise of expanding personal powers and responsibilities" replaced "traditional forms of communal discipline."[33] Londoners increasingly expected to hear the call to virtue and civility as a still small voice, such as Elijah hears in I Kings 19:12, rather than as inspired preachers and pan-pounding neighbours. As urban upheaval challenged right hearing, Milton and others bypassed the ear altogether and advocated hearing directly with the heart. In *Paradise Lost*, for instance, the Father asserts: "And I will place within them as a guide / My umpire conscience, whom if they will hear" will "safe arrive" (*PL* 3.194–5, 197). The "place" of right hearing is "within" Londoners, not in the city's streets or at its pulpits. With the Word of God thus resounding in their hearts, Londoners might "conuert in life," as Crooke writes, and at the end of days, hear divine music in the City of Heaven.

Right hearing became all the more difficult when sounds of real-world tragedy compounded London's quotidian cacophony. The executions of beloved leaders, civil war, foreign conflict, plague, fire – each of these events introduced England's subjects, but especially residents of London where these events took place, to the sounds of suffering. Some of these events elicited sounds of celebration as well as lamentation. Cromwell's exhumation and posthumous hanging, for example, met with cheering and revelry. It is tempting to imagine Milton, as he hid in Bartholomew Close, trying to drown out these riotous sounds with orderly music, oratory, and poetry. Only a few years later London resounded with the noises of catastrophic loss as the Great Fire swept through the city, followed by joyous sounds of rebuilding. London's destruction and reconstruction may be heard in the sermons, poems, and proclamations that I discuss in the next section. The metropolis during and after the Great Fire also resounds in *Samson Agonistes*, in which Milton confronts readers with a tragic representation of urban mismeasure. Once again we may imagine Milton, now dictating his dramatic poem to an amanuensis. As Milton sang, the other piped (as it were) with his quill, and together they set to paper the rough music that would alert readers to what it might mean to hear metropolitan tragedy rightly.

The Sounds of Fire

The cause of the Great Fire, which broke out in the early hours of Sunday, 2 September 1666, quickly became the subject of rumour. In a letter dated "London Sept: 17. 1666," Arthur Stanekey writes to his brother: "the fire began at a Bakers house in pudding Lane neare my fathers house by Accident for any thinge I can heare."[34] Conjecture of causes other than mischance spread almost as fast as the flames. A letter from John Tremayne to his father, dated "London Septemb*er* 22, 1666," cites two popular explanations for the Fire: divine punishment and foreign conspiracy. Although Tremayne claims to "thinke it gods Judgm*ent*," he also gives credence to rumours that the Fire was a precursor to a French invasion: "god be praysed the villans never gathered to any head the severall outcries were made to that purpose and one in the night; which forced vs to leave all in the fields & take Armes."[35] Ultimately, an official investigation cleared London's alien population of all responsibility; but during and immediately after the Fire, the confused sounds of a foreign threat could not be suppressed.[36] As a result of these rumours, several alien residents were arrested and others purportedly killed in the street.[37] How many Londoners actually died during the four days and nights of the Fire also remained a subject of speculation and hearsay.[38] Against the definitive ocular proof of the Fire's progress, rumours about its material and human causes and effects continued to resound well after the flames were extinguished.[39]

An emphasis on acoustics over spectacle has its basis in the Great Fire itself. Many accounts assert that the flames could be heard well before they could be seen – or as Joseph Guillim writes in *The Dreadful Burning of London* (1667), "How does the crackling noise first wound our ear, / E're that the dreadful sight doth urge our fear."[40] In their attempts to describe the sound of the Fire, writers employed onomatopoeic terms, including crackle, rattle, and roar. Samuel Rolle in *Shlohavot* (1667) calls upon readers to "Hear how it crackles like a Fire in thorns: Hear what a rattling noise there is with the crackling and falling of timber."[41] Whereas Rolle associates rattling with London's buildings and, as a synonym for crackling, with biblical bushes, Thomas Vincent in *Gods Terrible Voice in the City* (1667) associates it with ancient chariots: "*Rattle, rattle, rattle,* was the noise which the Fire struck upon the ear round about, as if there had been a thousand Iron Chariots beating upon the stones."[42] Other writers describe the roaring of the Fire as both nature's appropriation and its undoing. In *Annus Mirabilis* (1667) John Dryden claims that the Thames began "to roar" when the Fire reached its bank; yet in a sermon on the Great Fire recorded in the Rodeney family manuscripts at the British Library, the Fire is said to have "roared like ye waues of the sea."[43] The river loses this acoustic contest, according to Guillim: "*Neptune* look[ed] up on this insulting Fire, / Which higher than his Surges doth aspire: / Who with his swelling Tides could scarce out-roar, / Or drown the noise they sente down to the shore."[44] In John Crouch's *Londons second tears* (1666) the Fire's roaring signifies not a natural superiority but a perverse rapacity: "When (strangely) it from adverse Windows ror'd: / Neighbour his Neighbour kindl'd and devour'd."[45] In Samuel Wiseman's *A Short and Serious Narrative of Londons Fatal Fire* (1667) roaring is among a catalogue of sounds that suggests the Fire's excessive physical and psychological violence: it "Roars, racks, Rends, Murmurs, and Raves."[46] Strikingly evocative of Tragedy's description of her office in *A Warning for Fair Women*, as I discuss in chapter 3, this catalogue of sounds portrays the Great Fire as a kind of tyrant intent on exercising tragic authority over the metropolis.

In addition to the elemental noises of combustion and collapse, the real-world tragedy of the Fire resounded with human cries of terror and distraction. According to numerous accounts, frightened voices alerted Londoners to the flames. Wiseman's *A Short and Serious Narrative* describes the "dreadful, hideous" cries of "Fire!" "screem'd out with a deep-strain'd throat" and other "direful Exclamations" indicative of "Horror, and fear."[47] In Simon Ford's *The Conflagration of London* (1667) the bellman's "*affrighting cryes*" awaken residents, who stumble into "the *clamorous street*" to become part of the "*Distracted Crowds*."[48] The sounds of terrified Londoners become confused with those of the city's structural ruin in John Allison's Pindaric ode on the Fire (1667):

> The Watches now in every street
> Eccho the dreadful noyse of Fire,
> Which calls with the same energy from bed,
> As the last Trumpet shall the dead,
> And bids them all draw nigher,
> The shiv'ring multitudes in bodies meet
> And some it raiseth by its light, and others by its heat.[49]

Allison does not clarify whether the "Eccho" is an exact admonition (the watches call out "Fire!") or a general similitude (the call of the watches is a dreadful noise, like that produced by the Fire). In his diary entry for Monday, 3 September, John Evelyn also conjoins the acoustics of human and infrastructural upheaval:

> mine eyes ... saw above ten thousand houses all in one flame, the noise & crakling & thunder of the impetuous flames, the shreeking of Women & children, the hurry of people, the fall of towers, houses & churches was like an hideous storme, & the aire all about so hot & inflam'd that at the last one was not able to approch it.[50]

The sounds of the Fire, more so than the sight or the feel of the flames that appear almost as afterthoughts, convey the tragedy of the metropolis.

However bewildering the sounds of the Great Fire, they communicated a clear message to many Londoners: Judgment Day is near. Like Allison's reference to "the last Trumpet," allusions to Judgment Day appear as both illustration and admonition in numerous accounts of the Fire. The official state record describes the Fire, especially its sounds of human suffering, by analogy to Doomsday: "Had you been at Kensington, you would have thought for 5 days that it had been Doomsday, from the fire and cries and howlings of the people."[51] Elsewhere the Great Fire is not simply *like* the final conflagration; it is an indisputable precursor, a warning of what would come to pass if Londoners do not reform. In their sermons, preachers present the Great Fire as a clarion call to hear rightly and take Londoners to task for their auricular failures – failures, they claim, that led to the Fire in the first place. In the dedicatory epistle to *London's calamity by Fire bewailed and improved* (1666) Robert Elborough chastises Londoners for not hearing earlier summons for reformation:

> *God hath spoken in the voyce of* Mercy, *and thou hast not heard; in the voyce of* his Ministers, *and thou hast not heard; ... in the voyce of the* Plague, *and the* Sword, *and thou hast not heard; and now in this* dreadful Judgement of Fire, *and thou doest not hear; no, though the* Fire *hath burnt round about, and in the midst of* thee, *and there be such* sad *and* dismal effects *of it, yet thou dost not hear.*[52]

Over a decade later, Thomas Gilbert in *Englands Passing-Bell* (1679) continued to blame the Fire on Londoners who had turned a deaf ear to God's ministers: "Thy *Prophets* were not dumb, but thou wert deaf."[53] Auricular failure may have caused London's destruction, according to these writers, but its correction was also the city's cure. If previously Londoners were deaf and damned, now they would hear and be saved. The ruin of England's metropolis was punishment for its citizens' many sins. In order to escape the final conflagration and eternal Pandemonium, London's faithful would need to hear rightly God's judgment in the here and now.

What it means to hear rightly the sounds of real-world tragedy bears a striking similarity to the effects ascribed to theatrical tragedy. William Gearing's *Gods sovereignty* (1667) recalls early modern English tragic theory when it describes the Fire as God's attempt to remedy Londoners' deafness and to move them to "pitty and compassion."[54] Because "you had hearts of stone," Gearing charges,

> who could hear the cries of the oppressed ... and hear them sighing and bemoaning their extremities and yet your bowels yearned not over such; ... Therefore doth the Lord take away our houses, our goods, our dearest outward comforts sometimes, for this end, that we may have a fellow-feeling of others miseries.[55]

In Gearing's account of the Great Fire, the theatre of God's judgments is a tragic theatre that softens hearts and stirs up pity and fear. No one is immune to these effects, not even kings. Whereas defences of the stage touted the universal efficacy of theatrical tragedy even as tyrannical rulers evaded its effects, accounts of the Great Fire describe divine and earthly kings as models for urban audiences on how to hear, and thus to feel, rightly. *Londons Lamentations* (1666) taps into the belief that God suppressed the Fire in compassionate response to sounds of suffering: "What Adamantine heart could but relent / To hear what dismal cryes and shrieks went up, / Such as even pierc't the Heavens."[56] In the weeks and months that followed, imagery of divine hearing and feeling continued to exemplify how Londoners' ears and hearts ought to function. "[M]ethinks I hear poor souls crying out, *Bread, Bread for the Lords sake*," Robert Elborough exclaims, "cryes of poor oppressed soules so pierce Gods eares, as that they cannot but work upon Gods heart."[57] According to Dryden, who dedicated his *Annus Mirabilis* "To the metropolis of Great Britain," these sounds worked upon the heart of God's anointed, Charles II, as well: the "shrieks of subjects pierce[d] his tender breast."[58] An implicit goal of these sermons and poems, and many others like them that flew off the presses in the aftermath of the Great Fire, is not simply to describe these magisterial responses to London's destruction but also to move readers to respond in kind.

In Crooke's formulation, however, to attend with the ear and to receive with the heart are not sufficient. A conversion "in the life and conuersation" is required, as well. In the case of the Great Fire, this conversion means exchanging acquisitiveness for altruism. A royal proclamation conveying Charles II's "princely compassion and very tender care, taking into consideration the distressed condition of many his good Subjects," also ordered his subjects in and around London to supply "present remedy and redress" to "the said distressed persons."[59] *The Londoners Lamentation*, a broadside ballad to the tune of "When Troy town," urges Londoners not to take advantage of their fellow residents but to recognize their common plight:

I know each Citizen hath drank
a scalding draught of this hot Cup,
But let him not (to mend his bank)
use greedy Gains to get it up,
Let them consider what they do,
Their Customers are Sufferers too.[60]

The implication of both royal and popular writings is that benevolent action is the proper response to real-world tragedy. Yet these and other solicitations for compassionate aid also suggest that many Londoners remained close-fisted after the Great Fire, despite the resounding calls for reformation and charity. Like piping and rough music, the sounds of urban ruin could have contradictory effects.

In the destruction of the metropolis, some Londoners did not hear the trumpet of judgment but the chimes of opportunity. When flames swept through the City of London, appeals to help transport children, pregnant women, the elderly, and the infirm were often ignored unless the appellant could pay the exorbitant fees charged by those with carts, wagons, and strong backs.[61] Likewise, fire-fighting efforts were hampered by Londoners' attempts to transport property out of harm's way. Sometimes these goods belonged to the bearer, sometimes not: the Fire became an opportunity for the looting of homes and businesses abandoned by frightened citizens. While this uncharitable behaviour does not necessarily reflect insensitivity to the plight of others, at least one Londoner linked the looters' selfishness to their indifference. In *Annus Mirabilis* Dryden laments: "So void of pity is th' ignoble crowd, / When others ruine may increase their store."[62] Crackling flames, rattling buildings, and crying citizens – these sounds *ought* to have inspired noble affections and actions, Dryden's verse suggests, but they failed to do so.

The opportunistic indifference of Dryden's "ignoble crowd" reappears in accounts of London's reconstruction. Many descriptions of urban recovery disclose the extent to which the sounds of building drowned out all other sounds. Christopher Flower's *Mercy in the midst of judgment*, a sermon delivered on the third anniversary of the Great Fire, describes the noises that reverberated throughout London between 1666 and 1669: "*every* one said to his *Brother,* be of *good* courage; So the *Carpenter* encourag'd the *Goldsmith,* and he that *smootheth* with the *Hammer* him that smote the *Anvil,* saying, it is *ready* for the *Sodering.*"[63] According to Flower, restoration of the physical city occasioned restoration of the civic community, as the sounds of building echoed those of fraternity among London's tradesmen and merchants. However, this is an acoustic chimera; reconstruction efforts were often self-serving. Of course tradesmen and merchants were "of good courage" and "encourag[ing]," because they profited considerably from the Fire.[64] Historically, London's carpenters and goldsmiths may have heeded calls for aid, and out of Christian compassion or civic duty, shared their financial gains with the city's less fortunate denizens.[65]

Flower remains silent on this point – and not surprisingly so. In his sermon, post-Fire London resounds with industry and profit, muffling the call and answer of charity.

The cacophonous pursuit of London's infrastructural measure may have impeded the restoration of other kinds of measure in the metropolis. In *Londons Resurrection* (1669) Simon Ford writes: "Hark, how the clatt'ring *Tools* confused sound / Divides the Ear! ... Thus goes the *Building* on. Confused grounds / Just *Verdicts* part."[66] Cynthia Wall, reading Ford's poem in the context of literary representations of London's reconstruction, juxtaposes "confused sound" and "Confused grounds": the former represents "the stabilizing forces of rebuilding," whereas the latter, "left hanging at the end of the line only to be 'parted' rather than resolved or reconciled by the (surveyors' or Fire Court's) Verdicts in the next [line]," reflects the disordering effect of litigation.[67] Although metrically sensitive and historically informed, Wall's reading does not account fully for Ford's acoustic imagery. The phrase "Divides the Ear" suggests that urban repair led to auricular impairment. The "confused sounds" of reconstruction, like piping and rough music, should produce order; but like Comus's wild music, they yield disorder by parting Londoners from just measure: acoustic, affective, legal. The effects of impaired hearing on the metropolis become more explicit later in Ford's poem:

> *Lady Enchantress* of the *ravisht Ear*,
> Ne're did thy *Art* effect what *Chance* doth here!
> Whiles building *Noises* by the pleased Mind
> Are into all harmonious *Notes* combin'd,
> *Orpheus* to us would grate, *Apollo* jar:
> *Hammers* and *Truels* sweeter *Musick* are.[68]

Ford's account of carpenters and bricklayers seems intent on celebrating the commitment of London's citizens to urban restoration. These industrious artisans hear music in the pounding of hammers and the scraping of trawls, in comparison to which the music of the lyre is cacophonous. At best, this acoustic inversion represents ambivalent praise. Londoners "pleased" by the prospect of personal gain – or, to offer a more generous interpretation, of civic renewal – combine "building *Noises*" into "harmonious *Notes*." But what they ought to hear, and which they expressly reject, are the sounds of God (Apollo) and God's agents (Orpheus). The "sweeter *Musick*" of London's reconstruction, it would seem, is in fact the wild measure of a self-indulgent Bacchic rout.

Right hearing should lead to right feeling which should lead to right doing. This chain (of) reaction, although it did not necessarily work in practice, charts the desired effects of urban catastrophe and its literary representation. Samuel Rolle's *Shlohavot* (1667) registers this connection in terms directly relevant to Milton's *Samson Agonistes*. Rolle, who elsewhere compares the sound of London's ruin to that of a divine flame, illustrates his explanation of fire with analogies to the passions and the biblical story of Samson razing the temple. Just as agitated particles of sulphur will wreak destruction before consuming itself, Rolle writes, men "transported with pride or passion" will "*Sampson*-like … go about to destroy the *Philistines*" and "pluck the house (as he did) upon their own heads."[69] Like Rolle, Milton found in Samson's razing of the Gazan temple a tragedy of passions, and he sets *Samson Agonistes* in a metropolis that resounds with the noises of early modern London, including those of the Great Fire. From this urban soundscape emerges a sense of the earthly city as a preview of the "City and proud seat / Of Lucifer" (*PL* 10.424–5). It is not that other places cannot speak to the fallen human condition; rather, no place better epitomizes or is more axiomatic of that condition than the metropolis. In *Samson Agonistes* Milton takes the sounds of urban ruin and divine judgment, and of humanity's continued failure to hear, feel, and do rightly, as the subjects of metropolitan tragedy.

Tragedy in Gaza

Samuel Rolle's *Shlohavot* is just one of numerous writings that compare London's burning in 1666 and Samson's violence in the Book of Judges. Some accounts of the Great Fire liken Londoners to the Philistines, whose gates and fields Samson razes in accordance with God's will; others liken them to Samson, who is justly humbled for his disobedience to God. So, too, when writers compare England's capital to the Gazan temple that Samson pulls down, killing thousands of his enemy and himself, Londoners figure alternatively as victim and cause of urban ruin. The common thread in these comparisons is the culpability of Londoners in their metropolis's tragedy. Yet for which crime specifically God punished the city remained a subject of debate: "The Quakers say [the Fire occurred as a punishment] for their Persecution. The Fanaticks say tis for banishing & silencing their Ministers. Others say tis for the Murther of the King & Rebellion of the City. The Clergy lay the blame on Schism & Licentiousness, while the sectaries lay it on

Imposition and their Pride."[70] If Milton discerned God's hand in the Great Fire, it would likely have been for England's failure to maintain a republic and for London's celebration at the monarchy's restoration. In *Samson Agonistes* Milton uses a moment of urban catastrophe analogous to Samson's razing of the temple to comment on, as Laura Knoppers puts it, "the moral corruption that makes a nation self-enslaved."[71] A focus on the acoustics of Milton's dramatic poem shifts critical attention from the nation to the metropolis and expands moral corruption to include a corruption of sense and sensation.

In *Samson Agonistes* Milton represents sound to infuse both metropolitan place and tragic action with meaning and effect. The representation of ancient Gaza, its acoustics, and its ruin seems poised to produce the "just measure" that Milton describes in the prefatory epistle to his tragedy. Yet *Samson Agonistes* does not set the affections in right tune. Like the Great Fire, Samson's violence fails to produce "calm of mind all passion spent," as the Chorus insists (*SA* 1748). Rather, like the fire that sparked on Pudding Lane, Samson becomes increasingly *out* of measure, and just as Londoners worked to halt the flames by exploding buildings, the Hebrew champion becomes "spent" only when he destroys himself. This auricular failure is, I contend, by design: Milton uses the cacophony of a ruined metropolis to provide a sense of tragic *mis*measure. In *Samson Agonistes* poetic metre reveals the loss of measure – material, affective, moral, civic – that "actual" tragedy produces and theatrical tragedy remedies or ought to remedy.

Milton's tragedy, like the other plays examined in this book, is set emphatically in a metropolis. The short epic *Paradise Regained* that precedes *Samson Agonistes* in the 1671 volume transports readers to a series of locales, some of them urban. By contrast, *Samson Agonistes* adheres to a strict interpretation of the neoclassical rule dictating unity of place. Milton uses the word "place" no fewer than ten times in *Samson Agonistes*, usually to refer to one of two locations in the city of Gaza: the prison-side bank and the temple of Dagon. Most of the action takes place on the prison-side bank, where readers remain and hear – and hear about – what occurs in the temple. From Milton's representation of these places and their respective sounds emerges an ancient metropolis dominated by acoustic cacophony and semiotic confusion.

At first blush, the prison and the bank are starkly different locales. The prison, like Satan's urban hell, is a place of literal and figurative confinement. There Samson is "chain'd" in shackles, "enjoyn'd" to "Daily," "servile toyl," and "imprison'd" also by the "air," a "close and damp / Unwholesome draught" (*SA* 5–9). Samson's blindness relegates him to a kind of solitary confinement, worse than any "dungeon" (68). Yet even in his isolation, Samson suffers "daily" auditory assault in the form of "insult" (113–14). By contrast, like Adam and Eve's rural paradise, the bank promises temporary relief from the torments of incarceration. There Samson may "sit" (4) and rest from his labours, his limbs alternatively warmed by the sun and cooled by shade (3). Rather than gasp at unhealthy air, he draws in "breath" that is "fresh blowing, pure and sweet" (10). The bank also offers auditory relief from verbal taunts as well as pagan festivity. "This day a solemn feast the people hold / To Dagon their sea-idol," Samson explains, "hence with leave / Retiring from the popular noise, I seek / This unfrequented place to find some ease" (12–17). Restful, salutary, quiet – the bank promises an experience of place wholly unlike that of the prison.

That this binary is unsustainable becomes apparent in Milton's attention to the expressly urban location of the bank. "The Argument" and scenic direction that introduce *Samson Agonistes* establish the bank's geographical proximity to the prison: the bank is "*nigh*" and "*before*" the prison (69, 70, original emphasis). Samson's opening speech emphasizes this proximity through a series of deictic modifiers, including "yonder," "a little further," "there," and "here" (*SA* 3–11), and subsequent verbal gestures to "*this* loathsome prison-house" and "*this* jail" (922, 949, emphasis added) remind readers of the contiguity of these places of relief and oppression. Because it is adjacent to "the common prison" and "public mill" (6, 1327, 1393; cf. 41), in which "common" and "public" denote generally known and accessible, the bank, although described as "uncouth" and "unfrequented" (333, 17), proves anything but anonymous or empty. It is found easily by a series of Hebrew and Philistine visitors who intrude upon Samson's retirement. These signifiers of geographical proximity intimate that the bank is, simply and fundamentally, as much a part of the physical city as the prison. This is striking because, in the years before England's Civil Wars, the bank was one of only a few large stage properties used in London's commercial theatres, where it conventionally functioned as a material and visual signifier of the flight from city to country to facilitate comic resolution. In sharp contrast to these spatial and generic associations, *Samson Agonistes* glosses the bank as urban and tragic.

Repeatedly Milton reminds readers that his tragedy takes place in a metropolis. Both "The Argument" and scenic direction that introduce *Samson Agonistes* set the action in biblical Gaza. In the dramatic poem itself, Gaza (or Azza) is mentioned seven times, and there are references to four other major Philistine cities – Ascalon, Ecron, Asdod, and Gath – as well as to minor urban centres, including Hebron, Eshtaol, and Zora. In addition to these specific references, the word "city" appears five times, usually to refer to the immediate Gazan setting. In a dramatic poem of barely 1,758 lines, the number of references to the city, both specific and general, is truly impressive.[72]

Despite this emphatic urban setting, the representation of place in Milton's tragedy has received surprisingly little scholarly attention. *The Prison and the Pinnacle*, which gathers papers presented at a conference in celebration of the tricentennial anniversary of the publication of *Samson Agonistes* and *Paradise Regained*, suggests in its title an interest in the places of Milton's late poetry. Yet only one contributor takes on this subject: Balachandra Rajan explains the order of the 1671 volume in terms of the poems' spatial imagery. Rajan argues that in *Paradise Regained* Milton represents divine perfection standing atop the pinnacle, whereas in *Samson Agonistes* humanity stumbles towards understanding in the "'subjected plain' to which the fallen Adam must descend."[73] The upshot of this imagery is an enlightened sense of what it means to live after the fall. "If *Paradise Regained* is the first poem in the sequence," Rajan asserts, "it is so that we can stand on the hill and know what is happening better as we enter the blindness of experience in the valley below," as represented in *Samson Agonistes*.[74] In the almost thirty years since Rajan's initial presentation, there has been little discussion of the spatial imagery in *Paradise Regained* or *Samson Agonistes*, but recent scholarship on *Paradise Lost* resonates with Rajan's reading of the 1671 volume and illuminates the operations of place in Milton's tragedy. John Gillies argues that Milton rejects the seventeenth century's denigration of place as static and inefficacious "by intuiting place as a property of the body"; and Maura Brady claims that Milton "imagin[es] what it would be like to inhabit a world whose governing physical concept is space, and test[s] several different models for its viability."[75] Whether Miltonic place renders the mundane wondrous, or the wondrous mundane, the result is the same: *place* is the condition of the postlapserian world.

The understanding of place in *Paradise Lost* is generic in the sense of not specific. Once humanity is banished from Paradise, anywhere can be a place; like Satan, we take our sinfulness with us wherever we go. In *Samson Agonistes* place becomes generic in the sense of associated with particular literary genres. Milton appropriates the conventionally rural and comic associations of the bank to his representation of the metropolis, and in so doing, his tragedy refocuses what it means to live after the fall. Whereas the prison reveals the city as a locus of suffering, oppression, and isolation, the adjacent bank reflects the capacity of urban place to facilitate release and renewal.

In Milton's retelling of the Book of Judges, the urban bank affords Samson opportunities for bodily restoration and spiritual reconciliation that manifest as a command of place and sound. Prior to his imprisonment, Samson could turn any place into a field of successful battle, where his "deeds themselves, though mute, spoke loud the doer" (*SA* 248). When the Philistines "persisted deaf" to his deeds, and "with gathered powers / Entered Judea seeking [Samson]," he did not flee, "but forecasting in what place / To set upon them," slaughtered thousands of his enemies with only an ass's jawbone (251–5). Such resounding command of place compelled its own silence: "The dread of *Israel*'s foes," Samson "walk'd thir streets, / None offering to fight" (342–4). Upon his arrest, Samson ceases to exert this command over place and sound; in prison he is the one set upon physically and aurally. Initially this inversion persists beyond the place of his confinement. Samson retires to the bank to escape the taunts of triumphant Philistines, yet the moment he has visitors, he inquires into these sounds. "[T]ell me friends," Samson asks the Chorus, "Am I not sung and proverbd for a Fool / In every street, do they not say, how well / Are come upon him his deserts'?" (202–5). The Chorus, which earlier echoes the "report" of Samson's fallen state (117), replies that they "oft have heard men wonder" about his marital choices (215). In the same streets where once Samson commanded silence, he has become the subject of common gossip. Moreover, although Samson seeks out the bank to avoid the "popular noise" of pagan festivities, he endures here the sounds of Philistine celebration. As Samson's father, the well-meaning Manoa, reports: "Here ... in *Gaza*" may be heard proclamations and "Praises loud / To *Dagon*" for the deliverance of "Thee *Samson* bound and blind into thir hands" (435–8). The city's streets, formerly silent in awe of Samson's deeds, now buzz with disdainful gossip and triumphant revelry.

A recovery of spatial and acoustic control also begins on the urban bank during Samson's conversations with Dalila and Harapha. Dalila beseeches Samson to "hear" explanations for her betrayal (766) and to "Hear what assaults I had, what snares besides" (845), which are principally auricular in nature.[76] These appeals to Samson's hearing preface a temptation of his "other senses," as Dalila proposes to "fetch thee / From forth this loathsome prison-house, to abide / With me" (921–3). Dalila appears confident that, just as she intends to find a "favourable ear" among the Philistine authorities and thus to secure Samson's release (921), Samson will hear her with favour. However, he proves "deaf" to her entreaties (960) and refuses her temptations in a manner reminiscent of his former deeds. Samson transforms Dalila's home from a place of prospective ease and pleasure to one of persistent "insult" (944), such as he experiences in the prison, and the prison from a place of subjection to one of independence: "This jail I count the house of liberty / To thine whose doors my feet shall never enter" (949–50). In an earlier encounter on the bank, Samson responds to efforts to secure his release with passivity and despondency: "Here rather let me drudge," Samson tells his father, until "oft-invocated death / Hast'n the welcom end of all my pains" (573–6). Dalila's similar efforts occasion an alternative experience of activity and control. As if rekindling the flame of divine mission, albeit in a limited and preliminary manner, Samson exerts the power to define place and *not* to hear.

Samson's next encounter on the bank advances his reclamation of authority and mission. Harapha, the Philistine champion, mocks Samson with gossip about the Nazarite's former strength and triumphs: "Much I have heard / Of thy prodigious might and feats perform'd, … And now am come to see of whom such noise / Hath walk'd about, and each limb to survey, / If thy appearance answer loud report" (*SA* 1082–3, 1088–90). If what Harapha sees – a blind, disheveled, shackled prisoner – contradicts popular "loud report," what he hears confirms it. When Harapha laments that he "was never on the place / Of those encounters, where we might have tried / Each other's force" (1084–6), Samson voices his confidence that he could bring down this "pile high-built and proud" (1069), an epithet that compares the Philistine giant to a large urban edifice.[77] In Renaissance country house poems, "pile" tends to refer to rural structures; but in Milton's epic poems, it denotes specifically urban ones.[78] Twice Samson challenges this personification of the enemy city: first, to combat in "Some narrow place enclosed," where he "only with an Oak'n staff will meet thee, / And raise such outcries on thy clatter'd Iron, / Which long shall not with-hold mee from thy head" (1117, 1123–5), and again, despite his chains, to "lay [Harapha's] structure low," right there on the bank (1239). Harapha declines to fight Samson, but he cannot evade the Nazarite's auricular assault. Samson derides Harapha for "descant[ing] on my strength" but not daring to try it, to which Harapha replies that his "ears [are] unus'd [to] / Hear these dishonours" (1228, 1231–2). Defying the personification of the enemy city, challenging him to physical combat, both in prison-like enclosure and on the open bank, and assaulting his ears – Samson seems poised to reclaim his former role as God's agent with absolute command of place and sound.

As Samson transfers his aggression from one urban pile to another – from the "high-built" Harapha to the temple of Dagon, described similarly as a "building ... vaulted high" (*SA* 1595–6) – the complex implications of his restoration emerge. The temple is structurally and experientially evocative of both the bank and the prison. Like the bank, it is a "spacious Theatre" (1595) that affords occupants both sun and shade, though not equally to all: the Philistine aristocracy sits under cover of the vaulted roof, while "The other side was op'n, where the throng / On banks and scaffolds under Skie might stand" (1599–1600). The temple also offers holiday pleasures, albeit ones more decadent than Samson's modest "ease": "Feast ... and Sacrifice / Had fill'd [the Philistines'] hearts with mirth, high chear, & wine, / When to thir sports they turn'd" (1602–4). Even Samson finds a spot to rest under its "arched roof" (1624). At the same time, the temple is reminiscent of the prison. It is another place of confinement, where "armed guards" (1607) hem in Samson; "servile toil," albeit in the form of feats of strength; and auditory assault, as "clamouring" (1611) and other sounds of pagan festivity accost Samson's ears. In addition to its physical conditions, the spiritual associations of the temple evoke both the bank and the prison. Initially Samson identifies the temple with the spiritual stupor of the prison, calling it a "place abominable," and asserting that if "Present in the Temples at Idolatrous Rites," he would "never, unrepented, find forgiveness" (1349, 1378, 1376). Here place corresponds to grace; the temple jeopardizes Samson's chances for divine pardon. Only a moment later, however, he changes his mind. In perhaps the tragedy's most contested lines, "Some rouzing motions" (1382) cause Samson to reconceive the correspondence between the temple and inevitable corruption. He hints that, like the bank, the temple will afford him an opportunity to reclaim his prior command of place and sound. If in the temple a still small voice authorizes some deadly, destructive act, Samson will have proof of his return to divine favour.

The "interpretive uncertainty," to borrow Stanley Fish's phrasing, that characterizes Samson's bodily restoration and spiritual reconciliation is inherent to the Gazan temple and, more broadly, to the metropolis itself.[79] Evocative of places of confinement and release, the temple is part of the polysemous city that necessarily eludes semiotic singularity. This ambiguity is evident, as well, in Samson's descriptions of what he will do in the temple. He describes his impending action as "Nothing ... that may dishonour / Our Law, or stain my vow," "nothing ... Scandalous or forbidden in our Law," and "Nothing dishonourable, impure, unworthy" (*SA* 1385–6, 1408–9, 1424). In these lines Samson intends to communicate a positive outcome; but as Annabel Patterson argues, whereas in Milton's other writings negative linguistic constructions convey a positive if ineffable world view, in *Samson Agonistes* they signify negative things.[80] Also in these lines, uncertainty emerges from Samson's repetition of the conjunction "or." Used most often to juxtapose adverse alternatives, "or" implies that corruption is a possible result of his action in the temple. Even when used to denote a positive outcome, as when Samson foretells "some great act, or of my days the last" (1389), "or" conveys ambivalence, equivocation, and doubt. The repetition of the word "nothing" works likewise. In the temple Samson may do something remarkable; but just as likely, he will do nothing worth noting. To borrow a line from another tragic protagonist: in the temple, nothing may come of nothing.

The cacophony produced when Samson pulls down the temple compounds the representation of this urban place. Just as the self-satisfied Philistines echo Harapha's proud mockery, the sounds of their fall recall those with which Samson threatens their sheepish champion. More significantly, the noises that emanate from the temple provide readers with a direct acoustic experience of the city as a place of both eternal damnation and possible salvation. "The Argument" to *Samson Agonistes* points out that when Samson exits to the temple, readers "*remain on the place,*" meaning the bank (69). "[H]ere" they "hear" two noises (*SA* 1542–3). The first noise, like the earlier popular noises of gossip and revelry, confirms the temple as an immoral place in the ancient Philistine city; the second, which is the noise of urban catastrophe, seems designed to echo the sounds of divine punishment during the Great Fire of London. How readers hear these two noises determines the efficacy of Milton's tragedy to stir up, temper, and reduce their passions to just measure.

Although a closet drama, *Samson Agonistes* provides a direct experience of the catastrophe through the acoustic descriptions and affective responses of readers' fellow auditors on the bank. Manoa registers the first noise to emanate from the temple when he exclaims, "What noise or shout was that? It tore the sky" (*SA* 1472). The metrical regularity of this line – it is monosyllabic iambic pentameter – parallels the intelligibility of the noise itself, which the Chorus agrees and the Messenger confirms is the Philistines' exultant "shout" (1473, 1610) upon seeing the captive Samson. Also like the verse, the shout is contained: both Manoa's line and the Philistines' exclamation are of limited length. The second noise could not be more different. About thirty-five lines after Manoa registers the first "noise," he interrupts himself to exclaim, " – Oh what noise! / Mercy of Heav'n what hideous noise was that!" (1508–9). Metrically irregular and grammatically convoluted, Manoa's exclamation parallels the disorder of the sound itself.[81] The sound "continue[s]" (1516) for at least nine lines, during which the word "noise" is repeated five times (1508–16). This amplification does not, however, resolve the identity or meaning of the sound. The Chorus and Manoa do not know what they hear; they classify it variously as a "universal groan" and an "outcry," the sound of "Blood, death, and deathful deeds," as well as of "Ruin, destruction" (1511–24). Ultimately, they appear to settle on the ambiguous "Some dismal accident" (1519).

According to some scholars, these two noises produce the catharsis that Milton describes in the prefatory epistle to *Samson Agonistes*. Šárka Kühnová contends that when Manoa registers the Philistines' shout, the metrical regularity of his line "intensifies the haunting resonance of the startling yet well-timed 'tore.'"[82] Martin E. Mueller argues that "[i]n Aristotelian terms," the noise of the temple's fall functions as "dramatic mimesis," to which readers, like Manoa, respond with amazement and terror.[83] Certainly these sonic experiences stir up readers' passions, but what follows fails to temper and reduce these emotions to just measure. Milton does not provide the anticipated resolution – either acoustic, semiotic, or affective. Instead, he suspends the ordering effects of tragedy to confront readers with the same choices of interpretation and response that they had during and after the Great Fire.

Samson Agonistes models the failures to hear and feel rightly through the conventional figures of the Messenger and the Chorus. The Messenger, who enters from the temple, offers a definitive account of the second noise. Rather than resolve the ambiguity of Manoa's and the Chorus's description, however, the Messenger's account adds a conflicting layer to the tragic soundscape. Upon pulling down the pillars in the temple, the Messenger explains, Samson "drew / The whole roof after them, with a burst of thunder / Upon the heads of all who sate beneath, / Lords, Ladies, captains, Councellors, or Priests" (*SA* 1640–3). The Messenger describes only the noise of structural ruin; his account muffles, or even silences, the outcries and groans heard earlier on the bank.

The Messenger's allusion to "thunder" becomes the basis for yet another acoustic account of the temple's destruction. In a startling act of revisionism, the Chorus asserts that it is not the roof that bursts like thunder but Samson who "cloudless thunder bolted on [the Philistines'] heads" (1686). By modifying thunder from a descriptor of destructive sound to a destructive force itself, the Chorus imposes acoustic and semiotic resolution upon the catastrophe. As Sharon Achinstein has shown, "cloudless thunder" is a classical trope for divine omnipotence, for only God can cause thunder to resound in a clear sky.[84] In its appropriation of the Messenger's account, the Chorus portrays Samson as executor of such celestial power. However tempting this resolution, it depends, even more so than the Messenger's account, upon selective hearing. The Chorus conveniently forgets, or simply dismisses as contrary to its agenda, the sounds of human suffering and structural ruin that reverberate earlier on the bank. Even as readers face the same choices – how will they understand and respond to Samson's violence? – they receive no guide to right hearing and feeling. In his dramatization of urban ruin, Milton withholds from readers a definitive acoustic, semiotic, and thus affective experience.

Milton drives home the suspension of readers' "just measure" in the *Omissa*, a passage of ten lines printed not in its proper place but appended at the end of the 1671 volume. In the *Omissa* Manoa and the Chorus continue to conjecture on the nature and meaning of the second "noise." They imagine, and with what might strike readers as uncanny accuracy, Samson executing deadly destruction in the temple in accordance with divine will. This dialogue appears to bring determinacy to the acoustic experience of Samson's violence; but its material disorder undermines any impression of semiotic order: Manoa and the Chorus's conclusive interpretation of the sounds of urban ruin is literally out of place. Moreover, the speakers use sets of opposing terms to describe the imagined destruction: "fear," "dole," and "joy"; "know," "doubt," and "think"; "Hope" and "Belief"; "good" and "bad" (120). Like Samson's negative linguistic constructions and use of "or" and "nothing," the contradictory diction of the *Omissa* reveals Manoa and the Chorus's failure to hear rightly. They do not recognize that the noises resounding from the temple may signify not heavenly judgment upon the Philistine leadership but a critique of the Israelites' backsliding, which is, after all, the crucial message of the account of Samson's life in the Book of Judges.

I have argued that the frustration of acoustic and semiotic resolution at the end of *Samson Agonistes* obstructs readers' just affective measure.

The effects of Milton's tragedy thus run counter to the theory outlined in his prefatory epistle. Within the dramatic poem, the Chorus insists that Samson, upon pulling down the temple in Gaza, achieves "calm of mind all passion spent" (*SA* 1748). Not only has the Chorus shown itself at best hard of hearing and at worst willfully deaf; but Milton's metropolitan tragedy does not resolve into an acoustic experience capable of purging readers of pity, fear, "and such like passions" (66). *Samson Agonistes* stirs up the passions through representations of the sounds of rumour, celebration, suffering, and ruin. The resolution of readers' emotions requires that concord follow this discord, but Milton presents more discord. This affective dissonance persists at the conclusion of *Samson Agonistes.* Just as "dire imagination still persues" the Messenger with the "horrid spectacle" of Samson's violence (*SA* 1534, 1532), so, too, readers may continue to hear the sounds of tragedy after they put down Milton's volume.

In *Samson Agonistes* Milton uses the sounds of urban ruin to call readers' attention to what and how they hear. The underlying premise of this project is that poetry, and especially dramatic tragedy, can make readers better citizens. Not everyone agreed: in *The Country-Man's Fare-wel to London* (n.d.), a broadside ballad that blames the Great Fire on Londoners' pride, the speaker remains sceptical of poetry's capacity to set readers in right tune. He mocks himself as one of those who "think'st ... with soft scratches of a Pen / For to reclaim such *brutified* Men," and recalling the conclusion of *Samson Agonistes*, insists: "They'r resolutely *Deaf,* and it appears, / Before they'l *hear, thunder* must *bore* their *Ears.*"[85] The implication is that the noise of the Fire failed to penetrate the ears of hard-hearted Londoners, so it is unlikely they will hear a common ballad. In fact, poetry might make matters worse. In Walter George Bell's often quoted words, "the Fire of London inspired more bad poetry than happily was destroyed by it."[86] Sounding more like Comus's riotous noise than Orpheus's civilizing harmony, poems about the Great Fire may not simply fail to produce just measure but actively yield mismeasure.[87] In Milton's metropolitan tragedy, readers also found an invitation to hear anew these sounds of the Great Fire's aftermath, when London was rebuilt but not, as we will see next, put to just measure.

Measure Twice, Cut Once

For Milton, the capacity of tragedy to effect change hinges upon what he calls in *Paradise Lost* a "fit audience ... though few" (*PL* 7.31). Stephen Dobranski argues that by "fit audience," Milton means a group of judicious readers who are intellectually prepared for the rigorous activity of engaging with his poetry.[88] *Samson Agonistes* implies that it is no longer sufficient for this "fit audience" to be "few" in number. Rather, the entire urban community must become skillful auditors who can hear rightly the sounds of metropolitan tragedy.[89] Milton's dramatic poem would thus seem to evoke a vision of civic unity not unlike Stow's nostalgic *Survey of London*. More than a century later, Daniel Defoe in *A Journal of the Plague Year* could not imagine what this earlier era of metropolitan unity might have looked like. After the plague of 1665, "the City had a new Face," Defoe writes, although "it must be acknowledg'd that the general Practice of the People was just as it was before … Some indeed said Things were worse."[90] A year later, the Great Fire altered the face of the metropolis once more, and again, not for the better. Describing the sounds of London's burning, Simon Ford laments Londoners' failure to come together: "Here *ruinous cracks*, there *doleful shriekes* do sound, / And those that *danger* should *unite, confound*."[91] Repeatedly in his diary, John Evelyn registers the effects of London's loss of structural unity as a loss of urban identity. Reconstruction efforts restored or improved London's façades, but this urban facelift could not conceal the persistent mismeasure of the metropolis.

The numerous city portraits that poured from domestic and foreign presses after the Great Fire suggests that many in England and on the Continent shared Milton's vision of a unified metropolis. Take, for example, *Londinum Celeberrimum Angliae Emporium*, published in 1666 by the Dutch printer Clement de Jonghe (Figure 11). This print updates Rombout van den Hoeye's circa 1638 city portrait by the same name. Other than the addition of flames and smoke, de Jonghe's *Londinum* leaves van den Hoeye's image largely unchanged. De Jonghe's *Londinum*, like other images of London produced after the Great Fire, reveal the bind in which printers found themselves in 1666. On the one hand, printers were responding to a historically local event, which required up-to-the-minute text and images; on the other hand, they needed to keep pace with a geographically international market, which made time-consuming new commissions impractical. To balance these demands, printers tended to take a middle road by updating earlier city portraits. Although based in the pragmatics of early modern print culture, the decision to recycle text and images from the previous century had significant implications for how viewers, and Londoners in particular, understood the destruction of England's metropolis. The retention of London's pre-1666 cityscape conveyed a sense of permanence and

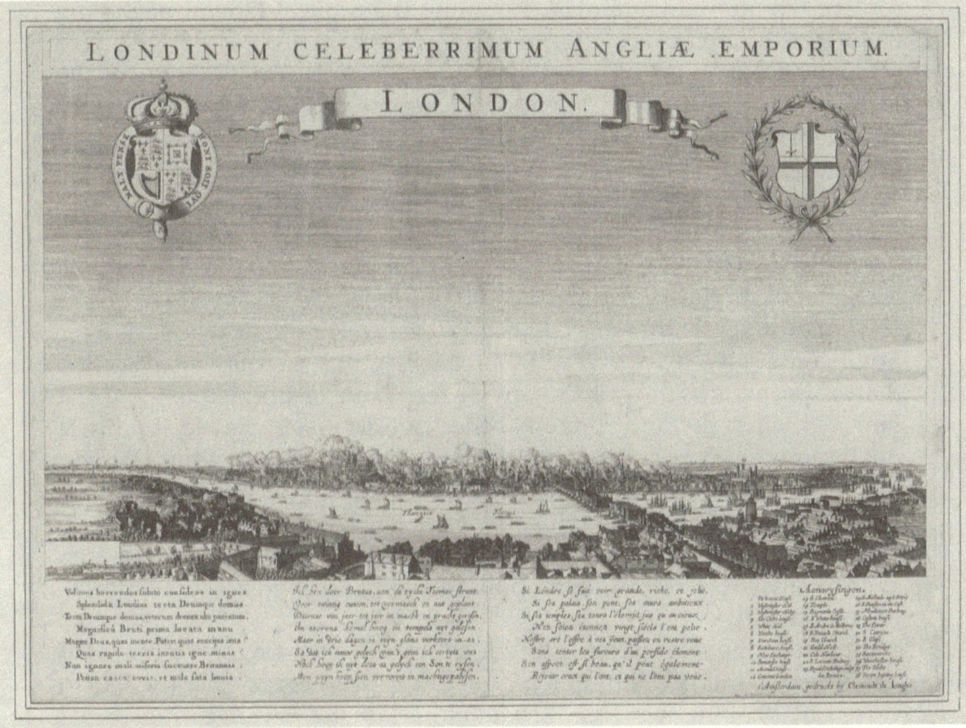

Figure 11: *Londinum Celeberrimum Angliae Emporium*, printed by Clement de Jonghe (Amsterdam, 1666). British Museum, Reg. No. 1880, 1113.1157 © The Trustees of the British Museum.

timelessness amidst radical change. For instance, de Jonghe's *Londinum* includes the Globe playhouse, which had been pulled down about two decades earlier. Rather than portray London as "no longer a Citty," stripped of the theatres and other definitive structures, this city portrait suggests the persistence of the erstwhile metropolis.

The legend that accompanies de Jonghe's *Londinum* complicates this sense of continuity amidst change. Like van den Hoeye's city portrait, de Jonghe's includes verses in Latin, Dutch, and French. However, only the last verse, which invites the viewer to rejoice in London's beauty, remains unaltered. Whereas the 1638 Latin and Dutch verses celebrate the city's unparalleled glories and illustrious past, those printed in 1666 replace tribute with jeremiad. Recalling the biblical lament of the fall of Judah, these verses attribute London's destruction to divine anger ("Magne Deus, quas mente, Pater, quas concipis iras?"), bemoan the loss of former power and splendor ("Daernae van jaer tot jaer in macht en pracht geresen"), and mourn the fall of the city that Brutus founded ("Magnifica Bruti prima locata manu," and "Ick ben door Brutus, aen de rycke Teemse strant"). De Jonghe's decision to retain van den Hoeye's multilingualism reflects the pan-European market for images of London after the Great Fire. In fact, since de Jonghe's shop did use English for some of its prints, the absence of an English-language verse on his *Londinum* suggests that this city portrait was not primarily intended for English markets. If we accept this scenario, then we may also assume that while many of the print's viewers may have responded to the Great Fire with empathy and sadness, others would have viewed it with, if not happiness, at least smug satisfaction. Indeed, Dutch public opinion tended to regard the Great Fire as divine retribution for Holmes's Bonfire in August 1666.[92] From this point of view, de Jonghe's reuse of van den Hoeye's cityscape emphasizes London's impending devastation, as if to say the glorious metropolis pictured in the earlier print was doomed to fall.

This city portrait alerts us to the ways in which English metropolitan tragedy emerged within a broader European context. In the Dutch verses of de Jonghe's 1666 *Londinum*, as in the revenge tragedies I discuss in chapter 2, London's ancient foundation ceases to signify the promise of metropolitan greatness and becomes an inauspicious model for civic leadership, which failed to prevent the city's ruination. Moreover, for many of its English viewers, de Jonghe's multilingual jeremiad, like Lavinia's signs in Shakespeare's *Titus Andronicus*, fails to translate the sounds of suffering into a sensible and singular narrative.[93] As we have seen in this chapter, Milton makes the frustration of definitive meaning the purposeful effect of *Samson Agonistes*. In doing so, he engages not only dramatic and non-dramatic works from ancient Greece and Renaissance England but also the writings of sixteenth- and seventeenth-century Dutch thinkers, including Joseph Scaliger, Daniel Heinsius, and Gerardus Joannes Vossius.[94] Milton's invitation to hear rightly the sounds of urban ruin, then, is not limited to his English audience but extends to all "fit" readers, regardless of national citizenship.

This expansion of Milton's audience is bound up with *Samson Agonistes* as a representation of not only the Great Fire but also its aftermath. Commissioned by Charles II to develop plans for London's reconstruction, Christopher Wren, John Evelyn, and others looked to the neoclassical infrastructure of other European cities. Their plans recall both James I's vision for London, which I discuss in relation to tyrant tragedy in chapter 3, and the fantasy of domestic tragedy that is the subject of chapter 1. Post-Fire urban planners called for brick buildings and wide thoroughfares arranged on a grid to replace London's formerly wooden edifices and convoluted topography. This uniform metropolis would, like another agent of royal authority, enforce law and order. As Cynthia Wall demonstrates, "the spatial arrangement of the city was designed to regulate or at least monitor the social and civic relationships of the inhabitants."[95] London's iconic punitive structures, including the scaffold and gallows on Tower Hill, are largely marginalized or absent from these plans. The implication is that the built environment will ensure the security of the city's law-abiding denizens. The reality of London's reconstruction did not live up to the designs of urban planners, any more than James I realized his vision for the city. In the City of London denizens rebuilt their homes and businesses out of available materials (i.e., wood, not brick) and literally along former lines rather than the network of broad streets and fashionable squares mapped out in print. Likewise, in the larger conurbation, plans for the modern cityscape were not immediately carried out. The practical, material changes that some authorities and citizens believed necessary to prevent real-world tragedy, both topographical ruin and urban crime, were repeatedly set aside in favour of individual convenience. Once again, and on a much grander scale, Londoners failed to heed the summons to come together for the welfare of the metropolis.

The relationship between metropolitan tragedy and the lived experience of post-Fire London is not as simple as cause and effect. Printed images of the metropolis in flames and plans for its reconstruction do not disclose the failure of dramatic tragedy to reform its audiences. Whether readers of *Samson Agonistes* trembled at Samson's violence or wept at his death did not dictate whether they (also) offered aid after the Great Fire or advocated for building reforms. Likewise, it is obvious that not everyone who gave charity to those who lost everything in the Fire or hoped to modernize the cityscape also read Milton's tragedy. Rather, images of post-Fire London, like earlier city portraits, demonstrate the pervasiveness of discourses of tragedy in the metropolis. The pursuit of justice, whether by preternatural or human means, remains crucial to tragic representations of London throughout an extended early modern moment.

These representations also engage with the pursuit of justice in other, future metropolises. In *Samson Agonistes* Milton alerts readers to what they cannot hear, even if they wished to: "the heavenly tune, which none can hear / Of human mould with gross unpurged ear" (*Arcades* [1632?; 1645], ll. 72–3). By purging the ear, metropolitan tragedy provides opportunities to "keep in tune with heaven" and eventually "To live" in the City of God itself ("At a Solemn Music," ll. 26, 28). As I have argued, *Samson Agonistes* frustrates the just measure of readers' passions *in order to* invite them to more measured hearing. This effect is not limited to "a fit audience … though few" of early modern readers, both in England and on the Continent; it extends to the faithful across time. In this sense, *Samson Agonistes* may be accurately described as a metropolitan tragedy that is also a *cosmopolitan* tragedy. Milton's is neither a secular nor an international cosmopolitanism.[96] Rather, it is an expressly Christian cosmopolitanism. Milton's tragedy prepares readers to hear the divine voice in the sounds of the earthly city and to make the necessary conversion for entrance to the heavenly metropolis.

Postscript

There are no manifestos in a flooded house,
and in the stolen narratives of your walls,
our neighborhood, I'm
a bag of stones with a mouth, silent
except in thought. The only history I trust
is painted on a filthy window.

– Erin Gendron, "In the House on Olympia Street" (2010)

Metropolitan tragedy – even when seemingly "about" sixteenth- and seventeenth-century London – often speaks to urban experiences that exceed its own temporality. In the classical sources and Christian cosmopolitanism of *Samson Agonistes*, for example, we find a desire to write to metropolises other than London circa 1666. Yet Milton's dramatic poem is far from unique: tragedy as an urban genre, in any given time period but especially the early modern, is marked by a tendency to inscribe itself within an extended history of form. In this postscript I focus on the Royal Shakespeare Company's 2002–3 production of Philip Massinger's *The Roman Actor* as an especially potent example of the way early modern English metropolitan tragedy (re)produces across time the connections among genre, justice, and the city that I trace throughout this book.

In my discussion of Massinger's *The Roman Actor* in chapter 3, I examined the historical resonances of the scene of Senators Rusticus and Sura's punishment, especially their entrance "bound back to back," and Caesar Domitian's comparison of the victims of torture to "double-faced Janus" (3.2.46 sd, 3.2.119). I argued that in this spectacle of tyrannical violence, Massinger underscores the extended histories – theatrical, judicial, urban – in which *The Roman Actor* participates and to which its original audiences would have been attuned. Even as the stage image of the senators bound back to back evokes popular print images of Marian martyrs with cityscapes in the background, the allusion to Janus, the Roman god of past and future, intimates that legal tyranny is not confined to an earlier period of English history, let alone ancient times, but will recur in states yet unknown. This ensuing age was closer than Massinger likely imagined. Little more than two decades after *The Roman Actor* premiered at Blackfriars, Parliament staged the logical if extreme outcome of the play's critique of the common lexicon of tragedy and tyranny on a scaffold outside Whitehall. *The Roman Actor* does not predict Charles I's execution; yet the play inscribes this future event into its representation of the urban scaffold as a stage on which tyrants meet tragedy.

At the end of the eighteenth century, Massinger's play promised – or threatened – to (re)produce these connections among genre, justice, and the city. John Philip Kemble prepared a version of *The Roman Actor* for the 1794–5 Drury Lane season that began with "a striking transposition from Massinger's text."[1] Whereas the 1629 printed text opens with a troupe of Roman actors discussing their repertoire, Kemble's version begins with four senators in dialogue about the regulation of political speech and the legal condemnation of all who stand fast against corruption. As David Worrall recently argued, this revised beginning resonated too closely with ongoing treason trials in England and, like other politically charged plays during this period, threatened to incite rioting in London's theatre district. As a result, in an "unprecedented" instance of self-censorship, Drury Lane pulled Kemble's version of *The Roman Actor* from its schedule.[2] Kemble's version of *The Roman Actor* would reach the stage in 1796, but its earlier stage history reveals the way Massinger's play is a product of and productive of not only Caroline London but the Georgian metropolis, as well.

In 2002–3 RSC director Sean Holmes illuminated how *The Roman Actor* (re)produces metropolitan tragedy for a post-9/11 world. Moreover, like Kemble, he did so not by adding to Massinger's play but by transposing its elements. Whereas Kemble moved dialogue, Holmes moved bodies. Specifically, in the scene of the senators' torture, Holmes deviated from the stage direction in the 1629 printing of *The Roman Actor* by positioning the senators side by side with their hands tied above them to a three-legged gallows. Holmes also cut Domitian's comparison of the senators to Janus (which would have been incongruent with the new staging). As a consequence of these directorial choices, the victims of torture faced downstage rather than to the sides of the stage, so that a majority of playgoers witnessed their suffering head-on. Figuratively, this new staging shifted the senators' gaze from the past and future to the present, as if to challenge playgoers to face – to acknowledge, to deal with – analogous spectacles of violence occurring outside the playhouse. Moments of direct address compounded this effect. When the senators shuddered but otherwise remained impassive in response to their torture, Domitian (played by Antony Sher) commanded the hangmen to "Torment 'em" and to "Search deeper," then turned to the audience and barked: "Who looks pale? Or thinks / That I am cruel?" (3.2.71, 3.2.79–80). These questions provoked the following response from Parthenius (Antony Byrne), spoken in an aside to the audience: "I dare not show / A sign of sorrow; yet my sinew shrink, / The spectacle is so horrid" (3.2.81–3). The 1629 edition of *The Roman Actor* also marks Parthenius's line as an aside, and it is quite possible that Domitian's line was also delivered likewise to the Blackfriars audience. In the context of Holmes's twenty-first-century staging, however, these moments of direct address took on a specific function. Like the positioning of the senators, they worked to compel the audience's engagement with injustice *in the present*.

The historical immediacy of the RSC production resulted, in large part, from the reactivation of Massinger's original tragic product. By telling playgoers how *not* to respond, Domitian/Sher called attention to sorrow and/or horror as the appropriate response to the torture depicted onstage. On the night I attended the production, members of the audience reacted in the same way as Parthenius/Byrne: many cringed, some turning away, others shutting their eyes. Whereas the senators remained impassive despite the violence done upon their bodies, the RSC audience responded viscerally to Holmes's staging of torture. In tormenting playgoers through dramatic representation, Holmes succeeded in activating the overlap between tyrannical and theatrical violence that is the basis for Massinger's critique of early modern English tragic theory. In the 1620s the scene recalled state-sanctioned abuses of power; in 2002–3 it did not yet evoke the state-sanctioned abuses of power that followed 9/11. But more than a decade later, it is impossible to consider Holmes's choices to attire the senators in their Roman robes, dirty and open at the back, and to arm the hangmen with meat hooks, which they thrust into the senators' exposed bodies, without reference to the photographs of physical and psychological abuse at the Abu Ghraib prison. The RSC production thus (re)produces the futurity of *The Roman Actor*, as well, in inscribing the debate about the legitimate uses of "extreme interrogation."

When the RSC produced *The Roman Actor*, these graphic images of torment, many carefully staged for the camera, still lay in the future. What Holmes's choices in the scene of the senators' torture evoked, however, were spectacles of violence in the present. For example, in the months preceding the opening of the RSC production of *The Roman Actor*, the kidnapping and murder of journalist Daniel Pearl was at the forefront of European and American news.[3] Photographs and video of Pearl's ordeal often disclose a Foucauldian strategy, such as staged in *The Roman Actor*, in which torture is used to discover inner "truth" and thus confirm the torturer's authority. In the popular American imagination, however, Pearl's capture, "confessions," and death were tragedies. Only days after US officials announced that the US had evidence of Pearl's death, *The New York Times* printed a group of letters to the editor under the title "The Tragic Story of Daniel Pearl," and a few months later, after CBS aired parts of the video that confirmed Pearl's death, the Pearl family released a statement that included: "it is beyond our comprehension that any mother, wife, father or sister should have to relive this horrific tragedy and watch their loved one being repeatedly terrorized."[4] Slippage between representation and reality, between story and history is nothing new in the idiomatic usage of *tragedy*, as we have seen. To the extent that this slippage is historically constructed, it is significant that journalistic coverage links Pearl's "tragedy" to urban injustice – not only the terrorist attacks of 9/11 on New York City and Washington, DC, but also the "civic nightmare" in Karachi, Pakistan, where Pearl was abducted, and other "metropolises," in which "poverty, chaos and corruption formed petri dishes for would-be radicals."[5] The RSC production of *The Roman Actor* did not make explicit reference to Daniel Pearl or the broader contexts in which his death would be understood. But by drawing on emergent experiences of spectacles of violence, it (re)produced the linkage among genre, justice, and the city inherent to Massinger's metropolitan tragedy.

On a more basic but no less significant level, Holmes's directorial choices constructed members of the audience as the urban crowd in attendance at the senators' torture. In doing so, the RSC production gestured to what W.B. Worthen, in his response to "A Forum on Theatre and Tragedy after 9/11" in a special volume of *Theatre Journal* (2002), called the "postmodern, globalized, polis."[6] To the extent that almost half of today's global population still does not live in cities, Worthen's comments disclose the various places in which real-world tragedy occurs.[7] Yet his reference to the *polis* shows that the city remains the point of reference for tragedy in our cultural imaginary, regardless of the actual locations of injustice. By (re)producing the metropolis as a locus of theatrical and "actual" tragedy, the RSC production of *The Roman Actor* resisted the distance implied by the play's ancient setting and early modern composition and invited an appreciation of the applicability of Massinger's portrayal of abusive authority for the twenty-first century.

A crucial argument of this book is that the metropolis is a significant tissue linking many early modern English tragedies. The RSC production of *The Roman Actor* highlights how early modern English tragedies also weave connections among moments in urban history. By inscribing their own futurity, the dramatic and non-dramatic writings examined in this book yield what we might call a transhistoriography of form. Early modern English metropolitan tragedy writes back to the dramatic and cultural legacy of which it is a part – by setting action in recognizable rather than mythic cityscapes, for example, and "correcting" Aristotle's occlusion of the *polis* from his theory of catharsis. It also writes forward, giving shape to emergent literary genres and urban experiences. The registers of early modern English metropolitan tragedy – imagined civic scopic regimes, anxieties about imperial ambition yielding metropolitan ruin, and calls to hear rightly the sounds of urban catastrophe – resonate in ensuing ages of metropolitan literature, including Arthur Conan Doyle's portraits of surveillance in Victorian London, Kurt Vonnegut's reimagining of the firebombing of Dresden in 1945, and the outpouring of poetry following Hurricane Katrina, such as the poem from which the epigraph to this postscript is taken.[8] These experiences of urban crime, suffering, and loss were still imminent in the sixteenth and seventeenth centuries, but they are always and already immanent in the metropolitan tragedies of early modern England.

Notes

Introduction

1 Heywood, *Apology*, sigs. A3r, C2r. In this tract, see also Heywood's discussion of how "playing is an ornament to the Citty, which strangers of all Nations, repairing hither, report of in their Countries, beholding them here with some admiration" (sig. F1r), and his reference to John Stow's *Chronicles*, which relates that Edward IV was "accustomed to see the Citty Actors" (sig. E1v).

2 Heywood's *London Ius Honorarium* features a personified London, "this faire lands Metropolis," surrounded by figures of "diverse others of the chiefe Cities of the Kingdome" (sig. B4r); his *Londini Artium & Scientiarum Scaturigo* lauds the "many Sciences, ... each Art and Trade" of which "London[,] which Metropolis we call[,]" is "Fount and Scaturigo" (sig. E2r); his *Londini Emporia* celebrates "this City [as] a Priority aboue any Metropolis in Europe" (sig. A2r); his *Londini Speculum* pays tribute to the Thames, St Paul's Cathedral, and the Tower of London, the last of which is described as "Of this Metropolis chiefe Generall" (sig. C2v); and his *Londini Status Pacatus* asserts: "the most famous Cities of the World, Athens, Thebes, Lacedemon, nor Rome it selfe the Metropolis of the Roman Empire, could ... in the least compare with London" (sig. A3r).

3 Heywood, *Challenge*, sig. B1v. Hereafter cited in-text.

4 *OED Online*, "civil, adj., n., and adv." esp. adj. I.4, 8, 9, and II.12.

5 Notable exceptions include Howard, "London and the early modern stage," 37–42, and Turner, *English Renaissance Stage*, 240–1. Other influential studies of literary London include Manley, *Literature and Culture*; Merritt, *Imagining Early Modern London*; Dillon, *Theatre, Court and City*; Smith, Strier, and Bevington, *The Theatrical City*; and Mullaney, *Place of the Stage*.

6 King James Bible, Genesis 4:11, 17.

7 In my use of "injustice" here, I follow Reiss, *Tragedy and Truth*, 19–21. On tragedy as a genre of the *polis* and of transition, see also Vernant and Vidal-Naquet, *Myth and Tragedy*; Felski, *Rethinking Tragedy*; and Brown and Silverstone, *Tragedy in Transition*.

8 Williams, *Modern Tragedy*, 13.

9 For an overview of London's demographic and geographic growth, and its impact on economic, social, political, and cultural life in the city, see Boulton, "London." On early modern London's two cities, see Archer, "London and Westminster"; Smuts, *Culture and Power*; and Dillon, *Theatre, Court and City*.

10 *OED Online*, "metropolitan, n. and adj." B2a. and "metropolis, n." 3a.

11 Fuller, *History of the Worthies*, 227; Howell, *Londinopolis*, 381–407. See also Slack, "Great and Good Towns"; Borsay and Proudfoot, "The English and Irish Urban Experience"; and Bartolovich, "'Baseless Fabric.'"

12 On the dualities of early modern London, see Manley, *Literature and Culture* and Paster, *Idea of the City*. On cities historically viewed as polysemous, see Hubbard, *City*. For an interrogation of the gendering of early modern London, see Bailey and Hentschell, *Masculinity and the Metropolis of Vice*.

13 Charles H. Mcllwain, ed., *The Political Works of James I* (Cambridge, MA: Harvard University Press, 1918), 343, quoted in Smuts, "The Court and Its Neighborhood," 119.

14 For example, Elyot's *Dictionary* defines "Matrix, cis, the mother or mattice in a woman, in the whyche the chylde is conceiued. also matrix is any female kynde that concenieth [i.e., conceives] and beareth. Also the citie in a countrey, where as is the archbishops sea, is callyd matrix vrbs, whiche in greke is callid Metropolis" (sig. Niir); Bilson's *Perpetual Governments* offers the appositives "*Metropolis* or *Mother citie*" (403 and, without emphasis, 407); Ainsworth, in *Annotations upon the Five Books of Moses*, explains "a *mother citie* (*Metropolis*) … for the chiefe-cities are counted as mothers, the villages about them as daughters, thorowout the Scriptures" (137); and Blount's *Glossographia* lists "Eardor-burh (Sax.) the Metropolis or chief City" (n.p.) and "Metropolis (Gr.) the chief, head, or Mother City or Town" (sig. Cc2r).

15 *OED Online*, "metro-, comb. form 1": "Forming nouns relating to poetic metre."

16 On metrology as subjective and relational, see Blank, *Shakespeare*.

17 Taylor argues that "different affective and epistemic positions" are revealed through a concerted attention to "live embodied behaviors"

rather than to scripted texts ("Remapping Genre through Performance," 1417–18).

18 For an opposing view, see Gellrich, *Tragedy and Theory*, which argues that in pre-Hegelian tragedy, theory and practice go in opposite directions: the former toward order, the latter toward disorder. For a view more in line with my own, see Lyne, "Neoclassicisms."

19 In "Doing Genre," the writing collective Group Phi draws a similar conclusion: describing genre as "that field of possible sentences, situations, or sentiments" (55), the group argues "genre offers an operational middle term between abstraction and instance," such that "genres invite taxonomy (in analysis, in reception) but they also frustrate it because their transactional nature renders them perpetually emergent" (64–5).

20 Jonson, *Every Man Out*, 1.2.123–6.

21 Garey, *Great Brittans little calendar*, 236. Sir Edward Coke made a similar point at the arraignment of Henry Garnet: the trial of the plotters "is but a latter Act of that heavy and woful Tragedy, which is commonly called the Powder-treason, wherein some have already played their parts, and, according to their demerits, suffered condign punishment and pains of death" (James I, Digby, and Barlow, *The Gunpowder-treason*, 75).

22 A sermon delivered on 10 October 1666, a national day of fasting in commemoration of the city's destruction, describes how the 1665 plague withdrew so "the Fire might come upon the Stage, to act its part too in the Tragoedy [*sic*] our sins have made among us: and I pray God this may be the last Act of it" (Stillingfleet, *Sermon*, 35–6). If London does not reform, another sermon warns, the city's ruins may serve as backdrop for subsequent scenes of deserved punishment, for "God will be sure to act a severer Tragedy upon us, then ever yet hath been acted" (Elborough, *London's Calamity*, 15–16).

23 Ford, *Londons Remains*, 11; also in Aubin, *London in Flames*, 101; Wiseman, *A Short and Serious Narrative*, 2; also in Aubin, *London in Flames*, 21; and Settle, *Elegy*, 5.

24 For example, *The London Gazette* 85 describes the fire as "a Sad and lamentable Accident of Fire" and "a Sad & Deplorable Fire." Below the anonymous print *Prospect of the Citty of London, as it appeared, in the time of its flames* appears an account of how the "dreadfull Fire" began; Vincent, *Gods Terrible Voice* describes "the late *Dreadful Fire*, which hath laid our *Jerusalem* in heaps" (sig. A4r); and in their private correspondence, Huffrey Giffard and George Smith each dubs the fire "dredfull" (Oxenden Papers, fo. 55 and 60). After the fire, the Crown issued "His

Majestie's Declaration to his City of London upon occasion of the late Calamit by the lamentable Fire," and on 4 October 1666, the Common Council of London ordered "an Expert and Speedy Survey of all Streets Lanes Allyes houses & places destroyed by the late dismall fire" (COL/SJ/03/004, London Metropolitan Archives). Sincera's *Observations* describes the fire as "so lamentable and dismal a Subject" (1).

In an examination of title pages from the sixteenth and early seventeenth centuries, Berek, "Tragedy" argues that the term *tragedy* became a marker of the emergence of a distinctly Protestant literary nationalism.

25 For an overview of the influence of Jonson's dramatic satire on the development of city comedy, see Ostovich's Introduction to Jonson, *Every Man Out*; James I, Digby, and Barlow, *The Gunpowder-treason* includes a prayer "to put it in his Majesties heart to make such a conclusion of this Tragedy to the Traytors, but Tragicomedy to the King and all his true Subjects" (71); and in his poem on the Great Fire, George Cartwright begins by lamenting the "dismal ... sight" of London in flames, then explains that the recollection of "King Charles his death, / How at thy very Gates he lost his breath, ... quickly chang'd my mind, & [I] sayd that fire, / Came down from Heav'n no doubt ... And now thou art iustly punished" (Cartwright, "Vpon the deplorable fire at London, / on September the second being Sunday / 1666," in *Brittish Rebellion*, fo. 57).

26 In chapters 3 and 4 I return to and complicate this overview of early modern debate over Aristotelian catharsis.

27 Bennett, "Making Up the Audience," 19.

28 See, among others, Craik and Pollard, *Shakespearean Sensations*; Gallagher and Ramon, *Knowing Shakespeare*; Steggle, *Laughing and Weeping*; and Paster, Rowe, and Floyd-Wilson, *Reading the Early Modern Passions*.

29 Menzer, "Crowd Control" and Steggle, "Notes." See also Lopez, *Theatrical Convention and Audience Response*.

30 These portraits include cartographic and architectural images as well as images in which a person is the primary or ostensible subject and the city's topography and structures seemingly secondary subjects. Whereas the tendency among literary scholars and historians alike has been to approach the pictorial as illustrative of or otherwise secondary to the textual, I work from the premise that visual images are associates of, and counterparts to, dramatic literature.

31 Stephen Cohen, in his Introduction to *Shakespeare and Historical Formalism*, describes this critical investment as follows:

> [E]nmeshed in a web of institutional and cultural as well as social and political histories, literary forms are overdetermined by their

> historical circumstances and thus multiple and variable in their results, neither consistently ideological nor inherently demystificatory but instead reacting unpredictably with each other and with other cultural discourses. (3)

See also Theile and Tredennick, *New Formalisms and Literary Theory*; Armstrong, "Form and History"; Levinson, "What Is New Formalism?"; Rasmussen, *Renaissance Literature*; Bruster, *Quoting Shakespeare*; and Rooney, "Form and Contentment."

32 Manley, *Literature and Culture*, 2. Earlier in the same decade, Denis Cosgrove confidently asserted "[a] widely acknowledged 'spatial turn' across arts and sciences" (Introduction to Cosgrove, *Mappings*, 7). In addition to the studies discussed below, see also Merritt, *Imagining*; Turner, *English Renaissance Stage*; and Sanders, *Cultural Geography*.

33 Howard, *Theater of a City*, 13 and 22. Throughout this book, I am indebted to Jean Howard's body of work at the intersections of form and history.

34 Zucker, *Places of Wit*, 86.

35 Bly, "Carnal Geographies," 91.

36 Stow, *Survey*, 1:129.

37 *OED Online*, "always, adv." 3.

38 Howell, *Londinopolis*, 26.

39 "Sr Jarvaise Elsies," fo. 1r.

40 For the complex historical, social, political, and theatrical associations of the Tower of London, see Deiter, *Tower of London*.

41 Howell, *Londinopolis*, 26.

42 Helwys, *The Lieutenant of the Tower*, sig. B2v.

43 On sites of punishment in early modern London, see Griffiths, *Lost Londons*; Harding, "Cheapside"; and Minson, "Public Punishment." See also my essay "Processions and History."

44 Journal of the Court of Common Council 26, fo. 145, COL/CC/01/01/027, London Metropolitan Archives.

45 Repertory of the Court of Aldermen 31, part 2, fo. 216, COL/CA/01/01/035, London Metropolitan Archives. These precepts echo earlier ones, such as the order made in April 1583 by the Court of Aldermen that "stronge and substanciall cages [are] to be made and sett vp in all the several wardes of this cyttye where cages are nowe wantinge and convenient place maye be found to sett them in" (Repertory of the Court of Aldermen 20, fo. 425, COL/CA/01/01/022, London Metropolitan Archives). And they were repeated subsequently, as in 1611 when county authorities ordered "that there shalbe made a Cage and a paire of Stockes for St. John's Streete, Cowcrosse and Charterlane" (*Middlesex Country Records*, 2:75).

46 Taylor, *The Praise and Virtue of a Jail and Jailers*, sig. B3v.
47 Griffiths, *Lost Londons.* I return to London's scopic regime in chapter 1.
48 Stow, *Survey*, 1:130. For the role of Tower Hill in ongoing tensions between City and Crown, see Griffiths, *Lost Londons*, 80–2.
49 Cartwright, *Brittish Rebellion*, fo. 34b–35.
50 For qualifications of Foucauldian paradigms as they relate to early modern England, see Hutson, "Rethinking the 'Spectacle of the Scaffold'"; Amussen, "Punishment"; and Laqueur, "Crowds, Carnival."
51 MacKay, *Persecution*, 3. In chapter 2 I use the image of Wentworth's execution to illustrate how early modern scaffold audiences did not necessarily accept condemnation as legal truth. Significantly, the word *scaffold*, which included purpose-built stands such as those featured in Hollar's print, was used interchangeably with *stage* in the early modern period.
52 Milton, *The 1671 Poems*, 66.
53 Milton, "At a Solemn Music," in Carey, *The Complete Shorter Poems*, l. 20.
54 In so doing, I am influenced by Goldhill, "Generalizing About Tragedy":

> The challenge for the critic remains to pay due attention to the specific socio-political context of [tragedy], while recognizing the drive toward transhistorical truth both in the plays' discourse and in the plays' reception. This double attentiveness should in turn inform each stage of the literary history of the genre – the fragmented and incremental development of the genre through social institutions of theatre, self-affiliation of writers, and the strictures of critics. Here too the local, the political, and the polemical are in tension with the grandest gesture toward the *longue durée* of the genre of tragedy. (61)

1. Topography, Murder, and Early Modern Domestic Tragedy

1 See n. 5 in the Introduction.
2 Collier, *History of English Dramatic Poetry*, 3:50. In the nearly two centuries since Collier's discussion of domestic tragedy as a generic group, scholars have continued to comment on the plays' fidelity to reality: in 1906 Symonds noted the plays' "somber realistic detail" (*Shakespeare's Predecessors*, 329); in 1975 Clark wrote about their "realism of the most unrefined and sensational kind" (*Domestic Drama*, 155); in the final decade of the twentieth century Dolan discussed their "grim journalistic detail" ("Gender," 211) and Holbrook their "quasi-documentary feel"

(*Literature and Degree*, 93); and at the turn of the twenty-first century, almost 170 years after Collier, Helgerson remains fascinated by domestic tragedy's "extraordinary realism" (*Adulterous Alliances*, 2).

3 Wall, *Staging Domesticity*, 12. Wall unpacks the term *fantasy* through reference to Jacqueline Rose, *States of Fantasy* (Oxford: Clarendon Press, 1996), 4, which discusses how fantasy provides both "fierce blockading protectiveness" and "grounds for license and pleasure."

4 In my discussion of cognitive mapping, I draw on Lynch's *Image of the City* and Jameson's "Cognitive Mapping." The postmodern model to which Jameson adopts Lynch's theory is not unlike the argument I mount in this chapter: both a socialist political project and early modern domestic tragedy are interested in imagining a utopian space, an idealized society that actual conditions repeatedly fail to achieve. My understanding of the roles of place-naming and spatial legibility in cognitive mapping is informed by de Certeau, *The Practice of Everyday Life* and Casey, *The Fate of Place*.

5 Turner, *English Renaissance Stage*, 195.

6 Zucker, *Places of Wit*; Howard, *Theater of a City*, ch. 1; and Bartolovich, "London's the Thing."

7 For a discussion of the representation of London in the domestic tragic plot of *Edward IV, part 1*, see my "Women and the Theatre."

8 For Symonds, *Shakespeare's Predecessors*, and Clark, *Domestic Drama*, among others, domestic tragedy's realism worked as a didactic strategy: if audiences could identify with the genre's middling-class protagonists who moved in recognizable settings and submitted to familiar temptations like lust and greed, the plays' moral content would be more readily brought home. For Mukherji, *Law and Representation*, ch. 3, and Floyd-Wilson, *Occult Knowledge*, ch. 2, domestic tragedy's realism is less an intentional pedagogical strategy than an unwitting cultural revelation, in which the plays reflect the quotidian quality of providence and the preternatural. For discussions of domestic tragedy, identity, and the household and the state, see Richardson, *Domestic Life*; Wall, *Staging Domesticity*; Whigham, *Seizures of the Will*; Comensoli, "*Household business*"; Dolan, *Dangerous Familiars*; Orlin, *Private Matters*; and Belsey, *Subject of Tragedy*.

9 Rowland, *Thomas Heywood's Theatre*, 99. Rowland argues that this alien setting is part of a larger project "to render strange and difficult every element of the burgeoning genre of domestic tragedy" (*Thomas Heywood's Theatre*, 99; see 97–154).

10 Wrightson, "'Decline of Neighbourliness' Revisited," 34.

11 Harding, "City," 215, 132. See also Orlin, "Boundary Disputes."
12 Stow, *Survey*, 1:127. On the growth of London into the suburbs, see Schofield, "Topography and Buildings," and Finlay and Shearer, "Population Growth and Suburban Expansion."
13 D. Maclean, "London in 1689–90 by the Revd R. Kirk," *Transactions of the London and Middlesex Archaeological Society* n.s., 6 (1929–33): 333, quoted in Boulton, *Neighbourhood*, 231.
14 See Slack, "Perceptions," and Lake, "From Troynouvant."
15 Harding, "City," 123, 130.
16 Griffiths, "Overlapping," 119, 117.
17 Quoted in Griffiths, "Overlapping," 119. The Crown expressed similar concerns: in a 1616 speech before the Star Chamber, for example, James I lamented how London's "overgrow[th]" and "increase" "in the suburbs" is "bringing miserie and surcharge to both Citie and Court" (*Political Works*, ed. McIlwain, 343).
18 Cf. Munro, *Figure of the Crowd*, in which the phrase "tangible referent" describes "the crowd … as the visible manifestations of an increasingly incomprehensible city" (1), as well as Howard, "London and the early modern stage," 39–42, and Richardson, *Domestic Life*.
19 Cannon, "*A Warning for Fair Women*," lines 96–7. Hereafter cited in text by line number.
20 Refusing to "go beyond the evidence and enter the realm of conjecture," Cannon cites an allusion to a "tobacco pipe" in *Warning* and concludes that the play was written between the mid-1580s, when tobacco smoking was introduced to England, and 1599, the date on the title page (Introduction to Cannon, "*A Warning for Fair Women*," 48).
21 Other publications include Arthur Golding's *A briefe discourse of the late murther of master George Sanders* (1573, 1577), Anthony Munday's *View of Sundry Examples* (1580), and Holinshed's *Chronicles* (1577). Most of these references have been noted previously: Orlin, *Private*; Marshburn, "'A Cruel Murder'"; and Nelson, *Monstrous Adversary*, 89–92. I have yet to find comment on the reference in Heywood, *Troia Britanica:* "now by the violent hand / Of one George Browne, who murdrous fury leads, / Was Maister Saunders slaine (the matter scand) / Anne Druery (for the fact) and Saunders wife, / George Browne, with trusty Roger lost his life" (Canto 17. Arg. 2. 123).
22 For comparative studies of early modern London and Dublin, see Borsay and Proudfoot, "The English and Irish Urban Experience," and Keene, "Growth."

23 Cf. Grantley, *London in Early Modern English Drama*, which argues that in *A Warning for Fair Women* the geographical specificity of Sanders's London itinerary creates a sense of character "in a landscape local to the audience that forges their familiarity and therefore sympathy with the murder victim" (58).
24 A similar comparison is subsequently made between George Sanders and the play's setting: Drury tells Browne that, "to his wife, in all this cittie, none [is] / More kinde, more loyall harted, or more firme" than George Sanders (*WFW*, ll. 515–16).
25 Howard, *Theater of a City*, 38.
26 Bartolovich, "London's the Thing," 146, 151.
27 Harding, "City," 137. For the "bounds" for Billingsgate and London's other wards, see Stow, *Survey*, 1:117, 205–6.
28 On the importance of domestic thresholds, see Gowing, "'The freedom of the streets.'" On women's surveillance of domestic spaces and activities more generally, see Korda, *Shakespeare's Domestic Economies*, esp. ch. 3.
29 Lake and Questier, *Antichrist's Lewd Hat*, 39.
30 Stow, *Survey*, 1:201.
31 Ibid., 1:210–11.
32 The Royal Exchange also stood in Cornhill, and Greenwich lies east of the City of London across the Thames.
33 The play's full title reads: *A warning for faire women Containing, the most tragicall and lamentable murther of Master George Sanders of London marchant, nigh Shooters hill. Consented vnto by his owne wife, acted by M. Browne, Mistris Drewry and Trusty Roger agents therin: with their seuerall ends. As it hath beene lately diuerse times acted by the right Honorable, the Lord Chamberlaine his Seruantes.*
34 On domestic crime rates in early modern England, see Sharpe, "Domestic Homicide"; Herrup, *Common Peace*; and Walker, *Crime, Gender*. For the way popular representations, including in domestic tragedy, shaped perception of domestic crimes rates see Dolan, *Dangerous Familiars*; see also Clark, *Women and Crime*.
35 Marshall, *Shattering of the Self*, 7.
36 Lake and Questier, *Antichrist's Lewd Hat*, xxiv–xxv; Owens, *Stages of Dismemberment*, 119–20.
37 According to Aristotle's *Poetics* (ch. 4), poetry satisfies humanity's general delight in imitation, including the representation of dead bodies; but as I return to in chapter 4, Aristotle omits all reference to the *polis* as the site and subject of theatrical tragedy.

38 Patenaude, "Critical," 359–60, 23. Henslowe's diary includes payments to John Day and William Haughton for "ther boocke called the tragedie of mereie" in November and December 1599; this play is most likely the same as "A Boocke called Beches tragedie," for which payment was made in January to the Master of the Revel (*Henslowe's Diary*, 128, 130; see also 62 and 127).

39 Patenaude, "Critical," 28. Possible sources include a presumed Italian source, an often-printed English ballad, and infamous English familial histories.

40 Richardson, *Domestic Life*, identifies a similar disparity in the play's "grammar of domestic organization": "Only the local strand of the narrative [i.e., the London plot] is interested in the particularising qualities of domestic settings, a feature which is given considerable prominence in contrast to the generalised sparseness of the Italian plot" (18, 130). However, from the play's disparities in spatial representation, she reaches a different conclusion than I do. Whereas Richardson detects "co-operation" between individual households, whose operations resist scrutiny, and the community, whose collective memory and efforts to interpret physical evidence facilitate discovery (144), I argue for the efficacy of urban place to reveal illicit activity, in which discovery the human *polis* is a secondary agent of justice.

41 Yarington, *Two Lamentable Tragedies*, sig. A3r. Hereafter cited in text by signature page.

42 Pertillo announces that Allenso gave him "[a] prettie Nag to ride to *Padua*," and later Pertillo's aunt relates that "the little boy / Was sent away, to keepe at *Padua*" (sigs. D4r, H1r).

43 Literary and political figures who spent time in Padua include Thomas Hoby, Thomas Wyatt, Cardinal Pole, Francis Walsingham, Philip Sidney, and Samuel Daniel. Dramatists may have learned about Padua from manuscript accounts by and conversations with these men, or "through casual conversations with fellow actors and other entertainers who had travelled there" (Brennan, "English Contact with Europe," 86).

44 In *Much Ado About Nothing* (1600) "Signor Benedick of Padua" is renowned for his wit (1.1.30); in *The Merchant of Venice* (1598) "the learned Bellario" sends from Padua the legal documents, apparel, and letter of introduction Portia needs to defend Antonio (4.1.162); and in *The Taming of the Shrew* (1592) Lucentio describes "fair Padua, nursery of the arts" as "[t]he pleasant garden of great Italy" (1.1.2, 1.1.4) – although *The Taming of the Shrew* is a significant point of comparison because its action

also takes place in two distinct settings, one English, the other Italian. But unlike Shakespeare's comedy, Yarington's tragedy does not designate one setting as real and the other as fictional.

45 Moryson describes "[t]he forme of the City" and specific buildings, including Livy's house and a former "publicke Inne, having the signe of an Oxe, which name it still retaineth," that was "seated over against Saint Martins church" (*Itinerary*, 1:151–6). Thomas Coryate describes Padua's topography, including the location and features of Livy's house; the city's "very auncient gate," which stood "hear to the signe of the Starre where [Coryate] lay being a very faire Inne"; and its covered streets, which provide "pleasant and safe shelter" from the sun in summer and injurious rains and "violent storms" in winter (*Coryats Crudities*, 135, 152, 155). Coryate also names towns around Padua and describes the many "pleasant and delectable Palaces and banqueting houses, which serue to hooses [*sic*] of retraite for the Gentlemen of Venice and Padua, wherein they solace themselues in the Sommer" (*Coryats Crudities*, 125).

46 Hoenselaars, "Italy staged"; Parolin, "'Not so Fitte a Place'"; Paster, *Idea of the City*; and Levith, *Shakespeare's Italian*.

47 Cave, "Ben Jonson's *Every Man in His Humour*," 287. According to the title page of the quarto version of *Every Man In*, the play was performed the same year as the printing of *A Warning for Fair Women*.

48 "The main accomplishment of Jonson's use of specific localities [in the 1616 *Every Man In*] is to map this practice of *moral* space onto the characters' practice of *civic* space" that was "recognizable from the audience's own experience" (Mardock, *Our Scene is London*, 51, original emphasis).

49 The Introduction to *Two Lamentable Tragedies* presents the Italian and English storylines as two halves of the same whole: Avarice boasts of "know[ing] *two* men" who will commit murder for lucre, Homicide gleefully announces that he and Avarice "will go make a *two-folde* Tragedie," and Truth warns audiences to "prepare [their] teare bedecked eyes, / To see *two shewes* of lamentation" (sigs. A2v–A3r, emphasis added).

50 These plays also, if less frequently, locate crime in terms of local extra-urban sites. In *Arden of Faversham*, for instance, Alice Arden and her lover commit adultery and then murder her husband in the Ardens' home, which the play situates in Faversham across from an inn named the Flower-de-Luce. Similarly, *The Witch of Edmonton* locates the scene of polygamy, witchcraft, and murder by naming sites topographically

proximate to Edmonton, including Waltham Abbey, Chessum Banks, and Enville Chase.

51 *Arden*, 2.98; 3.40, 123; 3.7, 32, 49, 100 and 6.3, 41.

52 Ibid., 2.107, 9.55; 7.18, 7.28; 9.56, 9.59, 9.91; 17.8, 17.12.

53 "This is no Paris-garden bandog," Young Banks claims, alluding to the vicious dogs seen bear-baiting in the Liberty of Paris-Garden (Rowley, Dekker, and Ford, *The Witch of Edmonton*, 4.1.258). "Neither is this the Black Dog of Newgate," he continues, referring to the ghostly canine that supposedly haunted the prison at Newgate prior to executions (4.1.261–2). Finally, Young Banks asserts, "The devil in St. Dunstan's will as soon drink with this poor cur as with any Temple-bar laundress that washes and wrings lawyers," thereby citing three additional sites in London: the Devil Tavern and the adjacent Temple Bar and St Dunstan's Church in the East (4.1.266–9).

54 In the introductory scene to *A Yorkshire Tragedy*, "from London" is repeated numerous times (ll. 9–10, 15 sd, 21, 29–30, 58, 58–9), as well as "at London" (l. 69), "in London" (l. 72), and "i' th' country" (l. 62). Cawley and Gaines argue that this prefatory scene was likely penned by a different writer than the rest of the play (Introduction to *A Yorkshire Tragedy*, 13–15). On the omission of the specific setting of the tragic action, see Hopkins, "*A Yorkshire Tragedy*."

55 Harris, "Ludgate Time," 13, and Lin, "Festivity."

56 On Bull Inns in London, see Lillywhite, *London Signs*, 78–82. See also Rogers, *Signs and Taverns*, and Heal, *Signboards*.

57 Lillywhite, *London Signs*, xvi. On signage in early modern English drama, see Gordon, "'If my sign could speak.'"

58 "[T]he boy … knew [Thomas Merry] fetcht his maister to [his] house," and "whereabouts [the Merrys] dwel" (*TLT*, sigs. C3r–C3v).

59 Walsham, *Providence*, 97; also 109. See also Maddern, *Violence and Social Order*, esp. 79–80; Lake and Questier, *Antichrist's Lewd Hat*; and Mukherji, *Law and Representation*.

60 The play cites two other place-based instances of preternatural justice, as well: one involves a grave in an unidentified location (ll. 2022–6); the other (which is retold in Heywood's *An Apology for Actors*, and which I discuss in chapter 3), a tragic performance in the town of Lynn (ll. 2036–47).

61 The Stationers' Register lists the following ballad, now lost: "7*d*. Septembris./. [1594]: Thomas Gosson/ Thomas Myllington/ Entred for their copie vnder the wardens handes, a ballad intituled/ *the pitifull lamentacon of RACHELL MERRYE whoo suffred in Smithfeild with her brother THOMAS MERRYE the vj*th *of September* 1594/ ... vj*d*." (Arber, *Transcript*, 659).

62 Bly, "Playing the Tourist," 69.

63 Ibid., 63.

64 Ibid., 62.

65 *A Warning for Fair Women* may have been performed at any or all of the theatres used by the Lord Chamberlain's Men in the mid- and late-1590s: the Curtain, the Theatre, and the Globe, none of which stood near the Sanderses' home or Shooter's Hill; and *Two Lamentable Tragedies* was likely performed at the Rose, which was not located within physical proximity of the Merrys' home, Smithfield, or Miles End Green, but perhaps at the Fortune, which at least stood on the same side of London (northerly) as Smithfield.

66 Berry, "View," contends it is the Curtain; Schlueter, "Rereading the Side Panels," 142–57, concurs. White, "London professional playhouses," 301, asserts that the *View* depicts the Theatre, not the Curtain.

67 Peacham, *The art of drawing*, 29.

68 On this print and the waning of traditional boundaries, see Berry, "View," esp. 209, 197; and Harding, "City," 135–6.

69 John Fitzherbert, *Here begynneth a ryght frutefull mater: and hath to name the boke of surueyeng and improumentes* (London, 1523), xxxiii, quoted in Gordon, "Overseeing," 84.

70 Holinshed, *The first volume of the chronicles*, 37v.

71 Digges, *The Complete Ambassador*, 347.

72 The adulterous murderers in domestic tragedy, including George Browne, tend to fill more than one of these categories; see Dolan, *Dangerous Familiars*.

73 Whetstone, *The Rock of Regard*, 101.

74 Harman, *A Caveat*, sigs. B1v–B2r.

75 Holinshed, *Chronicles*, 912.

76 Milton, *The Reason of Church Government* (1642), in Merritt, *John Milton*, 685. Milton links custom to tyranny again in the address "To the Parliament" that opens his *Doctrine and Discipline of Divorce* (1644) and in the opening lines of *The Tenure of Kings and Magistrates* (1650).

77 Zucker, *Places of Wit*, 91, 95.

78 Dolan, "Gender" argues that the "hybrid dramatic forms" of *A Warning for Fair Women*, which includes not only allegory but also the dumb show, "provide the perfect vehicles for competing, irreconciled interpretations of the events depicted" (201–2). Lopez, *Constructing the Canon* presents the "bifurcation" of form in *Two Lamentable Tragedies* in terms of Italian intrigue tragedy and "an English tragic idiom" defined by labor (179–81). A similar conjunction of domestic tragedy's innovative urban realism and

an established form, in this case the English history play, is evident in Heywood's *Edward IV, part 1.*

79 On city comedy's conjunction of innovative and established forms, see Lopez, *Constructing*, 181–2; Cave, "Ben Jonson's," 282–97; Morse, "What City, Friends"; and Manley, *Literature and Culture*, ch. 8.

80 See MacKay, *Persecution* and Paster, *Idea of the City*.

2. *Translatio Metropolitae* and Early English Revenge Tragedy

1 Goldhill, "Generalizing About Tragedy," 59.

2 Jones, *Metropolis*, 39. This is especially true of the imperial metropolis: "when cities-states became nation-states and then the centres of empire, then a true metropolis might emerge which towered over its contemporary cities" (Jones, *Metropolis*, 69).

3 See, for example, Bartolovich, "'Baseless Fabric'" and Barker, "London."

4 Herring, *Popish pietie*, n.p., st. 55.

5 Ibid., st. 61.

6 James, *Shakespeare's Troy* acknowledges that *Titus* takes up urban (and courtly) issues, but her analysis focuses on the play's caution against using ancient models as the basis for England's empire-building project. For other text-based approaches to *translatio imperii*, see de Grazia, *"Hamlet,"* esp. ch. 3; Keilen, *Vulgar Eloquence*, ch. 2; and Federico, *New Troy*.

7 Neill, *Issues of Death*, 251.

8 Through its interplay of formal, narrative, and theatrical return, revenge tragedy more broadly illustrates what we may call – by way of analogy to *topographesis*, Henry S. Turner's term for representations of place and their aesthetic and discursive functions – *choreographesis*, or the representations of movement and the formal and ideological purposes to which they are put (see Turner, *English Renaissance Stage*, esp. 30–3). I discuss *choreographesis* in my essay "Processions and History."

9 In mounting my argument, I bring together the work of scholars who emphasize words, etymologies, and linguistic materiality, on the one hand, and bodies, enactment, and theatrical materiality, on the other. In particular, Parker, *Shakespeare from the Margins*; Boedeker and Raabflaub, who suggest seeking out tragedy's urban resonances and civic functions in "the clues the poets themselves provide, not least in word choice and terminology" ("Tragedy and City," 125); Fletcher, *Time, Space, and Motion*; Smith, *Key of Green*; and Lin, *Shakespeare and the Materiality of Performance*.

10 De Certeau, *The Practice of Everyday Life*, 97. For the influence of de Certeau in early modern literary studies, see Howard, *Theater of a City;* Zucker, *Places of Wit*; Turner, *English Renaissance;* Harkness and Howard, "Places and Spaces"; Mardock, *Our Scene is London*; and Hopkins, *City/ Stage/Globe.*
11 Shakespeare, *Titus*, 1.1.33, 37, 67, 72, 76, 110, 162, 221.
12 To the stage direction for Titus's entrance, Wells and Taylor add "in his chariot" (Shakespeare, *The Complete Works*, ed. Wells and Taylor) and Waith adds "in a chariot" (Shakespeare, *Titus*, ed. Waith). On stage chariots in other plays, see Dessen and Thomson, *A Dictionary of Stage Directions*, 47–8. On theatrical and civic performances of triumphal processions, including in *Titus*, see Miller, *Roman Triumphs*, esp. 128–31.
13 On ancient Roman imagery in early modern English ceremony, see Miller, *Roman Triumphs.* Of course, other kinds of imagery shaped civic and royal pageantry, including English history, heraldry, and Christian imagery.
14 The prefix "re-" has "the general sense of 'back' or 'again,'" and in the seventeenth century was used "abundantly" as a prefix to verbs, "sometimes denoting that the action itself is performed a second time, and sometimes that its result is to reverse a previous action or process, or to restore a previous state of things" (*OED Online*, "re-," *prefix*). A review of "re-" words as catalogued in Spevack's *Concordance* does not suggest greater frequency of these words in *Titus* or Shakespeare's tragedies than in his other plays. I contend, however, that "re-" words would resonate with greater impact in revenge tragedies, such as *Titus*, than in other genres in which repetition is not a central feature of the plot; cf. Hammond, *Strangeness*, esp. 16, 33–6.
15 Shakespeare, *Complete Works*, ed. Dover Wilson, 754.
16 In the stage direction in Waith's edition of *Titus*, Tamora comes onstage "in a chariot." For a critique of this position, and a discussion of the performance of allegorical Revenge in *Titus* more generally, see Kiefer, *Shakespeare's Visual Theatre*, 43–54.
17 Her purpose in directing Saturninus to feign reconciliation is so that she may be "then let … alone" to "raze their faction and their family" (1.1.446–8) – that is, revenge.
18 Thomas Kyd, *The Spanish Tragedy*, in *Four Revenge Tragedies*, 1.2.102, 108–9. Hereafter cited in text as *ST.*
19 Beaumont and Fletcher, *The Maid's Tragedy*, 1.1.13–14.
20 Ibid., 4.2.0 sd.
21 Thomas Middleton, *The Revenger's Tragedy*, in *Four Revenge Tragedies*, 1.1.0 sd (see also 1.4.26–47), 1.1.117, 1.1.134. Hereafter cited in text as *RT*.

22 This juxtapositional strategy, like the implicit comparisons of Italian cities and London discussed in chapter 1, distinguishes *Hamlet* from revenge tragedies with no urban content whatsoever. In George Chapman's *The Revenge of Bussy D'Ambois*, for example, Clermont's adventures take him to a number of places but none of them an urban centre. Likewise, Cyril Tourneur's *The Atheist's Tragedy*, which is set in a generic France, abandons all sense of the city as the site of retributive violence.

23 In the opening scene alone, for example, the Ghost of King Hamlet enters and exits twice: after its initial entrance, it "stalks away" (*Hamlet* 1.1.48), and after its return, "it will not stand" but is "here," then "here," and "gone" (1.1.122–3). Later, after the Ghost "wafts [Hamlet] to a more removèd ground" (1.4.42), where it bids Hamlet to revenge his father's murder, it "cries ['Swear'] under the stage" four times (1.5.151 sd; see 1.5.151, 1.5.156, 1.5.162, 1.5.182), "remov[ing]" to "ground" each time (1.5.166, 1.5.158). On the theme of return in *Hamlet* more generally, see de Grazia, "*Hamlet*," ch. 2.

24 In the Arden Shakespeare edition of Quarto 2 of *Hamlet*, Thompson and Taylor annotate Hamlet's reference to "the city" as follows: "It is not clear which Danish city Hamlet might mean; again reference to London makes more sense" (2.2.298n). Thompson and Taylor's "again" points back to the mention of "the late innovation," which, they note by reference to the other texts of *Hamlet*, "could mean the revived fashion for children's companies" in London (2.2.295–6n). In the Pelican Shakespeare edition of *Hamlet*, Braunmuller glosses the words "city" as "London for Shakespeare's original audiences"; and "residence" as "for Shakespeare and his audience, this word would evoke the theatrical center, London" (2.2.304 and 2.2.299 nn.).

25 These repetitions function like linking analogues; see Dessen, *Elizabethan Drama*, 50–70.

26 Consequently, these scenes may be read in terms of the place-based analysis that *Titus* has recently attracted, according to which the juxtaposition of representational spaces debunks presumed ideological binaries, for example, between civilized Rome and barbarous foreign lands, and between *polis* and wilderness. See, e.g., Hutson, *Invention*, ch. 2; and Duncan, "'Sumptuously Re-edified.'"

27 On tragedy, and especially revenge tragedy, as a response to widespread interest in the pursuit of justice in the face of injustice and violence, see Reiss, *Tragedy and Truth* and Pollard, "Tragedy and Revenge."

28 For responses to Waith's suggestion in his edition that Titus's vow may involve "handshaking," see Bate, Introduction to *Titus*, 46, and James, *Shakespeare's Troy*, 74–5.

29 Similarly, in *The Spanish Tragedy*, after Hieronimo finds Bel-Imperia's letter that reveals his son's murderers, he "vow[s]" and Bel-Imperia "consent[s]" to avenge Horatio's death (*ST* 4.1.29–50). The combination of text and spoken word characterize the play-within-a-play "in sundry languages" by which Hieronimo and Bel-Imperia fulfill this vow (*ST* 4.4.9 sd). And in *The Revenger's Tragedy* Antonio, Piero, and Hippolito, with one or more swords in hand, make their "vow" and "swear" to avenge the Duchess's rape and death (*RT* 1.4.56–65). Yet it is fitting that Antonio is denied opportunity to fulfill his vow of extralegal violence, because at the end of *The Revenger's Tragedy* he assumes leadership of the court and punishes as treason Hippolito and Vindice's murder of the corrupt duke.
30 I discuss this archive in "Processions and History."
31 As I observed in the introduction, the place of punishment in Visscher's print is indeterminate, such that curators identify it variously as St Paul's Churchyard, Old Palace Yard, and a generic urban square.
32 T.W., *The arraignement and execution*, sig. B1r.
33 Compare the four copies of *Supplicium de octo coniuratis sumtum in Britannia* held in the collection of the British Museum: Reg. Nos. 1848, 0911.452 (shown here), 1919, 0513.1 (the preliminary drawing), 1892, 0817.2, and 1868, 0808.3208.
34 *A true and perfect relation*, sig. A2r.
35 The Foucauldian paradigm also involves the shift in the condemned's status from pariah to parishioner and from pollutant to prodigal. Disciplinary processions enacted this abstract progression between these social and spiritual states as a literal progression between geographical locations. In the case of the Gunpowder Plotters, however, there is little evidence of the offenders' restoration to the community and communion.
36 T.W., *The arraignement and execution*, sig. B1v.
37 See Howard, *Shakespeare's Art*. Rist goes further in his discussion of the early modern passions as dramatic speech and feeling, arguing that "contemporary theater (as written composition, performed speech, and audience experience) was inseparable from emotion, making performed plays an index to audiences' responses" ("Catharsis as 'Purgation,'" 141).
38 In *The Revenger's Tragedy*, audiences are invited to lament the death of Antonio's wife, whom they never meet but whose dead body is "discover[ed]" as an emblem of wifely virtue (*RT* 1.4.0 sd). In *Hamlet*, the Ghost of King Hamlet tells a tale of fratricide that is clearly meant to horrify his onstage auditor—and arguably the offstage audience, as well: the Ghost tells Hamlet to "Pity me not" but bewails his death, "O horrible, O horrible, most horrible!" (*Hamlet* 1.5.5, 1.5.80).

39 Explications of 3.1 in performance, including Howard, *Shakespeare's Art*, 153–6; Jones, *Scenic Form*, 8–13; and Teague, *Shakespeare's Speaking Properties*, 92–6, make at most passing reference to Titus's response to Lucius.

40 Shakespeare, *Titus*, ed. Bate, 3.1.32–48. The Norton edition omits the half-line "And bootless unto them."

41 Wentworth, *A true relation*, 7. This "wish" appears, as well, in two other versions of Wentworth final words: *The Earle of Straffords speech*, 3, and *The true speech of Thomas Wentworth*, sig. A3v.

42 Kilburn and Milton, "The public context," 232; and *A true relation of the manner of the execution of Thomas Earle of Strafford*, 8.

43 My reading of Wentworth's dying speech draws on the discussion of rhetoric, performance, and affect in Roach, *Player's Passion*. More recent work on rhetoric and affect in early modern England includes Enterline, *Shakespeare's Schoolroom*; Olmsted, *Imperfect Friend*; Cockcroft, *Rhetorical*; and Graham, *Performance of Conviction*.

44 In addition to an implicit pun on "groundlings" (Hamlet's term), there may have been an implied joke on "understanders," which was the more common term, as the playgoers in the yard (i.e., who stand under the stage) and Titus when he lies down (i.e., is not standing).

45 Bate includes the half-line, albeit "in wavy brackets to indicate a possible false start," because "both grammatical disintegration and blockage of the measured flow of the pentameters are singularly appropriate to the content of the speech" (Bate, *Titus*, 100–1).

46 *OED Online*, "bootless, adj.1," 3, and "bootless, adj.2."

47 Moreover, given Titus's description of the stones as lacking the "grave weeds" of the tribunes, "bootless" may also be a reference to the humble footwear of the groundlings.

48 Schoenfeldt, "Shakespearean Pain," citing the discussion of representations of cruelty making viewers cruel, humane, or indifferent in Susan Sontag, *Regarding the Pain of Others* (New York: Picador, 2003).

49 These responses were not unknown in the ancient theatre, where tragic witnessing (Easterling, "Weeping, Witnessing") and *eudaimonia* (partiality) (Nussbaum, *Upheavals of Thought*) may have undermined the force of compassionate response.

50 In their introduction to *Staging Pain*, Allard and Martin frame the essays in the collection in terms of the way scenes of suffering may yield "not tragic pleasure but either laughter or disgust" (3).

51 On the Clown's execution in *Titus* as a critique of excessive judicial violence, see Barker, *Culture of Violence*, 143–206. This moment in *Titus*

is also unlike Shakespeare's comedies and history plays, in which representations of the passage to the scaffold operate in the service of theatrical privilege and generic innovation; see my "Crossing from Scaffold to Stage."

52 Hutson, *Invention*, esp. ch. 2. Brooks considers sympathy as a cause of unease for its capacity to sway legal decisions in the context of modern psychotherapy and the confessions of victims (*Troubling Confessions*, 136–7).

53 See esp. Lake and Questier, "Agency"; Dolan, "'Gentlemen'"; Cunningham, "Renaissance Execution"; and Sharpe, "'Last Dying Speeches.'" Craik, "'A Lover's Complaint'" offers a more literary approach to the "narrative instability" (443) of criminal confessions.

54 The contest over the impact of Wentworth's death was highlighted by the joint publication of the Tower and scaffold speeches (*The two last speeches*). The popularity of this text is attested by its multiple printings: *Early English Books Online* lists seven editions (Wing S5799, S5799A, S5799B, S5799C, S5800, S5800A, and S5800B).

55 *Aeneid* 1.152–3, quoted in James, *Shakespeare's Troy*, 49.

56 Parker, *Shakespeare from the Margins*, 137–43 and ch. 5 passim.

57 Wallace, *Cambridge Introduction to Tragedy*, esp. "Case studies 2: Language"; Poole, *Tragedy*, esp. ch. 7; Silverstone, "Afterword"; and Hammond, *Strangeness*.

58 Although Enterline, *Rhetoric of the Body* makes only passing references to *Titus Andronicus*, her discussion of Ovidian narratives about the fragmentation of women's bodies and language, especially the story of Philomela, bears on my analysis of the judicial and affective dynamics of Lavinia's translation.

59 Bacon, *Essayes*, 19.

60 Marcus refers directly to "revenge" four times (*Titus* 4.1.73, 4.1.92, 4.1.127, 4.1.128). Chiron and Demetrius are silenced – first, gagged, then, their throats cut – at 5.2.157–205; their dismemberment takes place offstage.

61 See Turner, "Plotting"; Brückner and Poole, "The Plot Thickens"; Hutson "Fortunate Travelers"; Palfrey and Tiffany, *Shakespeare in Parts*, ch. 3 and 4; and Stern, *Documents of Performance*, ch. 7.

62 On erasable writing tables in the late sixteenth and early seventeenth centuries, see Stallybrass, Chartier, and Mowery, "Hamlet's Tables."

63 Perhaps the same "gates shut on [Lucius]" when he was "unkindly banished" (*Titus* 5.3.104, 5.3.103).

64 The reference to Tarquin also implicitly figures Lavinia's assault in terms of the rape of Lucrece.

65 In Shakespeare's England, "repair" meant physical return, moral rectification, and material reconstruction, specifically of a city (*OED Online*, "repair, v.2").

66 A slew of pastoral imagery situates Lucius and the Goth army outside of Rome, e.g., the Goth forces and Lucius are compared to "stinging bees in hottest summer's day / Led by their master to the flowered fields" (*Titus* 5.1.14–15), and Aaron uses of the word "trim" (5.1.93–6) to describe Lavinia's mutilation, recalling Marcus's forestry terms upon discovering his niece (2.3.16–51) as well as the sylvan setting of her assault (4.1.51–60).

67 On the remains of monasteries, churches, and other religious structures and architectural antiquarianism in post-Reformation England, see Aston, "English Ruins," and Walsham, "'Like Fragments of a Shipwreck.'"

68 Gerschow, "Diary," 59. According to the U.S. Naval Observatory, whose computations of sunrise and sunset are used by the Royal Observatory in Edinburgh, sunset in London on 27 September 2011 – the year 1602 was out of range – occurred at 6:48 p.m. (http://www.usno.navy.mil/USNO/astronomical-applications/data-services/rs-one-year-world; accessed 9 May 2011). Gerschow's observations are similar to those of Lupold von Wedel in his account of his journey through England and Scotland in 1584–5. Von Wedel describes the punishment of Dr William Parr and eighteen others condemned for attempted regicide, and notes that after the executions, "[t]he Doctor's head was fixed on the gate of London Bridge, where about thirty heads of noblemen and gentlemen were fixed who had sought to take the life of the queen" (Wedel, "Journey," 267).

69 Manley, *Literature and Culture*, 223.

70 Newman, *Cultural Capitals*, 53–9.

71 Norden, *The view of London Bridge*. The small boats that Norden shows traveling beneath and along the bridge's length evoke one creation myth related in the accompanying text: the daughter of a London ferryman, who became rich by "the transportation of Passengers, betweene the Citie and *Southwarke*," built the first timber bridge.

72 My discussion of the city portraits by Norden, Braun and Hogenberg, and Visscher is indebted to Hopkins, *City/Stage/Globe*.

73 Gordon, "Performing London," 81.

74 Manley shows that the growth of ornate pageantry for royal coronations in the fourteenth century and mayoral inaugurations in the sixteenth

century coincide not only with periods of "consolidation of London's status as a capital and dominant metropolis" but also heightened tensions between the City of London and the monarchy (*Literature and Culture*, 213; see also 267).

75 As the three existing plates of the copperplate map include only the northern-most part of London Bridge, we do not know if this city portrait also included the heads. But the parallels between this map and Braun and Hogenberg's, as well as the inclusion of body parts impaled on Moorsgate in the plate of the northern portion of the city, suggest that it did.

76 Frye, *Elizabeth I.*

77 Hopkins, *City/Stage/Globe*, 89.

78 Hunt, *Drama of Coronation*, ch. 5; and Lancashire, *London Civic Theatre.*

79 Hunt, ibid., 72.

80 Armitage, "*Procession Portrait*," 301.

81 Frye, *Elizabeth I*, 42–3.

82 Mardock, *Our Scene is London*; Hopkins, *City/Stage/Globe*; and Hill, "'Representing.'"

3. Tyrant Tragedy and the Tyranny of Tragedy in Stuart London

1 On the tradition of tyrant tragedy in early modern England, see Bushnell, *Tragedies of Tyrants.*

2 In his edition of Beaumont and Fletcher's *Philaster*, Andrew Gurr, citing the reference to "the new platform" in "the city" (5.3.2–3), a likely allusion to the main deck of the *Prince Royal* that launched in 1610, writes: "Although the setting of the play is Sicily, the citizens are unquestionably Londoners, and the 'city' identifiable as the City of London" (96). In Thomas Middleton's *Women, Beware Women*, a procession of the Duke, Cardinals, and "All our chief states of Florence" transforms the city into a kind of degraded extension of the Italian court (ed. John Jowitt, in Middleton *Collected Works*, 1.3.97; see 1.3.101 sd). "The Scene" of *The Tragedy of Albouine* is "Uerona," but its depiction of down-and-out soldiers, who rail against the city as "oregrowne" and "luxurious," evokes contemporary London at the conclusion of the Anglo-French War (sigs. A4v, C3r, H2v).

3 On *Coriolanus* as a tyrant tragedy, see Parker, *Plato's Republic.*

4 Chernaik, *Myth of Rome*, ch. 8.

5 Manley, *Literature and Culture*, 8, original emphasis.

6 Stow, *Survey*, 2:198–9.

7 In addition to Bushnell, *Tragedies of Tyrants*, see Patterson, *Censorship and Interpretation*; Butler, "Romans in Britain"; Hartley, "*The Roman Actor*"; and Reinheimer, "*The Roman Actor.*"

8 On plays, and especially *The Roman Actor*, as literary theory, see Barish, "Three Caroline Defenses"; Pastoor, "Metadramatic Performances"; and Delery, "Dramatic Instruction."

9 The repeated failures of tragedy to affect moral reformation leads Orgel to assert that *The Roman Actor* "acts out the charge that mimesis can only be pernicious, since we inevitably imitate the bad and ignore the good" ("Play of Conscience," 141). Anne Barton offers a more tempered response: "There is a sense in which *The Roman Actor* is more pessimistic about the power of art to correct and inform its audience than any other play written between 1580 and 1642. Yet there was something in Massinger which refused to abandon the effort, while insisting that the game should not be played with marked cards" ("The Distinctive Voice of Massinger," *Times Literary Supplement*, May 20, 1977, 623–4, repr. in Howard, *Philip Massinger*, 231).

10 Massinger, *The Roman Actor*, 3.2.19–21. Hereafter cited in text.

11 The Gemonies steps led to the Aventine Hill, where traitors were executed and their bodies displayed before being dragged on hooks to the Tiber River (Massinger, *Roman Actor*, 88n). For other references to this practice, see 1.1.94–5 and 4.2.294–5.

12 I find it likely, in fact, that the reference to the Gemonies in *The Roman Actor* functions in this way, preceding by over a quarter of a century the first example in the *Oxford English Dictionary*: Robert Fletcher's juxtaposition of the Gemonies to the "wrack" in *Ex otio negotium. Or, Martiall his epigrams translated. With sundry poems and fancies* (1656), 174; see *OED Online* "gemonies, n."

13 Rochester, *Staging Spectatorship*, 73 proposes the scene refers to the execution of Latimer and Ridley in Oxford in 1555. Regardless of any intended or perceived referent, the historically uncanny effect of this stage image works through reference to images of pairs of Marian martyrs "chained together to a stake, back-to-back amidst the flames" that were "somewhat 'generic' [in] appearance" (Jones, *The Print in Early Modern England*, 58; see images reproduced on 59).

14 King, *Foxe's "Book of Martyrs,"* 18 and ch. 3; see also Knott, *Discourses of Martyrdom*.

15 The hangmen and their victims exit at line 122; Domitia and other members of the court enter two lines later; and "Without more circumstance" than "a short flourish," *Iphis and Anaxarete* begins (3.2.148 and 3.2.148 sd).

16 On the westward trajectory of early modern city comedy, see Howard, *Theater of a City*, 209–15.

17 See, for example, the discussion of architectural imagery in the Earl of Rochester's revision of *Valentinia*, in Love, "Was Lucinda Betrayed at Whitehall?"

18 Moretti, "The Great Eclipse: Tragic Form as the Deconsecration of Sovereignty," in *Signs*, 42–82.

19 Wilks, "The Discourse of Reason," 133.

20 Philip Sidney, *An Apology for Poetry*, in Adams, *Critical Theory*, 152. Adams notes that Sidney's *Apology*, which was also published in 1595 under the title *A Defence of Poesie*, was written in 1583 (143).

21 *Aristotle's Theory of Poetry and Fine Art*, 4th ed., trans. S.H. Butcher (New York: Dover, 1955), repr. in Adams, *Critical Theory*, 53.

22 See Herrick, *Fusion*, esp. ch. 4. On the "double bind" into which the effort to reconcile Aristotelian and Horatian theories put Renaissance writers, see Matz, *Defending*, 23.

23 The continental interpretation of catharsis is found in Sidney's *Apology* and in John Milton's preface to *Samson Agonistes*, yet as I demonstrate, these constitute exceptions. On early modern interpretations of catharsis, see Orgel, "The Play of Conscience," 132–7; Weinberg, *History of Literary Criticism*; Spingarn, *History of Literary*; and Clayton, "Catharsis," a response to Orgel.

24 Orgel, "The Play of Conscience," 139, see also 139–42; Herrick, *Poetics*, 24–7, 49–50; and Hardison, "Three Types," esp. 4–8.

25 MacKay, *Persecution, Plague*, pt. 1.

26 Kelley, "Elizabethan Political Thought," 48.

27 Peck, "Kingship, Counsel," and Dzelzainis, "'Incendiaries of the State.'"

28 Bushnell, *Tragedies of Tyrants*, 9–20.

29 William Barclay is the best-known respondent to George Buchanan due to the citation of his *De regno* (1600) in John Locke's *Two Treatises of Government*. On Barclay's and others' responses to Buchanan's *De jure regni apud Scotos* (1579), see Burns, "George Buchanan."

30 Bodin, *The six bookes of a common-weale*, 210. Subsequent quotations appear on this page, as well. Bodin's treatise was printed initially in French (1576; repr. 1583) and then in a revised Latin edition (1586).

31 *Vindiciae*, sig. O2r. Hereafter cited in text. For an overview of the composition and print history of *Vindiciae contra tyrannos* and the evidence of its author's identity, see Kingdom, "Calvinism and Resistance Theory," 211–12.

32 Buchanan, *De jure regni*, 19, 85. Buchanan's treatise was originally published in Latin in 1579 (the same year as *Vindiciae contra tyrannos*) but "written ... a dozen years earlier" (Burns, "George Buchanan," 4).

33 Ibid., 85, 70, 94.

34 James VI and I, *Political Writings*, 20. The author's name given here acknowledges his dual role as King James VI of Scotland from 1567 to 1625 and as King James I of England from 1603 to 1625.

35 Ibid., 183.

36 Lemon, *Treason by Words*, 158.

37 Slights, *Casuistical Tradition*, 65.

38 Lukacher, *Daemonic Figures*, 154.

39 Goldberg, *James I*, 113–63. See also Gallagher, *Medusa's Gaze* on the subject of the royal conscience and the king's "spiritual colonization" of his subjects' consciences (6).

40 James I, *Political Writings*, 141.

41 Ibid.

42 Foucault, *Discipline and Punish*, 43.

43 Hanson, *Discovering*, 24. See also Langbein, *Torture*.

44 Quoted in Smith, *Elizabethan Critical Essays*, 2:209–10.

45 Sidney, *Apology for Poetry*, 152.

46 Herrick, *Poetics*, 27–78, and "Some Neglected." See Rubidge, "Catharsis Through Admiration" on "the discourse of admiration – all but the word itself" in *The Roman Actor* (329).

47 Heywood, *Apology*, sig. G1v.

48 Perkins, *Cases of Conscience*, 585–86. The analogous lexicons of Renaissance English tragedy and contemporary casuistic writings have not received critical attention, despite a recent outpouring of scholarship on the dynamic between early modern literature and casuistry: Gallagher, *Medusa's Gaze*; Lemon, *Treason by Words*: Lukacher, *Daemonic Figures*; Slights, *Casuistical Tradition*; and Kiefer, *Writing on the Renaissance Stage*, and "'Written Troubles.'" Cf. Wilks, *The Idea of Conscience*.

49 Heywood, *Apology*, sig. G1v; I.G., *Refutation*, 42–3.

50 I.G., *Refutation*, 42–3. I.G. also writes: "God onely gaue authority of publique instruction and correction but to two sorts of men: to his Ecclestasticall Ministers, and temporal Magistrates: hee neuer instituted a third authority of Players, or ordained that they should serue in his

Ministry: and therefore are they to bee reiected with their vse and quality" (57).

51 See Kelly, *Ideas and Forms.* Renaissance writers tended to privilege one or the other plotline. An exception is Sidney, who invokes both plotlines in his *Apology* when he writes that tragedy represents the punishment awaiting the tyrant and "the uncertainty of this world" (Sidney, *Apology,* in Adams, *Critical Theory,* 152).

52 Smith, "E/loco/com/motion," 144. As Nuttall points out, "'[m]ove', 'motion', 'emotion' are of course both etymologically and conceptually cognate" (*Why Does Tragedy Give Pleasure?,* 23). I return to the intersection of embodied sensation and affective sense in chapter 4.

53 Heywood, *Apology,* sig. F1v.

54 *OED Online* "touch, v." 8a., and "attach, v." I.a., 2; the sense of "attach" as "To join in sympathy or affection *to* a person, place, etc" did not emerge until the eighteenth century (7a).

55 Sidney, *Apology,* in Adams, *Critical Theory,* 150.

56 The *OED Online* definitions for folk include: "An aggregation of people in relation to a superior, *e.g.* God, a king or priest; the great mass as opposed to an individual; the people" ("folk, n." 2a). In his *Apology,* Sidney registers his frustration that the doors through which "evil men come to the stage" and "go out" represent multiple locations (Sidney, *Apology,* in Adams, *Critical Theory,* 159), although he dismisses as ridiculous the idea that playgoers would need signs announcing place-names to understand that the stage represents, but is not in fact, those locations (155).

57 Of course, to be "appal[led]" is considerably less harsh than madness. Yet the fact that Hamlet remains untroubled by the prospect of striking blameless souls, even mildly, with the performance of tragedy signals the impending loss of conscience observed by Belsey, "The Case of Hamlet's Conscience," 144.

58 As Pollard has recently shown ("Conceiving Tragedy," and "What's Hecuba"), this scene frames the effects of tragedy in relation to female bodies and effeminate emotions.

59 G. Smith, *Elizabethan Critical Essays,* 2:424; Cicero, *On Duties,* 72 (2.26).

60 Harington, in G. Smith, *Elizabethan Critical Essays,* 2:210; Heywood, *Apology,* sig. F4v.

61 Sidney, *Apology for Poetry,* in Adams, *Critical Theory,* 152.

62 Philemon Holland's translation of Plutarch's *Morals* (1603), quoted in Proudfoot, "'Play's the Thing,'" 161. Proudfoot, "Play's the Thing," 161–2, also reproduces corroborating if less-detailed accounts of Alexander's

affective and physical response to tragedy in Plutarch's *Lives* (trans. Thomas North [1576]), and Aelion's *Histories* (trans. Abraham Fleming [1570]).

63 Plutarch's *Morals*, quoted in Proudfoot, "'Play's the Thing,'" 161.

64 The threat of punishment for improperly responding to performance receives extended dramatization in the anonymous *The Tragedie of Nero*, when, for example, Nimphidius recounts his confinement in the playhouse where Nero was performing: "But when we once were forc't to be spectators, / Compel'd to that, which should haue bin a pleasure," and "there stood knaues / That put downe in their Tables all that stir'd, / And markt in each there cheerefulnesse, or sadnesse" (sig. D3r).

65 A similar moment occurs in Beaumont and Fletcher's *The Maid's Tragedy* when the Tyrant forces Govianus to see the pairing of the new king and the former king's betrothed:

> *Tyrant*: The banishment were gentle, were that all;
> But to afflict thy soul, before thou goest
> Thou shalt behold the heav'n that thou must lose
> In her that must be mine.
> Then to be banished, then to be deprived,
> Shows the Full torment we provide for thee.
> *Govianus*: Here's a right tyrant now ... (1.1.102–7)

66 Other classical writers, including Plutarch and Augustine, also argued that singing has emotional and physiological effects analogous to tragedy. On the common etymology and mythology of singing and tragedy, see Hall, "The Singing Actors of Antiquity," 4–5.

67 If Domitian directs this question to his guards and the playhouse audience, as Martin White posits, the play would point up that Lamia is not the only innocent spectator driven to admiration by the sudden deployment of tragic catharsis (Massinger, *Roman Actor*, 123n).

68 Clark, *Moral Art*, 59; Delery, "Instruction and Misinstruction," 113–14; Habicht, "Traps," 266; Hartley, "*The Roman Actor* and Censored Theater," 368–9; and Reimheiner, "*The Roman Actor*," 329.

69 On these aspects of Stoic philosophy, see Goldberg, *James I*; and Edwards, "Acting and Self-actualization," 377–94. Neill frames these aspects as elements of tragedy, which works "to contain the fear of death by staging fantasies of ending in which the moment of dying was transformed by the arts of performance, to a supreme demonstration of distinction" (*Issues of Death*, 32).

70 The fact that Domitian's cousin, Domitilla, is cast as Anaxarete points up that this play-within-a-play is not a public performance but a court

performance, such as those in which seventeenth-century aristocratic women routinely participated. See Brown and Parolin, *Women*.

71 A similar moment occurs in Marston's *The Insatiate Countess* (1610) when Isabella not only proves sexually "insatiate" but also presumes the godhead to attain her desire: "Is he not a god / That can command what other men would win / With the hard'st advantage? I must have him, / Or shadow-like follow his fleeting steps" (2.1.203–6). Isabella's subsequent distraction when waiting for her beloved (2.3) and her language of ravishment to refer to both music and love (3.2) are also similar to Massinger's portrait of the empress.

72 At the end of Beaumont and Fletcher's *The Maid's Tragedy*, Evadne describes her murder of the Tyrant as a physical and political purgative: "You are too hot, and I have brought you physic / To temper your high veins. ... [Y]ou must bleed" (5.1.53–4, 58). Denman, "Anatomizing," 327, explains "Evadne's role is now to let the blood from the person of the tyrant ['the state of my body,' 5.1.56] and by extension to deflate the tyranny he embodies," i.e., the body politic.

73 Heywood, *Apology*, sig. G2v.

74 Many scholars assert that Massinger's opening reference alludes to Euripides's play: Bushnell, *Tragedies of Tyrants*, 174; Clark, *Moral Art*, 67; Reinheimer, "*The Roman Actor*," 326; and Hogan, "Imagery," 274. A notable exception is Barish, "Three Caroline Defenses," 197. Pentheus's story appears in Ovid's *Metamorphoses* and other ancient plays, including Accius's *Bacchae*, Pacuvius's *Pentheus*, a trilogy by Aeschylus, and Statius's *Agave*. The likelihood that the opening of *The Roman Actor* refers to Euripides's *Bacchae* is supported by the ancient dramatist's reputation and popularity in early modern Europe.

75 Domitian puts off his "robe and wreath" and sports a "cloak and hat" that "fit the person" of a lord (4.2.224–8). On Domitian's costume as an anachronism that points up the overlap of fictional Rome and early modern London, see Rochester, *Staging Spectatorship*, 43.

76 Wallace, *Cambridge Introduction to Tragedy*, 106.

77 Seaford, "Tragedy and Dionysus," 32.

78 Poole, *Tragedy*, 118.

79 "Good kings are mourned for after life, but ill, / And such as governed only by their will, / And not reason, unlamented fall, / No good man's tear shed at their funeral" (Massinger, *Roman Actor*, 5.1.90–3).

80 Rochester, *Staging Spectatorship*, 46, proposes that Massinger intended the staging of Domitian's death to recall directly Julius Caesar's assassination in Shakespeare's play in performance. But Massinger could also be

alluding to an allusion: in Beaumont and Fletcher's *The Maid's Tragedy* (1611), for example, Amintor warns Evadne, "Mock not the powers above, that can and dare / Give thee a great example of their justice / *To all ensuing ages*, if thou playst / With thy repentance, the best sacrifice" (4.1.239–43, emphasis added). In his edition of the play, T.W. Craik accepts the emendation of "ages" from Quarto 1's "eies" (i.e., "eyes"), citing meter and sense.

81 Machacek, "Allusion," 534.

82 Ferguson, *Trials of Desire*, 165.

83 Adams and Stephens, *Select Documents*, 394.

84 My discussion of the Banqueting House is based on Thurley's comprehensive study, *Whitehall Palace.*

85 Thurley, *Whitehall Palace*, 45. As Anderson shows (*Inigo Jones*, 165–83), the actual construction of the Banqueting House necessarily assimilated native materials and conventions. On the dynamic between classical and native architecture, see Gent, ed., *Albion's Classicism.*

86 Anderson, *Inigo Jones*, 26.

87 Proclamation for Buildings, 16 June 1615, in *Stuart Royal Proclamations*, 346.

88 For an overview, see Peck, *Consuming Splendor*, esp. 201–5.

89 Gent, Introduction to *Albion's Classicism*, 12. On Jones's 1619 Banqueting House as an expression of monarchical authority, see Newman, "Inigo Jones." In towns and cities throughout England, the association between classical architecture and political power became a commonplace by the mid-seventeenth century (Howard, *Building*).

90 In this regard, it is not that James lacked awareness of "the importance of image" (as opposed to word) in the relationship between a ruler and the people (cf. Sharpe, *Selling* and *Image Wars*; quote appears in Sharpe, *Selling*, xxv). Rather, he failed to recognize the illegibility of classicism to most Londoners. This is evident not only in his architectural projects but also in the visual arts; see, for example, Paul van Somer's 1620 personal and architectural portraiture, *James I in front of the Banqueting House*, discussed in Anderson, *Inigo Jones*, 176, and Howarth, *Images of Rule*, 125–7.

91 For an argument that foregrounds architecture as a means of social control and improvement, see Lubbock, *Tyranny of Taste.*

92 Anderson, *Inigo Jones*, 41–7. For tensions between urban and royal regarding construction policy and planning during the reigns of James I and Charles I, see Smuts, "The Court and Its Neighborhood."

93 The installation of Rubens's ceiling paintings, which required the cessation of masquing in the Banqueting House, is often cited as a significant alteration in the building's operations. Yet reinforcing

continuity more than inciting change, Rubens's paintings were neoclassical expressions of divine right monarchy, and they loomed above a variety of state functions, including Charles's entertainment of foreign leaders and addresses to Parliament.

94 Griffiths, *The Print in Stuart Britain*, 17. Commenting on the scarcity of topical prints of Charles's execution, Malcolm Jones writes: "Astonishingly, even at the Restoration, there seem to have been very few graphic, single-sheet representations of what by then it was politically correct to think of as the martyrdom of Charles I, and for suitably shocking scenes of the king's execution modern historians are obliged to illustrate their books with [foreign prints]" (Jones, *Print*, 100).

95 For reproductions and discussions of this print, see Griffiths, *The Print in Stuart Britain* 154–5; and Jones, *Print*, 60–1, 63–8.

96 It was perhaps to avoid these associations that Royalist prints tend to represent the king's death in terms of traditional emblems, especially arboreal imagery. A visual metaphor for Charles's genealogical legitimacy, natural crown, and his own person, trees – either under assault or already chopped down – allowed artists and viewers to grapple with an unprecedented event in familiar terms (Jones, *Print*, 100–5).

97 Marvell, "An Horation Ode upon Cromwell's Return from Ireland" (1650), in *The Complete Poems*, ll. 57–8.

98 Morrill, *Nature of the English Revolution*, 288–9. Morrill cites five examples of Charles I's legal tyranny in the years 1626–9 (289–91).

99 Ibid., 295; see also 295–7.

100 Dzelzainis, "'Incendiaries of the State,'" 76–7.

101 Parliamentarians used theatrical language to portray Charles I as a tyrant justly punished for his crimes against the commonwealth; in contrast (and more successfully, Maguire posits), Royalists portrayed the king as a martyr wrongly persecuted upon the tragic scaffold (Maguire, "Theatrical Mask").

102 Marvell, "An Horation Ode," in *The Complete Poems*, ll. 53–6.

4. Noise, the Great Fire, and Milton's *Samson Agonistes*

1 Milton, *Samson Agonistes*, in *The 1671 Poems*, 66. Quotations from this edition refer to the prefatory materials by page number and to the dramatic poem by line number without l./ll.

2 Hall argues that Aristotle's silence in the *Poetics* on the subject of the *polis* implies a radical position, which she paraphrases as: *"poetry is not*

to be assessed by criteria to do with the polis" ("Is there a *Polis*," 302, original emphasis).

3 Knoppers, *Historicizing Milton*; Mueller, "The Figure and the Ground"; and Radzinowicz, *Toward Samson Agonistes*. For the longer discursive history of fire in London, see MacKay, *Persecution, Plague, and Fire*, pt. 3.

4 *OED Online* "topical, adj." 1a. The use of "topical" to mean "Of or pertaining to the topics of the day; containing local or temporary allusions" began only in the late nineteenth century (3b).

5 Vincent, *Gods Terrible Voice*, 61.

6 Settle, *An Elegy*, 5.

7 Quoted in Knoppers, General Introduction to *The 1671 Poems*, li.

8 Boal, *Theatre*, 27.

9 On Milton's identification with Orpheus, see, among others, Lieb, *Milton and the Culture of Violence* and Falconer, *Orpheus Dis(re)membered.*

10 Smith, *Literature and Revolution*; Skantze, *Stillness in Motion*; Clare, *Drama of the English Republic*; Norbrook, *Writing the English Republic*; and Randall, *Winter Fruit*.

11 The "affective turn" of early modern studies includes consideration of reading as well as enactment; see, for example, Craik, *Reading Sensations*. On sound in particular, see Smith, "'More Swete'"; Bloom, *Voice in Motion*; and Smith, *Acoustic World*.

12 In addition to Smith, *Literature and Revolution*, see his "Literature and London."

13 Milton, "At a Solemn Music," in Carey, *Milton*, l. 20.

14 On "measure" as a choreographic term, see Mullally, "*Measure*" and "More about the Measures," and Howard, *Politics of Courtly Dancing*, 13–17. On "measures" as a musical term, see Ward, "The English Measure."

15 Ben Jonson, *Pleasure Reconciled to Virtue* (1618), in *The Complete Masques*, ed. Stephen Orgel (New Haven: Yale University Press, 1969), l. 4, also quoted in Smith, "The Contest of Apollo," 93.

16 Richard Brathwait, *Whimzies: Or, A New Cast of Characters* (London: Ambrose Rithirdon, 1631), sigs. L11r–L11v, also quoted in Smith, *The Acoustic World*, 142, original emphasis.

17 *Colin Clouts Come Home Againe*, in Spenser, *Edmund Spenser's Poetry*, ed. Maclean and Prescott, l. 76.

18 "A reformed poet of eros, Colin now sings delightful love songs consistent with conscience and moral discipline conductive to the nation" (Cheney, "Spenser's pastorals," 99).

19 These early works thus align music's effects less with purgation than lustration, or an ethical and religious purification, which is how Milton

translates the Greek *catharsis* in the Latin tag featured on the title page of *Samson Agonistes*: "Tragœdia est imitation actionis seriæ, &c. Per misericordiuam & metum perficiens talium affectum *lustationem*" (Milton, *The 1671 Poems*, 65, and Knoppers, Notes to *The 1671 Poems*, 143–4, emphasis added).

20 Bloom, *Voice in Motion*, 112.

21 These and other impediments to proper reception of God's word are outlined in Egerton, *The boring of the eare.*

22 Richard Crooke, "To the Christian and beneuolent *READER*," prefacing Egerton, *The boring of the eare*, sig. A3v.

23 *OED Online* "dumb, adj." 5a.

24 Ingram, "Ridings," 86.

25 Thompson, "Rough Music," 3.

26 MacLean, Landry, and Ward, Introduction to *The Country and the City Revisited*, 4. On the importance of the suburbs to the construction of London identity, see also Ward, "Imagining the metropolis."

27 Sanders, *Cultural Geography*, esp. 157–63; Newman, *Cultural Capitals*, 73–5; and Manley, *Literature and Culture*, 507.

28 Smith, "'Making fire.'"

29 *OED Online*, "pandemonium, n." 2a; see also 2b. On the sounds of early modern London, see Smith, *The Acoustic World*, 49–71, and Cockayne, *Hubbub*, 106–30.

30 *Paradise Lost*, ed. Fowler, 10.439. Hereafter cited in-text.

31 Hiltner, "'Belch'd fire,'" 293.

32 Ibid.

33 Manley, *Literature and Culture*, 568. Manley understands the implications of this change in terms of sedentarism, by which he means a sense of physical and spiritual liberation from the city, "of no longer being tied to social or geographical 'place'" and "radical individualism" (*Literature and Culture*, 532–3, 579). By contrast, I am interested in the acoustic implications of this change.

34 COL/SJ/03/012, London Metropolitan Archives.

35 Ibid., COL/SJ/03/014.

36 *The London Gazette* for 3–10 September 1666 relates that "Divers Strangers, *Dutch* and *French*" were interrogated in connection with the Fire, but "notwithstanding which suspicions, the manner of the burning all along in a Train, and so blown forwards in all its way by strong Winds, makes us conclude the whole was an effect of an unhappy chance, or to speak better, the heavy hand of God upon us for our Sins, shewing us the terrour of his Judgment in thus raising the fire." For a recent

consideration of the rumours of Catholic involvement in the Great Fire, see Dolan, *True Relations*, 87–107.

37 Tremayne writes that "there were severall taken & killed outright … & any that had but the looke of a Frenchman was taken & caried to the prison, or cutt & slashed p[er] the people they were so violently bent ag[ains]t the French" (COL/SJ/03/014, London Metropolitan Archives).

38 The official Bill of Mortality for the three weeks ending 18 September 1666 records only four people "burnt at several places" and one "found dead in the street" (quoted in "1666 and other London Fires"). Yet word on the street varied from Tremayne's assertion that "ther were severall people burnt" to Gilbert Burnet's claim that he "could never hear of any one person that was either burnt or trode to death" (Burnet, *Bishop Burnet's History*, I.232).

39 In his account of the Fire, Samuel Pepys appears deeply suspicious of hearsay and insists upon seeing things for himself. In his diary entry for 2 September 1666, for example, Pepys writes of being awakened by his maid "about three in the morning, to tell us of a great fire they saw in the City. So I rose, and slipped on my night-gown and went to her window," and again, in the morning, when the maid told him "that she hears that above 300 houses have been burned down tonight by the fire we saw, … I made myself ready presently, and walked to the Tower; and there got up upon one of the high places, … and there I did see the houses at the end of the bridge all on fire, and an infinite great fire on this and the other side" (Pepys, *The Diary*, in *Norton*, 2134). Like Pepys's diary entries, poems, sermons, and official documents routinely describe what Londoners *saw* beginning in the early hours of that fateful Sunday morning. For example, in the ballad *London Undone*, an "Eye-witness" to the Fire exclaims, "Alas! we had no Night, / For a whole week together, 'twas too *light*." Other accounts observe that just as flames turned night into day, smoke transformed day into night. This subversion of the natural order did not prevent some observers from tracing the path of destruction. Many accounts offer precise mappings of the Fire as it blazed through the city as well as exact enumerations of the ruins that Londoners witnessed.

40 Guillim, *Dreadful Burning*, 2; also in Aubin, *London in Flames*, 35. Similarly, Dryden's *Annus Mirabilis* notes that "crackling noise" "Call'd up" Londoners (57, st. 225) to the Fire that "pulls us down" (54, st. 211).

41 Rolle, *Shlohavot*, III.24.

42 Vincent, *Gods Terrible Voice*, 52. Military acoustics appear, as well, in the account of Franciscus de Rapicano, principal confidential secretary of

Queen Christina of Sweden, who writes in his diary of being awakened in the early hours of 2 September 1666 by "a great sound of drums" (Harvey, "A Foreign Visitor's Account," 84).

43 Dryden, *Annus Mirabilis*, 59, st. 231; and Rodeney family mss, fo. 71b. This simile persists well into the next century. According to the anonymous *The Burning of London by the Papists*, the Fire "roar'd like the Waves of the Sea, that some who were Spectators think they can never say enough to express the Terror it carried with it, both to the Ear and to the Eye" (11).

44 Guillim, *Dreadful Burning*, 6; also in Aubin, *London in Flames*, 39.

45 Crouch, *Londons second tears*, 4; ibid., 49.

46 Wiseman, *A Short and Serious Narrative*, 8; ibid., 27.

47 Ibid., 2–3; ibid., 21.

48 Ford, *Conflagration of London*, 6; ibid., 7.

49 Allison, *Upon the Late Lamentable Fire*, 6; ibid., 77.

50 Evelyn, *Diary*, III. 453.

51 *Calendar of State Papers, Domestic*, 8 September 1666, *Addenda*, 1670, 713, quoted in Aubin, *London in Flames*, xii.

52 Elborough, *London's calamity*, sigs. A2–A2v.

53 Gilbert, *Englands Passing-Bell*, 9; also in Aubin, *London in Flames*, 114.

54 Gearing, *God's soveraignty*, 146.

55 Ibid., 146–7.

56 R.P., *Londons lamentations*, 1–2.

57 Elborough, *London's calamity*, 10.

58 Dryden, *Annus Mirabilis*, sig. A2; 60, st. 238.

59 Charles II, "Charles R. His Majesty." This assistance included making bread and other provisions available at markets throughout London, providing for "Publick places" where citizens could safely store their goods, and requiring "all Cities and Towns whatsoever shall without any contradiction [to] receive the said distressed persons, and permit them the free exercise of their Manual Trades."

60 *Londoners Lamentation*; also in Aubin, *London in Flames*, 88.

61 In *The Londoners Lamentation*, also in Aubin, *London in Flames*, 2, readers hear such appeals voiced, seemingly verbatim, and then ignored:

> Some cry, My children, Oh are they secure?
> And are none left i' th house still are you sure?
> Others, my Father, some, my Mother cry;
> Another sayes, he can't his wife espy.
> …

Another cryes, Oh help to save my Plate;
Another calls, a Cart at any rate;
...
Oh cryes another, I am quite undone;
To help to save my goods, I can get none.
Thus all are in a hurry, and some take
From others straits advantage, gain to make.

62 Dryden, *Annus Mirabilis*, 63, st. 250.

63 Flower, *Mercy in the midst of judgment*, sig. A3v–A4r.

64 As Defoe writes in *A Journal of the Plague Year*, 214–15, financial losses during the plague years were more than recuperated after the Fire.

65 Even if this were the case, appeals for charity continued – and continued to be ignored. On 26 September 1668, almost two years to the day after the Great Fire, Charles II issued "A Proclamation touching the charitable collections for relief of the poor distressed by the late dismal Fire in the City of London" because "the Collections intended by that Proclamation, have not been so made or answered as they ought to have been, but in many places omitted and not made at all, and from many parts no Returns at all made." Over half a century later, the speaker in Defoe's *Journal* contrasts the outpouring of relief for plague victims to the dearth of charity and misuse of funds in the aftermath of the Fire (214). Although published almost sixty years after the Fire, Defoe's *Journal* is considered one of the most accurate accounts of mid-seventeenth-century London.

66 Ford, *Londons Resurrection*, 8; also in Aubin, *London in Flames*, 139.

67 Wall, *Literary and Cultural Spaces*, 71–2.

68 Ford, *Londons Resurrection*, 8; also in Aubin, *London in Flames*, 139–40.

69 Rolle, *Shlohavot*, II.108.

70 "Letters concerning the Great Fire in London Sept. 1666," MS Gough London 14, fo. 38r, Bodleian Library, quoted in Smith, "'Making fire,'" 280.

71 Knoppers, General Introduction to *The 1671 Poems*, lvi.

72 This number includes the ten lines (*SA* 1527–35 and 1537) that do not appear in the 1671 text but are appended in the *Omissa*. From the Trinity manuscript, it would appear that Milton seemed intent on writing a tragedy set in a city: "nearly half (26 of 61) of the biblical plots [outlined in the Trinity manuscript] would have culminated in large-scale disasters, ones that often befall entire cities" (Burbery, *Milton the Dramatist*, 69).

73 Rajan, "'To Which is Added,'" 102.

74 Ibid., 98.

75 Gillies, "Space and Place," 32, and Brady, "Space," 168. Cf. Fenton, *Milton's Places*, epilogue, and Manley, *Literature and Culture*, ch. 10.

76 Dalila describes how "the Magistrates / And Princes ... Sollicited, commanded, threatn'd, urg'd, / Adjur'd" her and "the Priest / Was ... ever at [her] ear, / Preaching" (*SA* 850–9).
77 *OED Online*, "pile n5," 2a. In an earlier version of the *OED* (second edition, 1989), "pile, n3" points out that pile may mean not only a large building but also "[a] lofty mass of buildings" (4a) – i.e., a city – and cites this line from *SA* for its figurative use (4b).
78 In *Paradise Lost*, "The ascending pile" of Pandemonium is "Built like a temple" of "such magnificence" that it surpasses every building in the ancient cities of Babylon and Egypt (*PL* 1.722, 713, 718). It is also the principal structure the "city and proud seat / Of Lucifer," with his former peers "reduced in careful watch / Round their metropolis" (*PL* 10.424–5, 438–9). In *Paradise Regained* Satan brings the Son to stand upon the pinnacle of the highest "pile," also dubbed a "glorious Temple," in "The holy City" of Jerusalem (*PR* 4.545–7). Although not referred to as a pile, the temple of Dagon in *SA* recalls the temple-piles of *PL* and *PR*.
79 Fish, "'There Is Nothing,'" 257.
80 Patterson, "Milton's Negativity," esp. 98.
81 Netzley, "Reading Events," 520–1.
82 Kühnová, "'Inspired with Contradiction,'" 353.
83 Mueller, "*Pathos* and *Katharsis*," 169.
84 Achinstein, "Cloudless Thunder," esp. 5–7.
85 *Country-Man's Fare-wel.*
86 Bell, *The Great Fire*, 227.
87 Unlike *Samson Agonistes*, most poems about the Great Fire tend to follow strict metrical structures and include detailed lists of rubble-filled streets and fallen buildings. Wall, *Literary and Cultural Spaces*, 21–2, argues that the form and content of these poems conspire to impose conceptual order and shape upon a physically shambolic cityscape.

Manley's discussion of an earlier generation of London writers' epigrams, which also deployed repetitive schemes and lists of place names, suggest that poems about the Great Fire could, instead, "threaten to elude neat closure and to become instead an endless series" (*Literature and Culture*, 427).
88 Dobranski, "Milton's Ideal Readers." Likening himself to Orpheus, Milton glosses his "fit audience" by contrast to "*Bacchus* and his Revellers," whose "the barbarous dissonance" and "savage clamor [drown] / Both Harp and Voice" (*PL* 7.32–7).
89 Cf. Lewalski, "How Poetry Moves," 766: "After the Restoration Milton could no longer believe that the reformation of literature and culture

might help produce a free society and, conversely, that a free society would nurture good art. ... Nevertheless, along with his more universal aims, Milton attempted in his major poems to teach and move a 'fit' audience to think again, and think better, about some major issues of the revolution and interregnum."

90 Defoe, *Journal*, 219–20.

91 Ford, *Conflagration of London*, 10; also in Aubin, *London in Flames*, 9.

92 One striking example of this interpretation appears in a 1666 Dutch broadside, *Sinne-Beelt, op d'Engelfe Brandt-stichters, waar in aangewesen weidt haar grouwelijcke Tirannye gepleaght in 't Vlie, en aan d' inwoodners op 't Eylant ter Schelling; als meede de stratte Godts over 't verbranden der Stadt LONDEN* (Emblem of the English arsonists, in which is shown their brutal tyranny at the Vlie, and on the inhabitants of Terschelling Island, as well as the punishment of God in the burning of the town of London), which juxtaposes an image of London in flames with an image of the burning of Dutch ships and the town of Terschelling. I am grateful to Carmen Nocentelli for her translations of and insights into Dutch prints related to the Great Fire.

93 In this regard, the multilingual poem on de Jonghe's *Londinium* also recalls the Hieronimo's "tragedy" "*in sundry languages*," the meaning of which Hieronimo obscures further when, first, he bites off his own tongue to prevent himself from speaking under "tortures" and, then, uses the Viceroy's knife to kill himself rather than to "mend his pen" and "write the troth" (*ST* 4.4.1, 9 sd, 183, 199, 200).

94 See Leo, "Milton's Aristotelian Experiments"; Flower, "The Critical Context"; and Mueller, "Sixteenth-Century Italian Criticism."

95 Wall, *Literary and Cultural Spaces*, 41.

96 Cf. Hall's discussion of Aristotle's secular cosmopolitanism in "Is there a *Polis*" and the discussion of Sidney's international cosmopolitanism in Stillman, *Philip Sidney*.

Postscript

1 Worrall, *Celebrity*, 204.

2 Ibid., 204, and ch. 8 passim.

3 According to the Shakespeare Birthplace Trust Archive Catalogue, the RSC production of *The Roman Actor* opened at the Swan Theatre in Stratford-upon-Avon on 30 May 2002, and closed on 13 September 2002; it moved for three performances to the Newcastle Playhouse in Newcastle-upon-Tyne (2 October 2002–19 October 2002) and then to the

Geilgud Theatre in London (14 December 2002–19 March 2003). Jo Wilding, User Services librarian at the Shakespeare Centre Library and Archive, suggests that rehearsals began in mid-April of 2002.

According to BBC "Timeline: Daniel Pearl Kidnap," Pearl was reported missing on 23 January 2002; photographs were released to the media on 28 January; the US State Department confirmed Pearl's death on 21 February; US officials identified Pearl's body on 18 May; and all defendants charged in Pearl's kidnapping and murder were found guilty on July 10 and sentenced to either death or life in prison on 15 July.

4 "The Tragic Story"; Pearl family statement quoted in "CBS Sparks."

5 Moreau and Hussain, "Failed Cities," 39.

6 W.B. Worthen, in Romàn, "A Forum on Theatre," 100.

7 The report on "Urban Population Growth" for the World Health Organization (WHO) reads: "The urban population in 2014 accounted for 54% of the total global population, up from 34% in 1960, and continues to grow. The urban population growth, in absolute numbers, is concentrated in the less developed regions of the world. It is estimated that by 2017, even in less developed countries, a majority of people will be living in urban areas."

8 See Moretti, "Clues," in *Signs*, 130–56; McLaughlin, *Writing*; Fuchs, *After the Dresden Bombing*; and Salvaggio, *Hearing Sappho*.

Bibliography

Manuscripts and Printed Maps

British Library

Cartwright, George. *The Brittish Rebellion in Heroick Vers, or A short relation of the most remarkable passages happening in our Civil Wars, beginning in the year 1639 to the happy entrance of Charles the Second in sixty inst.* © The British Library Board, Add. 34363.

Oxenden Papers. Vol. 18. © The British Library Board, Add. 40713.

Rodeney family mss © The British Library Board, Add. 34239.

British Museum

Norden, John. *The view of London Bridge from East to West.* 1597. Copy *c.* 1803 of the original plate. Reg. No. 1880, 1113.1527. © Trustees of the British Museum.

Prospect of the Citty of London, as it appeared, in the time of its flames. 1667. Reg. no. 1880, 1113.1160. A separate impression of the second inset view from the top on the right of *A new and exact map of Great Britainnie*, print by Wenceslaus Hollar and published by John Overton (London, 1667). © Trustees of the British Museum.

Sinne-Beelt, op d'Engelfe Brandt-stichters, waar in aangewesen weidt haar grouwelijcke Tirannye gepleaght in 't Vlie, en aan d' inwoodners op 't Eylant ter Schelling; als meede de stratte Godts over 't verbranden der Stadt LONDEN. 1666. Reg. no. 1885,1114.149. © Trustees of the British Museum.

Huntington Library

"S*r* Jarvaise Elsies / Speech just before his / Execution on Tower Hill / 2*d*. Nov*r*. 1615." EL 5980.

London Metropolitan Archives

London City Records, COL/SJ/03/001–028.

Primary Printed Sources

A true and perfect relation of the whole proceedings against the late most barbarous traitors, Garnet a Iesuite, and his confederats contayning sundry speeches deliuered by the Lords Commissioners at their arraignments, for the better satisfaction of those that were hearers, as occasion was offered; the Earle of Northamptons speech hauing bene enlarged vpon those grounds which are set downe. And lastly all that passed at Garnets execution. London, 1606.

"A Warning for Fair Women": A Critical Edition. Ed. Charles Dale Cannon. The Hague: Mouton, 1975.

A warning for faire women Containing, the most tragicall and lamentable murther of Master George Sanders of London marchant, nigh Shooters hill. Consented vnto by his owne wife, acted by M. Browne, Mistris Drewry and Trusty Roger agents therin: with their seuerall ends. As it hath beene lately diuerse times acted by the right Honorable, the Lord Chamberlaine his Seruantes. London, 1599.

A Yorkshire Tragedy. Ed. A.C. Cawley and Barry Gaines. Manchester: Manchester University Press, 1986.

Ainsworth, Henry. *Annotations upon the five bookes of Moses, the booke of the Psalmes, and the Song of Songs, or, Canticles*. London, 1627.

Allison, John. *Upon the late lamentable fire in London in an humble imitation of the most incomparable Mr. Cowley his Pindarick strain*. London, 1667.

Arber, Edward, ed. *A Transcript of the Registers of the Company of Stationers of London, 1554–1640*. London, 1875–7, 1894.

Arden of Faversham. In *Plays on Women*. Ed. Kathleen E. McLuskie and David Bevington. Manchester: Manchester University Press, 1999.

Aubin, Robert Arnold, ed. *London in Flames, London in Glory: Poems on the Fire and Rebuilding of London 1667–1709*. New Brunswick, NJ: Rutgers University Press, 1943.

Bacon, Francis. *Essayes and counsels, civil and moral whereunto is newly added a table Of the colours of good and evil*. London, 1664.

Beaumont, Francis, and John Fletcher. *The Maid's Tragedy*. Ed. T.W. Craik. The Revels Plays. Manchester: Manchester University Press, 1988.

– *Philaster, or Love Lies a-Bleeding*. Manchester and New York: Manchester University Press, 1969, 2003.

Bilson, Thomas. *The perpetual gouernement of Christes Church*. London, 1593.

Bodin, Jean. *The six bookes of a common-weale ... Out of the French and Latine copies, done into English, by Richard Knolles*. London, 1606.

Buchanan, George. *De jure regni apud Scotos; or, A dialogue, concerning the due priviledge of government in the kingdom of Scotland ... translated out of the original Latine into English by Philalethes*. [n.p], 1680.

Burnet, Gilbert. *Bishop Burnet's History of His Own Time*. Ed. Thomas Burnet. 2 vol. London, 1724.

The Burning of London by the Papists: or, A Memorial to Protestants on the Second of September. Sed Furor Papisticus qui tam Dira / Patravit nondum restiguitur. Inscript. On the Monument. London, 1714.

Charles II. "Charles R. His Majesty in his princely compassion and very tender care …" London, [1666].

– "His Majestie's Declaration to his City of London upon occasion of the late Calamit by the lamentable Fire." London, 1666.

– "A Proclamation touching the charitable collections for relief of the poor distressed by the late dismal Fire in the City of London." [London], 1668.

Cicero. *On Duties*. Ed. M.T. Griffin and E. M. Atkins. Cambridge Texts in the History of Political Thought. Cambridge: Cambridge University Press, 1991.

Coryate, Thomas. *Coryats Crudities*. London, 1611.

The Country-Man's Fare-wel to London. or, A Broad-side against Pride [London], [c. 1670].

Crouch, John. *Londineses lacrymae Londons second tears mingled with her ashes: a poem*. London, 1666.

D'Avenant, William. *Tragedy of Albouine, King of the Lombards*. London, 1629.

Digges, Sir Dudley. *The compleat ambassador, or, Two treaties of the intended marriage of Qu. Elizabeth of glorious memory comprised in letters of negotiation of Sir Francis Walsingham, her resident in France: together with the answers of the Lord Burleigh, the Earl of Leicester, Sir Tho. Smith, and others: wherein, as in a clear mirror, may be seen the faces of the two courts of England and France, as they then stood, with many remarkable passages of state*. London, 1655.

Dryden, John. *Annus Mirabilis: The year of wonders, 1666. An historical poem containing the progress and various successes of our naval war with Holland, under the conduct of His Highness Prince Rupert, and His Grace the Duke of Albemarl: and describing the fire of London*. London, 1667.

Egerton, Stephen. *The boring of the eare contayning a plaine and profitable discourse by way of dialogue: concerning 1. Our preparation before hearing, 2. Our demeanour in hearing, 3. Our exercise after we haue heard the Word of God*. London, 1623.

Elborough, Robert. *London's calamity by Fire bewailed and improved, in a sermon preached at St. James Dukes-Place; wherein the Judgements of God are asserted, the times of those judgments specified, the reasons for those judgments assigned, and all in some measure suitably applied*. London, 1666.

Elyot, Thomas. *The dictionary of syr Thomas Elyot*. London, 1538.

Fitzherbert, John. *Here begynneth a ryght frutefull mater: and hath to name the boke of surueyeng and improumentes*. London, 1523.

Flower, Christopher. *Mercy in the midst of judgment with a glimpse of, or a glance on, London's glorious resurrection like a Phoenix out of it's ashes delivered in a sermon preach'd at St. Dunstans in the West, Sept. 2, 1669 being the day of publick fasting and humilation in consideration of the late dreadful fire*. London, 1669.

Ford, Simon. *Conflagratio Londinensis poetice depicta* [*Conflagration of London poetically described*]. [2nd ed.] London, 1667.

– *Londini quod reliquum, or, Londons remains in Latin and English*. London, 1667.

– *Londons resurrection, poetically represented and humbly presented to His Most Sacred Majesty*. London, 1669.

Four Revenge Tragedies. Ed. Katharine Eisaman Maus. Oxford and New York: Oxford University Press, 1995.

Fuller, Thomas. *The history of the worthies of England who for parts and learning have been eminent in the several counties: together with an historical narrative of the native commodities and rarities in each county*. London, 1662.

G., I. *A refutation of the Apology for actors Diuided into three briefe treatises. Wherein is confuted and opposed all the chiefe groundes and arguments alleaged in defence of playes: and withall in each treatise is deciphered actors, 1. heathenish and diabolicall institution. 2. their ancient and moderne indignitie. 3. the wonderfull abuse of their impious qualitie*. London, 1615.

Garey, Samuel. *Great Brittans little calendar: or, Triple diarie, in remembrance of three daies Diuided into three treatises. 1. Britanniae vota: or God saue the King: for the 24. day of March, the day of his Maiesties happy proclamation. 2. Caesaris hostes: or, the tragedy of traytors: for the fift of August: the day of the bloudy Gowries treason, and of his Highnes blessed preseruation. 3. Amphitheatrum scelerum: or, the transcendent of treason: the day of a most admirable deliuerance of our King ... from that most horrible and hellish proiect of the Gun-Powder Treason Nouemb. 5. Whereunto is annexed a short disswasiue from poperie*. London, 1618.

Gearing, William. *God's soveraignty displayed from Job 9.12.: Behold he taketh away, who can hinder him? &c., or, A discourse shewing, that God doth, and may take away from his creatures what hee pleaseth, as to the matter what, the place where, the time when, the means and manner how, and the reasons thereof: with an application of the whole, to the distressed citizens of London, whose houses and goods were lately consumed by the fire: an excitation of them to look to the procuring causes of this fiery tryal, the ends that God aims at in it, with directions how to behave themselves under their losses.* London, 1667.

Gilbert, Thomas. *ΘΡΗΝΩΔΗ: Or, Englands Passing-Bell.* London, 1679.

Guillim, Joseph. *Ακάματον Πῦρ. Or, the Dreadful Burning of London: Described in a Poem.* London, 1667.

Harman, Thomas. *A caueat for commen cursetors vvlgarely called uagabones, set forth by Thomas Harman, esquiere, for the vtilite and proffyt of his naturall cuntrey [sic].* London, 1573; 1566, 1567.

Helwys, Sir Gervase Helwys. *The Lieutenant of the Tower His Speech and Repentance.* [London], [1615].

Henslowe, Philip. *Henslowe's Diary.* Ed. R.A. Foakes and R.T. Rickert. Cambridge and New York: Cambridge University Press, 1961.

Herring, Francis. *Popish pietie, or The first part of the historie of that horrible and barbarous conspiracie, commonly called the powder-treason nefariously plotted against Iames King of great Britaine, Prince Henrie, and the whole state of that realme assembled in Parliament; and happily discouered, disappointed, and frustrated by the powerfull and sole arme of the Almightie, the fifth of Nouember, anno 1605. Written first in Latin verse by F. H. [...] in physicke: and translated into English by A.P.* London, 1610.

Heywood, Thomas. *An Apology for Actors. Containing three briefe treatises. 1 Their antiquity. 2 Their ancient dignity. 3 The true vse of their quality* London, 1612.

– *A challenge for beautie as it hath beene sundry times acted, by the Kings Majesties Servants: at the Blacke-friers, and at the Globe on the Banke-side.* London, 1636.

– *Londini artium & scientiarum scaturigo. Or, Londons fountaine of arts and sciences Exprest in sundry triumphs, pageants, and showes, at the initiation of the Right Honorable Nicholas Raynton into the Maiorty of the famous and farre renowned city London. All the charge and expence of the laborious proiects both by water and land, being the sole vndertaking of the Right Worshipfull Company of the Haberdashers.* London, 1632.

– *Londini emporia, or Londons mercatura Exprest in sundry triumphs, pageants and showes, at the inauguration of the Right Honorable Ralph Freeman into the Maiorty of the famous and farre renowned citty London. All the charge and expence of the laborious proiects, both by water and land, being the sole vndertaking of the Right Worshipfull Company of the Cloath-Workers.* London, 1633.

– *Londini speculum: or, Londons mirror exprest in sundry triumphs, pageants, and showes, at the initiation of the right Honorable Richard Fenn, into the Mairolty*

[sic] *of the famous and farre renowned city London. All the charge and expence of these laborious projects both by water and land, being the sole undertaking of the Right Worshipful Company of the Habberdashers*. London, 1637.

– *Londini status pacatus: or, Londons peaceable estate Exprest in sundry triumphs, pageants, and shewes, at the innitiation of the right Honourable Henry Garvvay, into the Majoralty of the famous and farre renowned city London. All the charge and expence, of the laborious projects both by water and land, being the sole undertakings of the Right Worshipfull Society of Drapers*. London, 1639.

– *London ius honorarium Exprest in sundry triumphs, pagiants, and shewes: at the initiation or entrance of the Right Honourable George Whitmore, into the Maioralty of the famous and farre renouned city of London. All the charge and expence of the laborious proiects, and obiects both by water and land, being the sole vndertaking of the Right Worshipfull, the society of the Habburdashers*. London, 1631.

– *Troia Britanica: or, Great Britaines Troy A poem deuided into XVII. seuerall cantons, intermixed with many pleasant poeticall tales. Concluding with an vniuersall chronicle from the Creation, vntill these present times*. London, 1609.

Holinshed, Raphael. *The firste volume of the Chronicles of England, Scotlande, and Irelande Conteyning, the description and chronicles of England, from the first inhabiting vnto the conquest. The description and chronicles of Scotland, from the first originall of the Scottes nation, till the yeare of our Lorde. 1571. The description and chronicles of Yrelande, likewise from the firste originall of that nation, vntill the yeare. 1547*. London, 1577.

Howell, James. *Londinopolis, an historicall discourse or perlustration of the city of London, the imperial chamber, and chief emporium of Great Britain whereunto is added another of the city of Westminster, with the courts of justice, antiquities, and new buildings thereunto belonging*. London, 1657.

James VI and I. *The Political Works of James I*. Ed. Charles Howard McIlwain. New York: Russell and Russell, 1965.

– *Political Writings*. Ed. Johann P. Sommerville. Cambridge: Cambridge University Press, 1994.

James I, Sir Everard Digby, and Thomas Barlow. *The Gunpowder-treason with a discourse of the manner of its discovery, and a perfect relation of the proceedings against those horrid conspirators, wherein is contained their examinations, tryals, and condemnations: likewise King James's speech to both houses of Parliament on that occasion, now reprinted: a preface touching that horrid conspiracy, by the Right Reverend Father in God, Thomas, Lord Bishop of Lincoln: and by the way of appendix, several papers or letters of Sir Everard Digby, chiefly relating to the gunpowder-plot, never before printed*. London, 1679.

Jonson, Ben. *Every Man Out of His Humor*. 1599. Ed. Helen Ostovich. Manchester: Manchester University Press, 2001.

The London Gazette 85. London, 1666. Facsimile rpt. London: Her Majesty's Stationery Office, 1965.

London undone; or, A reflection upon the late disasterous fire. London, 1666.

The Londoners lamentation. Wherein is contained a sorrowfull description of the dreadful fire which happened in Pudding-Lane ... on the second of Septemb. 1666 ... With an account of the King and the Duke of York's indeavors ... for the quenching of the same ... and the name of every particular place where the fire did stop. Tune is, When Troy town, &c. London, [1666].

Marston, John. *The Insatiate Countess.* In *Four Jacobean Sex Tragedies*. Ed. Martin Wiggins. Oxford and New York: Oxford University Press, 1998.

Marvell, Andrew. *The Complete Poems.* Ed. Elizabeth Story Donno. England: Penguin, 1972.

Massinger, Philip. *The Roman Actor: A Tragedy.* Ed. Martin White. Manchester: Manchester University Press, 2007.

Middleton, Thomas. *The Collected Works.* Ed. Gary Taylor and John Lavagnino. Oxford: Clarendon Press, 2007.

Middlesex Country Records. Ed. John Cordy Jeaffreson. London: Middlesex County Records Society, 1887.

Milton, John. *The Complete Works of John Milton, Volume II: The 1671 Poems: "Paradise Regain'd" and "Samson Agonistes."* Ed. Laura Lunger Knoppers. Oxford: Oxford University Press, 2008.

– *John Milton: Complete Poems and Major Prose.* Ed. Merritt Y. Hughes. Indianapolis and Cambridge: Hackett, 1957.

– *Milton: The Complete Shorter Poems.* Ed. John Carey. 2nd ed. Harlow, England: Pearson Longman, 2007.

– *Paradise Lost.* Ed. Alastair Fowler. 2nd ed. Harlow, England: Pearson Longman, 2007.

Moryson, Fynes. *An Itinerary.* 1617. 4 vols. Glasgow: MacLehose; New York: Macmillan, 1907–8.

The Norton Anthology of English Literature. 8th ed. Ed. Stephen Greenblatt et al. New York and London: W.W. Norton, 2006.

P., R. *Londons lamentations. Or, Some affectionate breathings forth on London's late Ruines by Fire, Begun Septemb. 2. 1666. about Two of the Clock in the morning. With Twenty lessons to be learned by this severe Rod of the Fire.* London, 1666.

Peacham, Henry. *The art of drawing with the pen, and limming in water colours more exactlie then heretofore taught and enlarged with the true manner of painting vpon glasse, the order of making your furnace, annealing, &c. Published, for the behoofe of all young gentlemen, or any els that are desirous for to become practicioners in this excellent, and most ingenious art.* London, 1606.

Perkins, William. *The whole treatise of the cases of conscience distinguished into three books*. Cambridge, 1606.

Rapicani, Francisco de. "A Foreign Visitor's Account of the Great Fire, 1666." Ed. P.D.A. Harvey. *Transactions of the London and Middlesex Archaeological Society* 20. 1960.

Rolle, Samuel. *Shlohavot, or, The burning of London in the year 1666 commemorated and improved in CX. discourses, meditations, and contemplations: divided into four parts, treating of I. The sins, or spiritual causes procuring that judgment, II. The natural causes of fire, morally applyed, III. The most remarkable passages and circumstances of that dreadful fire, IV. Counsels and comfort unto such as are sufferers by the said judgment*. London, 1667.

Rowley, William, Thomas Dekker, and John Ford. *The Witch of Edmonton*. Ed. Peter Corbin and Douglas Sedge. Manchester: Manchester University Press, 1999.

Settle, Elkanah. *An elegie on the late fire and ruines of London*. London, 1667.

Shakespeare, William. *The Complete Works*. Ed. Stanley Wells and Gary Taylor. Oxford: Clarendon Press, 1986, 2005.

– *The Complete Works of Shakespeare*. Ed. John Dover Wilson. London: Cambridge University Press, 1921–66. Rpt. Octopus Books Ltd., 3rd impression, 1983.

– *Hamlet*. Ed. Ann Thomson and Neil Taylor. The Arden Shakespeare, Third Series. London: Thomson Learning, 2006.

– *Hamlet*. Ed. A.R. Braunmuller. The Pelican Shakespeare. New York: Penguin, 2001.

– *The Norton Shakespeare: Based on the Oxford Edition*. Ed. Stephen Greenblatt, Walter Cohen, Jean E. Howard, and Katharine Eisaman Maus. New York and London: W.W. Norton, 1997.

– *Titus Andronicus*. Ed. Jonathan Bate. The Arden Shakespeare, Third Series. London and New York: Routledge, 1995.

– *Titus Andronicus*. Ed. Eugene M. Waith. Oxford: Clarendon Press, 1984, 2008.

Sincera, Rege. *Observations both historical and moral upon the burning of London, September 1666. With an account of the losses. And a most remarkable Parallel between London and Mosco [sic], both as to the plague and fire. Also an essay touching the easterly-winde. Written by way of narrative, for satisfaction of the present and future ages*. London, 1667.

Smith, G. Gregory, ed. *Elizabethan Critical Essays*. 2 vols. London: Oxford University Press, 1904.

Spenser, Edmund. *Edmund Spenser's Poetry: Norton Critical Edition*. 3rd ed. Ed. Hugh Maclean and Anne Lake Prescott. New York and London: W.W. Norton, 1993.

Stillingfleet, Edward. *A sermon preached before the honourable House of Commons at St. Margarets Westminster, Octob. 10, 1666 being the fast-day appointed for the late dreadfull fire in the city of London*. London, 1666.

Stow, John. *A Survey of London*. 1598, 1603. Ed. Charles Lethbridge Kingsford. 2 vols. Oxford: Clarendon Press, 1908.

Stuart Royal Proclamations, vol. 1: Royal Proclamations of James I, 1603–1625. Ed. James F. Larkin and Paul L. Hughes. Oxford: Clarendon Press, 1973.

Taylor, John. *The praise and vertue of a iayle, and iaylers With the most excellent mysterie, and necessary vse of all sorts of hanging. Also a touch at Tyburne for a period, and the authors free leaue to let them be hanged, who are offended at the booke without cause*. London, 1623.

Vincent, Thomas. *Gods terrible voice in the city of London wherein you have the narration of the two late dreadful judgements of plague and fire, indicted by the Lord upon that city, the former in the year 1665, the latter in the year 1666*. London, 1667.

Vindiciae contra tyrannos: a defence of liberty against tyrants. Or, of the lawfull power of the prince over the people, and of the people over the prince. Being a treatise written in Latin and French by Junius Brutus, and translated out of both into English. London, 1648.

W., T. *The arraignement and execution of the late traytors with a relation of the other traytors, which were executed at Worcester, the 27. of Ianuary last past*. London, 1606.

Wedel, Lupold von. "Journey Through England and Scotland Made by Lupold von Wedel in the Years 1584 and 1585." Trans. Gottfried von Bülow. *Transactions of the Royal Historical Society* 9 (1895): 223–70.

Whetstone, George. *The rocke of regard diuided into foure parts. … with diuers other morall, natural, & tragical discourses: documents and admonitions*. London, 1576.

Wiseman, Samuel. *A short and serious narrative of Londons fatal fire with its diurnal and nocturnal progression, from Sunday morning (being) the second of September, anno mirabili 1666, until Wednesday night following: a poem: as also London's lamentation to her regardless passengers*. London, 1667.

Wentworth, Thomas, Earl of Stafford. *The Earle of Straffords speech on the scaffold before he was beheaded on Tower-hill, the 12. of May 1641*. London, 1641.

– *The two last speeches of Thomas Wentworth, late Earle of Strafford, and Deputy of Ireland, the one in the Tower, the other on the scaffold on Tower-Hill, May 12, 1641*. London, 1641.

– *A true relation of the manner of the execution of Thomas Earle of Strafford with the severall passages and circumstances, together with his speech to the people on the scaffold, the 12. of May, 1641*. [London], 1641.

– *The true speech of Thomas Wentworth, late Earle of Strafford upon the scaffold, the twelfth of May. 1641. With a true relation of the manner of his execution: Together vvith a letter to His Maiestie*. [n.p.], 1641.

Yarington, Robert. *Two lamentable tragedies. The one, of the murther of Maister Beech a chaundler in Thames-streete, and his boye, done by Thomas Merry. The other of a young childe murthered in a wood by two ruffins, with the consent of his vnckle*. London, 1601.

Secondary Sources

"1666 and other London fires." Exhibition Catalog. 18 August–16 September 1966. Guildhall Art Gallery.

Achinstein, Sharon. "Cloudless Thunder: Milton in History." *Milton Studies* 48 (2008): 1–12.

Adams, George B., and Henry M. Stephens, eds. *Select Documents of English Constitutional History*. New York and London: Macmillan, 1920.

Adams, Hazard, ed. *Critical Theory Since Plato*. Rev. ed. Fort Worth, TX: Harcourt Brace Jovanovich College Publishers, 1992.

Allard, James Robert, and Mathew R. Martin. *Staging Pain, 1580–1800: Violence and Trauma in British Theater*. Surrey, England: Ashgate, 2009.

Amussen, Susan Dwyer. "Punishment, Discipline, and Power: The Social Meanings of Violence in Early Modern England." *Journal of British Studies* 34. 1 (January 1995): 1–34.

Anderson, Christy. *Inigo Jones and the Classical Tradition*. Cambridge and New York: Cambridge University Press, 2007.

Archer, Ian W. "London and Westminster." In *A Companion to Renaissance Drama*. Ed. Arthur Kinney. Oxford and Malden, MA: Blackwell, 2002. 68–82.

Armitage, David. "The *Procession Portrait* of Queen Elizabeth I: A Note on a Tradition." *Journal of the Warburg and Courtauld Institutes* 53 (1990): 301–7.

Armstrong, Paul A. "Form and History: Reading as an Aesthetic Experience and Historical Act." *Modern Language Quarterly* 69. 2 (June 2008): 195–219.

Aston, Margaret. "English Ruins and English History: The Dissolution and the Sense of the Past." *Journal of the Warburg and Courtauld Institutes* 36 (1973): 231–55.

Atherton, Ian, and Julie Sanders, eds. *The 1630s: Interdisciplinary Essays on Culture and Politics in the Caroline Era*. Manchester: Manchester University Press, 2006.

Bailey, Amanda, and Roze Hentschell, eds. *Masculinity and the Metropolis of Vice, 1550–1650*. New York: Palgrave Macmillan, 2010.

Barish, Jonas. "Three Caroline Defenses of the Stage." In *Comedy from Shakespeare to Sheridan: Change and Continuity in English and European Dramatic Tradition*. Ed. A.R. Braunmuller and J.C. Bulman. Newark: University of Delaware Press, 1986. 194–212.

Barker, Francis. *The Culture of Violence: Essays on Tragedy and History*. Chicago: University of Chicago Press, 1993.

Barker, Theo. "London: A Unique Megalopolis?" In *Megalopolis: The Giant City in History*. Ed. Theo Barker and Anthony Sutcliffe. New York: St Martin's Press; Houndmills: Macmillan Press, 1993. 43–60.

Bartolovich, Crystal. "'Baseless Fabric': London as a 'World City.'" In *"The Tempest" and Its Travels*. Ed. Peter Hulme and William H. Sherman. Philadelphia: University of Pennsylvania Press, 2000. 13–26.

– "London's the Thing: Alienation, the Market, and *Englishmen for My Money*." *Huntington Library Quarterly* 71. 1 (2008): 137–56.

Beier, A.L., and Roger Finlay, eds. *The Making of the Metropolis: London 1500–1700*. London: Longman, 1986.

Bell, Walter George. *The Great Fire of London in 1666*. London: John Lane, the Bodley Head, 1920.

Belsey, Catherine. "The Case of Hamlet's Conscience." *Studies in Philology* 76. 2 (1979): 127–48.

— *The Subject of Tragedy: Identity and Difference in Renaissance Drama*. New York: Methuen, 1985.

Bennett, Susan. "Making Up the Audience: Spectatorship in Historical Context." *Theatre Symposium* 20. 1 (2012): 8–22.

Berek, Peter. "Tragedy and Title Pages: Nationalism, Protestantism, and Print." *Modern Philology* 106. 1 (2008): 1–24.

Berry, Herbert. "The View of London from the North and the Playhouses in Holywell." *Shakespeare Survey* 53 (2000): 196–212.

Blank, Paula. *Shakespeare and the Mismeasure of Renaissance Man*. Ithaca: Cornell University Press, 2006.

Bloom, Gina. *Voice in Motion: Staging Gender, Shaping Sound in Early Modern England*. Philadelphia: University of Pennsylvania Press, 2007.

Bly, Mary. "Carnal Geographies: Mocking and Mapping the Religious Body." In Bailey and Hentschell, *Masculinity and the Metropolis of Vice*, 89–113.

– "Playing the Tourist in Early Modern London: Selling the Liberties Onstage." *PMLA* 122. 1 (2007): 61–71.

Boal, August. *Theatre of the Oppressed*. Trans. Charles A. McBride, Maria-Odilia Leal McBride, and Emily Fryer. London: Pluto Press, 2008. Originally published in 1974 as *Teatro del Oprimido*.

Boedeker, Deborah, and Kurt Raabflaub. "Tragedy and City." In Bushnell, *A Companion to Tragedy*, 109–27.

Borsay, Peter, and Lindsay Proudfoot. "The English and Irish Urban Experience, 1500–1800: Change, Convergence and Divergence." In Borsay and Proudfoot, *Provincial Towns*, 1–27.

– eds. *Provincial Towns in Early Modern England and Ireland: Change, Convergence and Divergence*, Proceedings of the British Academy 108. Oxford and New York: Oxford University Press for the British Academy, 2002.

Boulton, Jeremy. "London 1540–1700." In Clark, *Cambridge Urban History*, 315–46.

– *Neighbourhood and Society: A London Suburb in the Seventeenth Century.* Cambridge: Cambridge University Press, 1987.

Brady, Maura. "Space and the Persistence of Place in *Paradise Lost.*" *Milton Quarterly* 41. 3 (2007): 167–82.

Brennan, Michael G. "English Contact with Europe." In Hadfield and Hammon, *Shakespeare and Renaissance Europe*, 53–97.

Brooks, Peter. *Troubling Confessions: Speaking Guilt in Law and Literature.* Chicago and London: University of Chicago Press, 2000.

Brown, Pamela Allen, and Peter Parolin, eds. *Women Players in England, 1500–1660: Beyond the All-Male Stage.* Aldershot, England: Ashgate, 2005.

Brown, Sarah Annes, and Catherine Silverstone, eds. *Tragedy in Transition.* Malden, MA: Blackwell, 2007.

Brückner, Martin, and Kristen Poole. "The Plot Thickens: Surveying Manuals, Drama, and the Materiality of Narrative Form in Early Modern England." *English Literary History* 69. 3 (2002): 617–48.

Bruster, Douglas. *Quoting Shakespeare: Form and Culture in Early Modern Drama.* Lincoln: University of Nebraska Press, 2000.

Burbery, Timothy J. *Milton the Dramatist.* Pittsburgh: Duquesne University Press, 2007.

Burns, J.H., ed. *The Cambridge History of Political Thought 1450–1700.* Cambridge: Cambridge University Press, 1991.

– "George Buchanan and the Anti-monarchomachs." In *Political Discourse in Early Modern Britain.* Ed. Nicholas Phillipson and Quentin Skinner. Cambridge: Cambridge University Press, 1993. 3–22.

Bushnell, Rebecca, ed. *A Companion to Tragedy.* Malden, MA: Blackwell, 2005.

– *Tragedy: A Short Introduction.* Malden, MA: Blackwell, 2008.

– *Tragedies of Tyrants: Political Thought and Theater in the English Renaissance.* Ithaca: Cornell University Press, 1990.

Butler, Martin. Introduction to *The Roman Actor* by Philip Massinger, for the RSC. London: Nick Hern, 2002.

– "Romans in Britain: *The Roman Actor* and the Early Stuart Classical Play." In Howard, *Philip Massinger*, 139–70.

Campbell, Gordon, and Thomas N. Corns. *John Milton: Life, Work, and Thought.* Oxford: Oxford University Press, 2008.

Casey, Edward S. *The Fate of Place: A Philosophical History.* Berkeley, Los Angeles, and London: University of California Press, 1997.

Cave, Richard Allen. "Ben Jonson's *Every Man in His Humour*: A Case Study." In Milling and Thomson, *The Cambridge History of British Theatre*, 282–97.

"CBS Sparks Outrage by Airing Pearl Death Video." *The New York Post*. 15 May 2002: 2.

Cheney, Patrick. "Spenser's pastorals: *The Shepheardes Calender* and *Colin Clouts Come Home Againe*." In *The Cambridge Companion to Spenser*. Ed. Andrew Hadfield. Cambridge: Cambridge University Press, 2001. 79–105.

Chernaik, Warren L. *The Myth of Rome in Shakespeare and His Contemporaries*. Cambridge and New York: Cambridge University Press, 2011.

Clare, Janet, ed. *Drama of the English Republic*. Manchester: Manchester University Press, 2002.

Clark, Andrew. *Domestic Drama: A Survey of the Origins, Antecedents, and Nature of the Domestic Play in England, 1500–1640*. Salzburg, Austria: Universität Salzburg, Institut für Anglistik und Amerikanistik, 1975.

Clark, Ira. *The Moral Art of Philip Massinger*. Lewisburg, PA: Bucknell University Press; London: Associated University Presses, 1993.

Clark, Peter, ed. *The Cambridge Urban History of Britain, II: 1540–1840*. Cambridge: Cambridge University Press, 2000.

Clark, Peter, and Raymond Gillespie, eds. *Two Capitals: London and Dublin 1500–1840*. Proceedings of the British Academy 107. Oxford and New York: Oxford University Press for the British Academy, 2001.

Clark, Sandra. *Women and Crime in the Street Literature of Early Modern England*. Houndmills, England, and New York: Palgrave Macmillan, 2003.

Clayton, Thomas. "Catharsis in Aristotle, the Renaissance, and Elsewhere." *Journal of the Rocky Mountain Medieval and Renaissance Association* 2 (1981): 87–95.

Cockayne, Emily. *Hubbub: Filth, Noise and Stench in England, 1600–1770*. New Haven and London: Yale University Press, 2007.

Cockcroft, Robert. *Rhetorical Affect in Early Modern Writing: Renaissance Passions Reconsidered*. New York: Palgrave Macmillan, 2003.

Cohen, Stephen, ed. *Shakespeare and Historical Formalism*. Aldershot, England: Ashgate, 2007.

Collier, John Payne. *The History of English Dramatic Poetry to the Time of Shakespeare*. 3 vols. London: Murray, 1831.

Comensoli, Viviana. *"Household Business": Domestic Plays of Early Modern England*. Toronto: University of Toronto Press, 1996.

Cormack, Bradin. *A Power to Do Justice: Jurisdiction, English Literature, and the Rise of Common Law, 1509–1625*. Chicago and London: University of Chicago Press, 2007.

Corns, Thomas N., ed. *The Royal Image: Representations of Charles I*. Cambridge: Cambridge University Press, 1999.

Cosgrove, Denis, ed. *Mappings*. London: Reaktion Books, 1999.

Crace, John Gregory. *A Catalogue of Maps, Plans, and Views of London, Westminster and Southwark Collected and Arranged by Frederick Crace*. 1878.

Craik, Katharine A. "'A Lover's Complaint' and Early Modern Criminal Confession." *Shakespeare Quarterly* 53. 4 (2002): 437–59.

– *Reading Sensations in Early Modern England*. Houndmills, England, and New York: Palgrave Macmillan, 2007.

Craik, Katharine A., and Tanya Pollard, ed. *Shakespearean Sensations*. Cambridge: Cambridge University Press, 2013.

Cunningham, Karen. "Renaissance Execution and Marlovian Elocution: The Drama of Death." *PMLA* 105. 2 (1990): 209–22.

De Certeau, Michel. *The Practice of Everyday Life*. Trans. Steven Rendall. Berkeley: University of California Press, 1985.

De Grazia, Margreta. *"Hamlet" Without Hamlet*. Cambridge and New York: Cambridge University Press, 2007.

Defoe, Daniel. *A Journal of the Plague Year*. 1722. Ed. Cynthia Wall. London: Penguin, 2003.

Deiter, Kristen. *The Tower of London in English Renaissance Drama: Icon of Opposition*. New York: Routledge, 2008.

Delery, Clayton. "Dramatic Instruction and Misinstruction in Philip Massinger's *The Roman Actor*." In *Search for Meaning: Critical Essays on Early Modern Literature*. Ed. Paula Harms Payne. New York: Peter Lang, 2004. 105–14.

Deleuze, Gilles. *Foucault*. 1986. Trans. and ed. by Seán Hand. Minneapolis and London: University of Minnesota Press, 1988.

Denman, Jason R. "Anatomizing the Body Politic: Corporeal Rhetoric in *The Maid's Tragedy*." *Philological Quarterly* 84. 3 (2005): 311–31.

Dessen, Alan C. *Elizabethan Drama and the Viewer's Eye*. Chapel Hill: University of North Carolina Press, 1977.

Dessen, Alan C., and Leslie Thomson. *A Dictionary of Stage Directions in English Drama, 1580–1642*. Cambridge: Cambridge University Press, 1999.

Devereaux, Simon, and Paul Griffiths, eds. *Penal Practice and Culture, 1500–1900: Punishing the English*. Houndmills, England, and New York: Palgrave Macmillan, 2004.

Dillon, Janette. *Theatre, Court and City, 1595–1610: Drama and Social Space in London*. Cambridge: Cambridge University Press, 2000.

Dobranski, Stephen B. "Milton's Ideal Readers." In Pruitt and Durham, *Milton's Legacy*, 191–207.

Dolan, Frances E. *Dangerous Familiars: Representations of Domestic Crime in England, 1550–1700*. Ithaca: Cornell University Press, 1994.

– "Gender, Moral Agency, and Dramatic Form in *A Warning for Fair Women*." *Studies in English Literature* 29 (1989): 201–18.
– "'Gentlemen, I Have One More Thing to Say': Women on Scaffolds in England, 1563–1680." *Modern Philology* 92.2 (1994): 157–78.
– *True Relations: Reading, Literature, and Evidence in Seventeenth-Century England*. Philadelphia: University of Pennsylvania, 2013.
Duncan, Helga L. "'Sumptuously Re-edified': The Reformation of Sacred Space in *Titus Andronicus*." *Comparative Drama* 43. 4 (2009): 425–53.
Dzelzainis, Martin. "'Incendiaries of the State': Charles I and Tyranny." In Corns, *The Royal Image*, 74–95.
Eagleton, Terry. *Sweet Violence: The Idea of Tragedy*. Malden, MA: Blackwell, 2003.
Easterling, P.E., and Edith Hall, eds. *Greek and Roman Actors: Aspects of an Ancient Profession*. Cambridge: Cambridge University Press, 2002.
Easterling, P.E. "Weeping, Witnessing, and the Tragic Audience: Response to Segal." In Silk, *Tragedy and the Tragic*, 173–81.
Edwards, Catharine. "Acting and Self-actualization in Imperial Rome: Some Death Scenes." In Easterling and Hall, *Greek and Roman Actors*, 377–94.
Enterline, Lynn. *Rhetoric of the Body from Ovid to Shakespeare*. Cambridge Studies in Renaissance Literature and Culture 35. Cambridge: Cambridge University Press, 2000.
– *Shakespeare's Schoolroom: Rhetoric, Discipline, Emotion*. Philadelphia: University of Pennsylvania Press, 2011.
Euben, J. Peter. *The Tragedy of Political Theory: The Road Not Taken*. Princeton: Princeton University Press, 1990.
Evelyn, John. *The Diary of John Evelyn*. Ed. E.S. de Beer. 6 vols. Oxford: Clarendon Press, 1951; rpt. 2000.
Falconer, Rachel. *Orpheus Dis(re)membered: Milton and the Myth of the Poet-Hero*. Sheffield, England: Sheffield Academic Press, 1996.
Federico, Sylvia. *New Troy: Fantasies of Empire in the Late Middle Ages*. Medieval Cultures, Vol. 36. Minneapolis and London: University of Minnesota Press, 2003.
Felski, Rita, ed. *Rethinking Tragedy*. Baltimore: Johns Hopkins University Press, 2008.
Fenton, Mary C. *Milton's Places of Hope: Spiritual and Political Connections of Hope with Land*. Aldershot: Ashgate, 2006.
Ferguson, Margaret W. *Trials of Desire: Renaissance Defenses of Poetry*. New Haven and London: Yale University Press, 1983.
Finlay, Roger, and Beatrice Shearer, "Population Growth and Suburban Expansion." In Beier and Finlay, *The Making of the Metropolis*, 37–59.

Fish, Stanley. "'There Is Nothing He Cannot Ask': Milton, Liberalism, and Terrorism." In Lieb and Labriola, *Milton in the Age of Fish*, 243–64.

Fitzpatrick, Joan, ed. *The Idea of the City: Early-Modern, Modern and Post-Modern Locations and Communities*. Newcastle: Cambridge Scholars Publishing, 2009.

Fletcher, Angus. *Time, Space, and Motion in the Age of Shakespeare*. Cambridge, MA, and London: Harvard University Press, 2007.

Flower, Annette C. "The Critical Context of the Preface to *Samson Agonistes*." *Studies in English Literature* 10 (1970): 409–23.

Floyd-Wilson, Mary. *Occult Knowledge, Science, and Gender on the Shakespearean Stage*. Cambridge: Cambridge University Press, 2013.

Foucault, Michel. *Discipline and Punish: The Birth of the Prison*. 1975. Trans. Alan Sheridan. New York: Vintage Books, 1977.

Fuchs, Anne. *After the Dresden Bombing: Pathways of Memory, 1945 to the Present*. Houndmills, England, and New York: Palgrave Macmillan, 2012.

Frye, Susan. *Elizabeth I: The Competition for Representation*. New York: Oxford University Press, 1996,

Gadd, Ian, and Alexandra Gillespie, eds. *John Stow (1525–1605) and the Making of the English Past*. London: British Library, 2004.

Gallagher, Lowell. *Medusa's Gaze: Casuistry and Conscience in the Renaissance*. Stanford: Stanford University Press, 1991.

Gallagher, Lowell, and Shankar Ramon, eds. *Knowing Shakespeare: Senses, Embodiment and Cognition*. Houndmills, England, and New York: Palgrave Macmillan, 2010.

Garrett, Martin. *"A diamond, though set in horn": Philip Massinger's Attitude to Spectacle*. Salzburg Studies in English Literature/Jacobean Drama Studies 72. Universität Salzburg: Institute für Anglistik und Amerikanistik, 1984.

Gellrich, Michelle. *Tragedy and Theory: The Problem of Conflict since Aristotle*. Princeton: Princeton University Press, 1988.

Gent, Lucy, ed. *Albion's Classicism: The Visual Arts in Britain, 1550–1660*. New Haven: Yale University Press for the Paul Mellon Centre for Studies in British Art, 1995.

Gerschow, Frederic. "Diary of the Journey of Philip Julius, Duke of Stettin-Pomerania, through England in the Year 1602." Ed. Gottfried von Bülow. *Transactions of the Royal Historical Society* 6 (1892): 1–67.

Gillies, John. "Space and Place in *Paradise Lost*." *English Literary History* 74 (2007): 27–57.

Goldberg, Jonathan. *James I and the Politics of Literature: Jonson, Shakespeare, Donne, and Their Contemporaries*. Baltimore: Johns Hopkins University Press, 1983.

Goldhill, Simon. "Generalizing About Tragedy." In Felski, *Rethinking Tragedy*, 45–65.

Gordon, Andrew. "'If my sign could speak': The Signboard and the Visual Culture of Early Modern London." *Early Theatre* 8. 1 (2005): 35–51.

– "Overseeing and Overlooking: John Stow and the Surveying of the City." In Gadd and Gillespie, *John Stow*, 81–8.

– "Performing London: The Map and the City in Ceremony." In Gordon and Klein, *Literature, Mapping*, 69–88.

Gordon, Andrew, and Bernhard Klein, eds. *Literature, Mapping, and the Politics of Space in Early Modern Britain*. Cambridge: Cambridge University Press, 2001.

Gowing, Laura. "'The Freedom of the Streets': Women and Social Space, 1560–1640." In Griffiths and Jenner, *Londinopolis*, 115–33.

Graham, Kenneth J.E. *The Performance of Conviction: Plainness and Rhetoric in the Early English Renaissance*. Ithaca and London: Cornell University Press, 1994.

Grantley, Darryll. *London in Early Modern English Drama: Representing the Built Environment*. Houndmills, England, and New York: Palgrave Macmillan, 2008.

Greenberg, Marissa. "Crossing from Scaffold to Stage: Execution Processions and Generic Conventions in *The Comedy of Errors* and *Measure for Measure*." In Cohen, *Shakespeare and Historicist Formalism*, 183–209.

– "Processions and History in Shakespeare and Fletcher's *Henry VIII*." *English Literary Renaissance* 45. 2 (2015).

– "Women and the Theatre in Thomas Heywood's London." In *The Idea of the City: Early-Modern, Modern and Post-Modern Locations and Communities*. Ed. Joan Fitzpatrick. Newcastle: Cambridge Scholars Publishing, 2009. 79–89.

Griffiths, Antony. *The Print in Stuart Britain, 1603–1689*. London: British Museum Press, 1998.

Griffiths, Paul. *Lost Londons: Change, Crime and Control in the Capital City, 1550–1660*. Cambridge: Cambridge University Press, 2008.

– "Overlapping Circles: Imagining Criminal Communities in London, 1545–1645." In *Communities in Early Modern England: Networks, Places, Rhetoric*. Ed. Alexandra Shephard and Phil Withington. Manchester: Manchester University Press, 2000. 115–33.

Griffiths, Paul, and Mark S.R. Jenner, eds. *Londinopolis: Essays in the Cultural and Social History of Early Modern England*. Manchester: Manchester University Press, 2000.

Group Phi. "Doing Genre." In Theile and Tredennick, *New Formalisms and Literary Theory*, 54–68.

Habicht, Werner. "Traps of Illusion in Massinger's *The Roman Actor.*" In Laroque, *The Show Within*, 359–68.

Hadfield, Andrew, and Paul Hammon, eds. *Shakespeare and Renaissance Europe.* London: Arden, 2005.

Hall, Edith. "Is there a *Polis* in Aristotle's *Poetics*?" In Silk, *Tragedy and the Tragic*, 295–309.

– "The Singing Actors of Antiquity." In Easterling and Hall, *Greek and Roman Actors*, 3–38.

Hammond, Paul. *The Strangeness of Tragedy.* Oxford and New York: Oxford University Press, 2009.

Hanson, Elizabeth. *Discovering the Subject in Renaissance England.* Cambridge: Cambridge University Press, 1998.

Harding, Vanessa. "Cheapside: Commerce and Commemoration." *Huntington Library Quarterly* 71. 1 (2008): 77–95.

– "City, Capital, and Metropolis: The Changing Shape of Seventeenth-century London." In Merritt, *Imagining Early Modern London*, 117–43.

Hardison, O.B. "Three Types of Renaissance Catharsis." *Renaissance Drama* (1969): 3–22.

Harkness, Deborah, and Jean E. Howard, eds. "The Places and Spaces of Early Modern London," special volume of *Huntington Library Quarterly* 71. 1 (2008).

Harris, Jonathan Gil. "Ludgate Time and *The Shoemaker's Holiday.*" *Huntington Library Quarterly* 71. 1 (2008): 11–32.

– *Untimely Matters in the Time of Shakespeare.* Philadelphia: University of Pennsylvania Press, 2009.

Hartley, Andrew James. "*The Roman Actor* and Censored Theater." *English Literary History* 68. 2 (2001): 359–76.

Harvey, P.D.A. "A Foreign Visitor's Account of the Great Fire." *Transactions of the London and Middlesex Archaeological Society* 20 (1959–60): 76–87.

Heal, Ambrose. *The Signboards of Old London Shops.* London: Batsford, 1947.

Helgerson, Richard. *Adulterous Alliances: Home, State, and History in Early Modern European Drama and Painting.* Chicago: University of Chicago Press, 2000.

– *Forms of Nationhood: The Elizabethan Writing of England.* Chicago: University of Chicago Press, 1992.

Herrick, Marvin T. *The Fusion of Horation and Aristotelian Literary Criticism, 1531–1555.* Illinois Studies in Language and Literature 32. 1. Urbana: University of Illinois Press, 1946.

– *The Poetics of Aristotle in England.* New Haven: Yale University Press, 1930.

– "Some Neglected Sources of *Admiratio.*" *Modern Language Notes* 62. 4 (1947): 222–6.

Herrup, Cynthia B. *The Common Peace: Participation and the Criminal Law in Seventeenth-Century England*. Cambridge: Cambridge University Press, 1987.

Hill, Tracey. "'Representing the awefull authorities of soveraigne Majestie': Monarchs and Mayors in Anthony Munday's *The Triumphes of Re-united Britania*." In *The Accession of James I: Historical and Cultural Consequences*. Ed. Glenn Burgess, Rowland Wymer, and Jason Lawrence. Houndmills, England, and New York: Palgrave Macmillan, 2006. 15–33.

Hiltner, Ken. "'Belch'd fire and rowling smoke': Air Pollution in *Paradise Lost*." In Tournu and Forsyth, *Milton, Rights and Liberties*, 293–302.

– *What Else Is Pastoral? Renaissance Literature and the Environment*. Ithaca and London: Cornell University Press, 2011.

Hoenselaars, A.J. "Italy Staged in English Renaissance Drama." In Marrapodi, Hoenselaars, Cappuzo, and Santucci, *Shakespeare's England*, 30–48.

Hogan, A.P. "The Imagery of Acting in *The Roman Actor*." *The Modern Language Review* 66. 2 (1971): 273–81.

Holbrook, Peter. *Literature and Degree in Renaissance England: Nashe, Bourgeois Tragedy, Shakespeare*. Newark: University of Delaware Press, 1994.

Holland, Peter, and Stephen Orgel, eds. *From Script to Stage in Early Modern England*. Houndmills, England, and New York: Palgrave Macmillan, 2004.

Holliday, Richard. "Hostage at Gunpoint or a Callous Hoax?" *Evening Standard* 28 January 2002.

Hopkins, D.J. *City/Stage/Globe: Performance and Space in Shakespeare's London*. New York: Routledge, 2008.

Hopkins, Lisa. "*A Yorkshire Tragedy* and Middleton's Tragic Aesthetic." *Early Modern Literary Studies* 8. 3 (2003): 2.1–15.

Howard, Douglas, ed. *Philip Massinger: A Critical Reassessment*. Cambridge: Cambridge University Press, 1985.

Howard, Jean E. "London and the Early Modern Stage." In Manley, *The Cambridge Companion to the Literature of London*, 34–49.

– "Other Englands: The View from the Non-Shakespearean History Play." In *Other Voices, Other Views: Expanding the Canon in English Renaissance Studies*. Ed. Helen Ostovich, Mary V. Silcox, and Graham Roebuck. Newark: University of Delaware Press; London: Associated University Presses, 1999. 135–53.

– *Shakespeare's Art of Orchestration: Stage Technique and Audience Response*. Urbana and Chicago: University of Illinois Press, 1984.

– "Shakespeare, Geography, and the Work of Genre on the Early Modern Stage." *Modern Language Quarterly* 64. 3 (2003): 299–322.

– "The New Historicism in Renaissance Studies," *English Literary Renaissance* 16. 1 (1986): 13–43.

– *Theater of a City: The Places of London Comedy, 1598–1642*. Philadelphia: University of Pennsylvania Press, 2007.

Howard, Maurice. *The Building of Elizabethan and Jacobean England*. New Haven: Yale University Press for the Paul Mellon Centre for Studies in British Art, 2007.

Howard, Skiles. *The Politics of Courtly Dancing in Early Modern England*. Amherst: University of Massachusetts Press, 1998.

Howarth, David. *Images of Rule: Art and Politics in the English Renaissance, 1485–1649*. Berkeley and Los Angeles: University of California Press, 1997.

Hubbard, Phil. *City*. Key Ideas in Geography. London and New York: Routledge, 2006.

Hunt, Alice. *The Drama of Coronation: Medieval Ceremony in Early Modern England*. Cambridge: Cambridge University Press, 2008.

Hunter, Michael, ed. *Printed Images in Early Modern Britain: Essays in Interpretation*. Farnham, England: Ashgate, 2007.

Hutson, Lorna. "Fortunate Travelers: Reading for the Plot in Sixteenth-Century England." *Representations* 41 (1993): 83–103.

– *The Invention of Suspicion: Law and Mimesis in Shakespeare and Renaissance Drama*. New York: Oxford University Press, 2007.

– "Rethinking the 'Spectacle of the Scaffold': Juridical Epistemologies and English Revenge Tragedy." *Representations* 89 (2005): 30–58.

Ingram, Martin. "Ridings, Rough Music, and the 'Reform of Popular Culture.'" *Past and Present* 105 (1984): 79–113.

James, Heather. *Shakespeare's Troy: Drama, Politics, and the Translation of Empire*. Cambridge: Cambridge University Press, 1997.

Jameson, Frederic. "Cognitive Mapping." 1988. *The Jameson Reader*. Ed. Michael Hardt and Kathi Weeks. Oxford: Blackwell, 2000. 277–87.

Jones, Emrys. *Metropolis*. Oxford and New York: Oxford University Press, 1990.

– . *Scenic Form in Shakespeare*. Oxford: Clarendon Press, 1971.

Jones, Malcolm. *The Print in Early Modern England: An Historical Oversight*. New Haven and London: Yale University Press for the Paul Mellon Centre for Studies in British Art, 2010.

Keene, Derek. "Growth, Modernisation and Control: The Transformation of London's Landscape, c. 1500–c. 1760." In Clark and Gillespie, *Two Capitals*, 7–38.

Keilen, Sean. *Vulgar Eloquence: On the Renaissance Invention of English Literature*. New Haven and London: Yale University Press, 2006.

Kelley, David B. "Elizabethan Political Thought." In Pocock, *The Varieties of British Political Thought*, 47–79.

Kelly, Henry Ansgar. *Ideas and Forms of Tragedy from Aristotle to the Middle Ages.* Cambridge: Cambridge University Press, 1993.

Kiefer, Frederick. *Shakespeare's Visual Theatre: Staging the Personified Characters.* Cambridge: Cambridge University Press, 2003.

– *Writing on the Renaissance Stage: Written Words, Printed Pages, Metaphoric Books*. Newark: University of Delaware Press, 1996.

– "'Written Troubles of the Brain': Lady Macbeth's Conscience." In *Reading and Writing in Shakespeare*. Ed. David Bergeron. Newark: University of Delaware Press, 1996. 64–81.

Kilburn, Terence, and Anthony Milton. "The Public Context of the Trial and Execution of Strafford." In Merritt, *The Political World of Thomas Wentworth*, 230–51.

King, John N. *Foxe's "Book of Martyrs" and Early Modern Print Culture.* Cambridge and New York: Cambridge University Press, 2006.

Kingdom, Robert M. "Calvinism and Resistance Theory, 1550–1580." In Burns, *Cambridge History of Political Thought*, 194–218.

Knoppers, Laura Lunger, ed. *The Complete Works of John Milton, Volume II: The 1671 Poems: "Paradise Regain'd" and "Samson Agonistes."* Oxford: Oxford University Press, 2008.

Knoppers, Laura Lunger. "The Politics of Portraiture: Oliver Cromwell and the Plain Style." *Renaissance Drama* 51. 4 (1988): 1283–1319.

– *Historicizing Milton: Spectacle, Power, and Poetry in Restoration England.* Athens and London: The University of Georgia Press, 1994.

Knott, John R. *Discourses of Martyrdom in English Literature, 1563–1694.* Cambridge: Cambridge University Press, 1993.

Korda, Natasha. *Shakespeare's Domestic Economies: Gender and Property in Early Modern England.* Philadelphia: University of Pennsylvania Press, 2002.

Kühnová, Šárka. "'Inspired with Contradiction': Milton's Language of Liberty." In Tournu and Forsyth, *Milton, Rights and Liberties*, 345–54.

Lake, Peter. "From Troynouvant to Heliogabulus's Rome and Back: 'Order' and Its Others in the London of John Stow." In Merritt, *Imagining*, 217–49.

Lake, Peter, and Michael Questier. "Agency, Appropriation and Rhetoric under the Gallows: Puritans, Romanists and the State in Early Modern England." *Past and Present* 153 (1996): 64–107.

– *The Antichrist's Lewd Hat: Protestants, Papists, and Players in Post-Reformation England.* New Haven: Yale University Press, 2002.

Lancashire, Anne. *London Civic Theatre: City Drama and Pageantry from Roman Times to 1558.* Cambridge: Cambridge University Press, 2002.

Langbein, John H. *Torture and the Law of Proof: Europe and England in the Ancien Regime.* Chicago: University of Chicago Press, 1977.

Laqueur, Thomas W. "Crowds, Carnival and the State in English Executions, 1604–1868." In *The First Modern Society: Essays in English History in Honour of Lawrence Stone*. Ed. A.L. Beier, David Cannadine, and James M. Rosenheim. Cambridge and New York: Cambridge University Press, 1989. 305–55.

Laroque, François, ed. *The Show Within: Dramatic and Other Insets: English Renaissance Drama (1550–1642)*. Montpellier, France: Paul-Valéry University Press, 1990.

Lemon, Rebecca. *Treason by Words: Literature, Law, and Rebellion in Shakespeare's England*. Ithaca: Cornell University Press, 2006.

Leo, Russ. "Milton's Aristotelian Experiments: Tragedy, *Lustratio*, and 'Secret refreshings' in *Samson Agonistes* (1671)." *Milton Studies* (2011): 221–52.

Levinson, Marjorie. "What Is New Formalism?" *PMLA* 122. 2 (March 2007): 558–69.

Levith, Murray J. *Shakespeare's Italian Settings and Plays*. New York: St Martin's Press, 1989.

Lewalski, Barbara Kiefer. "How Poetry Moves Readers: Sidney, Spenser, and Milton." *University of Toronto Quarterly* 80. 3 (2011): 756–68.

Lieb, Michael. *Milton and the Culture of Violence*. Ithaca and London: Cornell University Press, 1994.

Lieb, Michael, and Albert C. Labriola, eds. *Milton in the Age of Fish: Essay on Authorship, Text, and Terrorism*. Pittsburgh: Duquesne University Press, 2006.

Lillywhite, Bryant. *London Signs*. London: Allen and Unwin, 1972.

Lin, Erika T. "Festivity." In *Early Modern Theatricality*. Ed. Henry S. Turner. Oxford: Oxford University Press, 2013. 212–29.

– *Shakespeare and the Materiality of Performance*. New York: Palgrave Macmillan, 2012.

Lopez, Jeremy. *Constructing the Canon of Early Modern Drama*. Cambridge: Cambridge University Press, 2014.

– *Theatrical Convention and Audience Response in Early Modern Drama*. Cambridge: Cambridge University Press, 2007.

Love, Harold. "Was Lucinda Betrayed at Whitehall?" In *That Second Bottle: Essays on John Wilmot, Earl of Rochester*. Ed. Nicholas Fisher. Manchester and New York: Manchester University Press, 2000. 179–90.

Low, Jennifer A., and Nova Myhill, eds. *Imagining the Audience in Early Modern Drama, 1558–1642*. New York : Palgrave Macmillan, 2011.

Lubbock, John. *The Tyranny of Taste: The Politics of Architecture and Design in Britain, 1550–1960*. New Haven and London: Yale University Press for the Paul Mellon Center for Studies in British Art, 1995.

Lukacher, Ned. *Daemonic Figures: Shakespeare and the Question of Conscience*. Ithaca and London: Cornell University Press, 1994.

Lynch, Kevin. *The Image of the City*. Cambridge, MA: MIT Press, 1960.
Lyne, Raphael. "Neoclassicisms." In Browne and Silverstone, *Tragedy in Transition*, 123–40.
Machacek, Gregory. "Allusion." *PMLA* 122. 2 (2007): 522–36.
MacKay, Ellen. *Persecution, Plague, and Fire: Fugitive Histories of the Stage in Early Modern England.* Chicago and London: University of Chicago Press, 2011.
MacLean, Gerald, Donna Landry, and Joseph P. Ward, eds. *The Country and the City Revisited: England and the Politics of Culture, 1550–1850*. Cambridge: Cambridge University Press, 1999.
Maddern, Philippa C. *Violence and Social Order: East Anglia, 1422–1442*. Oxford: Clarendon Press, 1992.
Maguire, Nancy, "The Theatrical Mask/Masque of Politics: The Case of Charles I." *Journal of British Studies* 28 (1989): 1–22.
Manley, Lawrence, ed. *The Cambridge Companion to the Literature of London*. Cambridge: Cambridge University Press, 2011.
– *Literature and Culture in Early Modern London*. Cambridge: Cambridge University Press, 1995.
Mardock, James D. *Our Scene is London: Ben Jonson's City and the Space of the Author*. New York: Routledge, 2008.
Marrapodi, Michele, A.J. Hoenselaars, Marcello Cappuzzo, and L. Falson Santucci, eds. *Shakespeare's Italy: Functions of Italian Locations in Renaissance Drama*. Manchester: Manchester University Press, 1993,
Marshall, Cynthia. *The Shattering of the Self: Violence, Subjectivity, and Early Modern Texts*. Baltimore: Johns Hopkins University Press, 2002.
Marshburn, Joseph H. "'A Cruel Murder Donne in Kent' and its Literary Manifestations." *Studies in Philology* 46 (1949): 131–40.
Matz, Robert. *Defending Literature in Early Modern England: Renaissance Literary Theory in Social Context*. Cambridge: Cambridge University Press, 2000.
McDonald, Marianne, and J. Michael Walton, eds. *The Cambridge Companion to Greek and Roman Theatre*. Cambridge: Cambridge University Press, 2007.
McLaughlin, Joseph. *Writing the Urban Jungle: Reading Empire in London from Doyle to Eliot*. Charlottesville: University Press of Virginia, 2000.
Menzer, Paul. "Crowd Control." In Low and Myhill, *Imagining the Audience*, 19–36.
Merritt, J.F. ed. *Imagining Early Modern London: Perceptions and Portrayals of the City from Stow to Strype, 1598–1720*. Cambridge: Cambridge University Press, 2001.
– ed. *The Political World of Thomas Wentworth, Earl of Strafford, 1621–1641*. Cambridge: Cambridge University Press, 1996.

Miller, Anthony. *Roman Triumphs and Early Modern English Culture*. Houndmills, England: Palgrave Macmillan, 2001.

Milling, Jane, and Peter Thomson. *The Cambridge History of British Theatre, Volume 1: Origins to 1660*. Cambridge: Cambridge University Press, 2004.

Minson, Stuart. "Public Punishment and Urban Space in Early Tudor London." *London Topographical Record* 30 (2010): 1–16.

Monteyne, Joseph. *The Printed Image in Early Modern London: Urban Space, Visual Representation, and Social Exchange*. Aldershot, England: Ashgate, 2007.

Moreau, Ron, and Zahid Hussain. "Failed Cities: Terror's Urban Jungle." *Newsweek* 14 October 2002: 39.

Moretti, Franco. *Signs Take for Wonders: On the Sociology of Literary Forms*. London and New York: Verso, 1983, 2005.

Morrill, John. *The Nature of the English Revolution*. London: Longman, 1993.

Morse, Ruth. "What City, Friends, Is This?" In *Plotting Early Modern London: New Essays on Jacobean Comedy*. Ed. Dieter Mehl, Angela Stock, and Anne-Julia Zwierlein. Aldershot, England and Burlington, VT: Ashgate, 2004. 177–91.

Mueller, Janel. "The Figure and the Ground: Samson as a Hero of London Nonconformity, 1662–1667." In *Milton and the Terms of Liberty*. Ed. Graham Parry and Joad Raymond. Rochester, NY: D. S. Brewer, 2002. 137–62.

Mueller, Martin E. "*Pathos* and *Katharsis* in *Samson Agonistes*." *English Literary History* 31. 2 (1964): 156–74.

– "Sixteenth-Century Italian Criticism and Milton's Theory of Catharsis." *Studies in English Literature* 6. 1 (1966): 139–50.

Muir, Edward. *Ritual in Early Modern Europe*. Cambridge: Cambridge University Press, 1997.

Mukherji, Subha. *Law and Representation in Early Modern Drama*. Cambridge: Cambridge University Press, 2006.

Mullally, Robert. "*Measure* as a Choreographic Term in the Stuart Masque." *Dance Research* 16. 1 (1998): 67–73.

– "More about the Measures." *Early Music* 22. 3 (1994): 417–38.

Mullaney, Steven. *The Place of the Stage: License, Play, and Power in Renaissance England*. Chicago: University of Chicago Press, 1988.

Munro, Ian. *The Figure of the Crowd in Early Modern London: The City and Its Double*. Houndmills, England, and New York: Palgrave Macmillan, 2005.

Neill, Michael. *Issues of Death: Mortality and Identity in English Renaissance Tragedy*. Oxford: Oxford University Press, 1997.

Nelson, Alan M. *Monstrous Adversary: The Life of Edward de Vere, 17th Earl of Oxford*. Liverpool: Liverpool University Press, 2003.

Netzley, Ryan. "Reading Events: The Value of Reading and the Possibilities of Political Action and Criticism in *Samson Agonistes*." *Criticism* 48. 4 (2007): 509–33.

Newman, J. "Inigo Jones and the Politics of Architecture." In *Culture and Politics in Early Stuart England*. Ed. Kevin Sharpe and Peter Lake. Stanford: Stanford University Press, 1993. 229–55.

Newman, Karen. *Cultural Capitals: Early Modern London and Paris*. Princeton and Oxford: Princeton University Press, 2007.

Norbrook, David. *Writing the English Republic: Poetry, Rhetoric and Politics, 1627–1660*. Cambridge: Cambridge University Press, 1999.

Nussbaum, Martha. *Upheavals of Thought: The Intelligence of the Emotions*. New York: Cambridge University Press, 2001.

Nuttall, A.D. *Why Does Tragedy Give Pleasure?* Oxford: Clarendon Press, 1996.

O'Connell, Sheila. *The Popular Print in England, 1550–1850*. London: British Museum, 1999.

Olmsted, Wendy. *The Imperfect Friend: Emotion and Rhetoric in Sidney, Milton, and Their Contexts*. Toronto: University of Toronto Press, 2008.

Orgel, Stephen. "The Play of Conscience." In *The Authentic Shakespeare and Other Problems of the Early Modern Stage*. New York: Routledge, 2002. 129–42.

Orlin, Lena Cowen. "Boundary Disputes in Early Modern London." In Orlin, *Material London*, 344–76.

– ed. *Material London, ca. 1600*. Philadelphia: University of Pennsylvania Press, 2000.

– *Private Matters and Public Culture in Post-Reformation England*. Ithaca: Cornell University Press, 1994.

Owens, Margaret E. *Stages of Dismemberment: The Fragmented Body in Late Medieval and Early Modern Drama*. Newark: University of Delaware Press, 2005.

Oxford English Dictionary Online. March 2014.

Palfrey, Simon, and Tiffany Stern. *Shakespeare in Parts*. Oxford and New York: Oxford University Press, 2007.

Parker, Barbara L. *Plato's Republic and Shakespeare's Rome: A Political Study of the Roman Works*. Newark: University of Delaware Press, 2004.

Parker, Patricia. *Shakespeare from the Margins: Language, Culture, Context*. Chicago and London: University of Chicago Press, 1996.

Parolin, Peter Alexander. "'Not so Fitte a Place': English Identity and Italian Difference in Early Modern England." Dissertation. University of Pennsylvania, 1997.

Parshall, Peter. "Prints as Objects of Consumption in Early Modern Europe." *Journal of Medieval and Early Modern Studies* 28. 1 (1998): 19–36.

Paster, Gail Kern. *The Idea of the City in the Age of Shakespeare*. Athens: University of Georgia Press, 1985.

Paster, Gail Kern, Katherine Rowe, and Mary Floyd-Wilson, eds. *Reading the Early Modern Passions: Essays in the Cultural History of Emotion*. Philadelphia: University of Pennsylvania, 2004.

Pastoor, Charles. "Metadramatic Performances in *Hamlet* and *The Roman Actor*." *Philological Review* 32. 1 (2006): 1–20.

Patenaude, Anne Weston. "A Critical Old Spelling Edition of Robert Yarington's *Two Lamentable Tragedies*." Dissertation. University of Michigan, 1978.

Patterson, Annabel. *Censorship and Interpretation: The Conditions of Writing and Reading in Early Modern England*. Madison: University of Wisconsin Press, 1984.

– "Milton's Negativity." In Lieb and Labriola, *Milton in the Age of Fish*, 81–102.

Peck, Linda Levy. *Consuming Splendor: Society and Culture in Seventeenth-Century England*. Cambridge: Cambridge University Press, 2005.

– "Kingship, Counsel and Law in Early Stuart Britain." In Pocock, *Varieties of British Political Thought*, 80–115.

Pocock, J.G.A., ed. *The Varieties of British Political Thought, 1500–1800*. Cambridge: Cambridge University Press, in association with the Folger Institute, 1993.

Pollard, Tanya. "Conceiving Tragedy." In Craik and Pollard, *Shakespearean Sensations*, 85–100.

– "A Kind of Wild Medicine: Revenge as Remedy in Early Modern England." *Revista Canaria de Estudio Ingleses* 50 (2005): 57–69.

– "Tragedy and Revenge." In Smith and Sullivan, *The Cambridge Companion to English Renaissance Tragedy*, 58–72.

– "What's Hecuba to Shakespeare?" *Renaissance Quarterly* 4 (2012): 1060–93.

Poole, Adrian. *Tragedy: A Very Short Introduction*. Oxford: Oxford University Press, 2005.

Proudfoot, Richard. "'The Play's the Thing': Hamlet and the Conscience of the Queen." In *"Fanned and Winnowed Opinions": Shakespearean Essays Presented to Harold Jenkins*. Ed. John W. Mahon and Thomas A. Pendleton. London: Methuen, 1987. 160–5.

Pruitt, Kristin A., and Charles W. Durham, eds. *Milton's Legacy*. Selinsgrove, PA: Susquehanna University Press, 2005.

Radzinowicz, Mary Ann. *Toward Samson Agonistes: The Growth of Milton's Mind*. Princeton: Princeton University Press, 1978.

Rajan, Balachandra, ed. *The Prison and the Pinnacle*. Toronto: University of Toronto Press, 1973.

– "'To Which is Added *Samson Agonistes*—.'" In Rajan, *The Prison and the Pinnacle*, 82–100.

Randall, Dale B.J. *Winter Fruit: English Drama 1642–1660.* Lexington: University Press of Kentucky, 1995.

Rasmussen, Mark D., ed. *Renaissance Literature and Its Formal Engagements.* New York: Palgrave Macmillan, 2002.

Reinheimer, David R. "*The Roman Actor,* Censorship, and Dramatic Autonomy." *Studies in English Literature* 38. 2 (1998): 317–32.

Reiss, Timothy J. *Tragedy and Truth: Studies in the Development of a Renaissance and Neoclassical Discourse.* New Haven and London: Yale University Press, 1980.

Richardson, Catherine. *Domestic Life and Domestic Tragedy in Early Modern England: The Material Life of the Household.* Manchester: Manchester University Press, 2006.

Rist, Thomas. "Catharsis as 'Purgation' in Shakespearean Drama." In Craik and Pollard, *Shakespearean Sensations,* 138–53.

– *Revenge Tragedy and the Drama of Commemoration in Reforming England.* Aldershot, England, and Burlington, VT: Ashgate, 2008.

Roach, Joseph R. *The Player's Passion: Studies in the Science of Acting.* Newark: University of Delaware Press; London: Associated University Presses, 1985.

Rochester, Joanne. *Staging Spectatorship in the Plays of Philip Massinger.* Aldershot, UK: Ashgate, 2010.

Rogers, Kenneth. *Signs and Taverns Round about Old London Bridge.* London: Homeland Assn., 1937.

Romàn, David, ed. "A Forum on Theatre and Tragedy in the Wake of September 11, 2001." *Theatre Journal* 54. 1 (2002): 95–138.

Rooney, Ellen. "Form and Contentment." *Modern Language Quarterly* 61. 1 (2000): 17–40.

Rowland, Richard. *Thomas Heywood's Theatre, 1599–1639: Locations, Translations, and Conflict.* Farnham, England: Ashgate, 2010.

Rubidge, Bradley. "Catharsis Through Admiration: Corneille, Le Moyne, and the Social Uses of Emotion." *Modern Philology* 95. 3 (1998): 316–33.

Salvaggio, Ruth. *Hearing Sappho in New Orleans: The Call of Poetry from Congo Square to the Ninth Ward.* Baton Rouge: Louisiana State University Press, 2012.

Sanders, Julie. *The Cultural Geography of Early Modern Drama, 1620–1650.* Cambridge: Cambridge University Press, 2011.

Saunders, Ann, and John Schofield, eds. *Tudor London: A Map and a View.* London Topographical Society Publication 159. 2001.

Schlueter, June. "Rereading the Side Panels in *The View of London from the North.*" *Medieval and Renaissance Drama in England* 23 (2010): 142–57.

Schoenfeldt, Michael. "Shakespearean Pain." In Craik and Pollard, *Shakespearean Sensations*, 191–207.

Schofield, John. "The Topography and Buildings of London, ca. 1600." In Orlin, *Material London*, 296–321.

Schwartzstät, Georg von. "England in 1609." Trans. G.P.V. Akrigg. *Huntington Library Quarterly* 14 (1950): 75–94.

Seaford, Richard. "Tragedy and Dionysus." In Bushnell, *A Companion*, 25–38.

Sennett, Richard, ed. *Classic Essays on the Culture of Cities*. New York: Appleton-Century-Croft, 1969.

Shakespeare Birthplace Trust Archive Catalogue. http://calm.shakespeare.org.uk/dserve.

Sharpe, J.A. "Domestic Homicide in Early Modern England." *The Historical Journal* 24. 1 (1981): 29–48.

– "'Last Dying Speeches': Religion, Ideology and Public Execution in Seventeenth-Century England." *Past and Present* 107 (1985): 144–67.

Sharpe, Kevin. *Image Wars: Promoting Kings and Commonwealths in England, 1603–1660*. Yale University Press, 2010.

– *Selling the Tudor Monarchy: Authority and Image in Sixteenth-century England*. New Haven and London: Yale University Press, 2009.

Shephard, Alexandra, and Phil Withington, eds. *Communities in Early Modern England: Networks, Places, Rhetoric*. Manchester: Manchester University Press, 2000.

Silk, M.S., ed. *Tragedy and the Tragic: Greek Theatre and Beyond*. Oxford: Clarendon Press, 1996.

Silverstone, Catherine. "Afterword: Ending Tragedy." In Brown and Silverstone, *Tragedy in Transition*, 277–86.

Skantze, P.A. *Stillness in Motion in the Seventeenth-Century Theatre*. London and New York: Routledge, 2003.

Slack, Paul. "Great and Good Towns 1540–1700." In Clark, *Cambridge Urban History*, 347–76.

Slack, Paul. "Perceptions of the Metropolis in Seventeenth-Century England." In *Civil Histories: Essays Presented to Sir Keith Thomas*. Ed. Peter Burke, Brian Harrison, and Paul Slack. Oxford: Oxford University Press, 2000. 161–80.

Slights, Camille Wells. *The Casuistical Tradition in Shakespeare, Donne, Herbert, and Milton*. Princeton: Princeton University Press, 1981.

Smith, Bruce R. *The Acoustic World of Early Modern England: Attending to the O-factor*. Chicago: University of Chicago Press, 1999.

– "The Contest of Apollo and Marsyas: Ideas About Music in the Middle Ages." In *By Things Seen: Reference and Recognition in Medieval Thought*. Ed. David L. Jeffrey. Ottawa: University of Ottawa Press, 1979. 81–108.

– "E/loco/com/motion." In Holland and Orgel, *From Script to Stage*, 131–50.

– *The Key of Green: Passion and Perception in Renaissance Culture*. Chicago and London: University of Chicago Press, 2009.

Smith, David L., Richard Strier, and David Bevington, eds. *The Theatrical City: Culture, Theatre and Politics in Shakespeare's London, 1576–1649*. Cambridge and New York: Cambridge University Press, 1995.

Smith, Emma and Garrett A. Sullivan Jr., eds. *The Cambridge Companion to English Renaissance Tragedy*. Ed. Cambridge: Cambridge University Press, 2010.

Smith, Helen. "'More Swete Vnto the Eare / Than Holsome for Ye Mynde': Embodying Early Modern Women's Reading." *Huntington Library Quarterly*, special issue on The Textuality and Materiality of Reading in Early Modern England 73. 3 (2010): 413–32.

Smith, Nigel. "Literature and London." In *The Cambridge History of Early Modern English Literature*. Ed. David Loewenstein and Janel Mueller. Cambridge: Cambridge University Press, 2002. 714–36.

– *Literature and Revolution in England, 1640–1660*. New Haven: Yale University Press, 1994.

– "'Making Fire': Conflagration and Religious Controversy in Seventeenth-Century London." In Merritt, *Imagining Early Modern London*, 273–93.

Smuts, R. Malcolm. "The Court and Its Neighborhood: Royal Policy and Urban Growth in the Early Stuart West." *Journal of British Studies* 30. 2 (1991): 117–49.

– *Culture and Power in England, 1585–1685*. New York: St Martin's Press, 1999.

Spevack, Marvin. *A Complete and Systematic Concordance to the Works of Shakespeare*. Hildesheim: Georg Olms, 1968–80.

Spingarn, J.A. *A History of Literary Criticism in the Renaissance*. 2nd ed. New York: Cornell University Press, 1908.

Stallybrass, Peter, Roger Chartier, and J. Franklin Mowery. "Hamlet's Tables and the Technologies of Writing in Renaissance England." *Shakespeare Quarterly* 55. 4 (2004): 379–419.

Steggle, Matthew. *Laughing and Weeping in Early Modern Theatres*. Basingstoke, England: Ashgate, 2007.

– "Notes Towards an Analysis of Early Modern Applause." In Craik and Pollard, *Shakespearean Sensations*, 118–37.

Stern, Tiffany. *Documents of Performance in Early Modern England*. Cambridge: Cambridge University Press, 2009.

– *Rehearsal from Shakespeare to Sheridan*. Oxford: Clarendon Press, 2000.

Stillman, Robert E. *Philip Sidney and the Poetics of Renaissance Cosmopolitanism*. Aldershot, England: Ashgate, 2008.

Strong, Roy C. *Britannia Triumphans: Inigo Jones, Rubens, and Whitehall Palace*. [London]: Thames and Hudson, 1980.

Swiss, Margo, David A. Kent, and Ralph Houlbrooke, eds. *Speaking Grief in English Literary Culture: Shakespeare to Milton*. Pittsburgh: Duquesne University Press, 2002.

Symonds, John Addington. *Shakespeare's Predecessors*. London: Smith, Elder, 1906.

Tanner, Laura E. "Holding On to 9/11: The Shifting Ground of Materiality." *PMLA* 127.1 (2012): 58–76.

Taylor, Diana. "Remapping Genre through Performance: From 'American' to 'Hemispheric' Studies." *PMLA* 122. 5 (2007): 1416–30.

Teague, Frances. *Shakespeare's Speaking Properties*. Cranbury, NJ: Associated University Presses, 1991.

Theile, Verena, and Linda Tredennick, eds. *New Formalisms and Literary Theory*. Houndmills, England, and New York: Palgrave Macmillan, 2013.

Thompson, E.P. "Rough Music Reconsidered." *Folklore* 103. 1 (1992): 3–26.

Thurley, Simon. *Whitehall Palace: An Architectural History of the Royal Apartments, 1240–1698*. New Haven and London: Yale University Press, 1999.

"Timeline: Daniel Pearl Kidnap." BBC News World Edition. 15 July 2002. http://news.bbc.co.uk/2/hi/south_asia/1835065.stm. Accessed 27 May 2014.

Tittler, Robert. *The Face of the City: Civic Portraiture and Civic Identity in Early Modern England*. Manchester and New York: Manchester University Press, 2007.

Tournu, Christophe, and Neil Forsyth, eds. *Milton, Rights and Liberties*. Bern: Peter Lang, 2005.

"The Tragic Story of Daniel Pearl." *The New York Times*. 23 February 2002. A14.

Turner, Henry S., ed. *The Culture of Capital: Property, Cities, and Knowledge in Early Modern England*. New York: Routledge, 2002.

– *The English Renaissance* Stage*: Geometry, Poetics and the Practical Spatial Arts*. Oxford: Oxford University Press, 2006.

– "Plotting Early Modernity." In Turner, *Culture of Capital*, 85–127.

"Urban Population Growth," Global Health Observatory (GHO), World Health Organization (WHO). http://www.who.int/gho/urban_health/situation_trends/urban_population_growth_text/en/. Accessed 14 September 2014.

Vernant, Jean-Pierre, and Pierre Vidal-Naquet. *Myth and Tragedy in Ancient Greece*. 1972, 1986. Trans. Janet Lloyd. New York: Zone Books, 1988.

Walker, Garthine. *Crime, Gender, and Social Order in Early Modern England*. New York: Cambridge University Press, 2003.

Wall, Cynthia. *The Literary and Cultural Spaces of Restoration London*. Cambridge: Cambridge University Press, 1998.

Wall, Wendy. *Staging Domesticity: Household Work and English Identity in Early Modern Drama*. Cambridge: Cambridge University Press, 2002.

Wallace, Jennifer. *The Cambridge Introduction to Tragedy*. Cambridge: Cambridge University Press, 2007.

Ward, John M. "The English Measure." *Early Music* 14. 1 (1986): 15–21.

Ward, Joseph P. "Imagining the Metropolis in Elizabethan and Stuart London." In MacLean, Landry, and Ward, *The Country and the City Revisited*, 24–40.

Walsham, Alexandra. *Providence in Early Modern England*. Oxford: Oxford University Press, 1999.

– "'Like Fragments of a Shipwreck': Printed Images and Religious Antiquarianism in Early Modern England." In Hunter, *Printed Images*, 87–109.

Weinberg, Bernard. *A History of Literary Criticism in the Italian Renaissance*. 2 vols. Chicago: University of Chicago Press, 1961.

Whigham, Frank. *Seizures of the Will in Early Modern English Drama*. Cambridge: Cambridge University Press, 1996.

White, Martin. "London Professional Playhouses and Performance." In Milling and Thomson, *The Cambridge History of British Theatre*, 298–338.

Wilding, Jo (User Services Librarian at the Shakespeare Centre Library and Archive). Email message to author, 11 March 2009.

Wilks, John S. "The Discourse of Reason: Justice and Erroneous Conscience in *Hamlet*." *Shakespeare Studies* 18 (1986): 117–44.

– *The Idea of Conscience in Renaissance Tragedy*. London: Routledge, 1990.

Williams, Raymond. *Modern Tragedy*. Stanford: Stanford University Press, 1966.

Wittreich, Joseph. *Shifting Contexts: Reinterpreting "Samson Agonistes."* Pittsburgh: Duquesne University Press, 2002.

Wood, Derek N.C. *Exiled from the Light: Divine Law, Morality, and Violence in Milton's "Samson Agonistes."* Toronto and Buffalo: University of Toronto Press, 2001.

Woodward, David, ed. *The History of Cartography, Vol. 3: Cartography in the European Renaissance*. Chicago and London: University of Chicago Press, 2007.

Worrall, David. *Celebrity, Performance, Reception: British Georgian Theatre as Social Assemblage*. Cambridge: Cambridge University Press, 2013.

Wrightson, Keith. "The 'Decline of Neighbourliness' Revisited." In *Local Identities in Late Medieval and Early Modern England*. Ed. Norman L. Jones and Daniel Woolf. Houndmills, England: Palgrave Macmillan, 2007. 19–49.

Zucker, Adam. *The Places of Wit in Early Modern English Comedy*. Cambridge: Cambridge University Press, 2011.

Zucker, Adam, and Alan B. Farmer, eds. *Localizing Caroline Drama: Politics and Economics of the Early Modern English Stage, 1625–1642*. New York and Houndmills, England: Palgrave Macmillan, 2006.

Index

Page numbers in *italics* and followed by "f" (e.g., *101f*) represent illustrations and captions.

www.ingramcontent.com/pod-product-compliance
Lightning Source LLC
LaVergne TN
LVHW090157080826
844660LV00013B/842/J

* 9 7 8 1 4 4 2 6 4 8 8 0 7 *